History of Early
REYNOLDS COUNTY
MISSOURI

by
JAMES E. BELL

THE AUTHOR

JAMES E. BELL

Turner Publishing Company

Copyright © 1986 by
James E. Bell

Library of Congress Catalog
Card Number 86-051181

Limited Edition of 1000 copies
of which this copy is number _____.

ISBN: 978-1-68162-368-9

PREFACE

A serious effort to research and record the history of Reynolds County has never been attempted even though the need for a comprehensive examination of its past has long existed.

All records of Reynolds County were lost twice in disastrous fires. Also, parent counties Wayne and Shannon lost old records due to courthouse fires. Most of pre-Reynolds County has not been recorded in any form; and those early pioneer day which hold such fascination for all of us has been lost forever.

This book is being dedicated to the seven men who formed the first county government in 1845. And it was hoped that we could find a descendant of each of these men, who would write the history and genealogy of his founding father. We have been only partially successful in this endeavor.

Devoted researchers know of the many difficulties encountered in undertaking a work such as this, and how elusive and time-consuming one simple fact may be. Only the die-hard will survive the adversities of publishing a book. Disappointment and frustration often beset us and we are tempted to toss the unfinished manuscript in the trash. Only the thought of preserving our heritage sustains us and causes us to push relentlessly onward to reach our goal. The author has written this book with the full knowledge that it may have only limited interest to those who do not have Reynolds County "roots". However few these may be, we are still desirous of preserving the heritage for them.

The name "Reynolds County" is relatively new, but the 817 square miles of Ozark Mountains which lies within its boundaries are very old. One cannot help but wonder as he gazes at this majestic beauty of the many events this land has witnessed since the beginning of time. Yet, for the most part, the hills remain silent, guarding its vast secrets with selfish indifference.

The author has attempted to show how the original five counties in 1812 were divided and sub-divided until, by 1862, 114 counties had emerged. Reynolds County at one time, at least in part, has been a portion of seven counties; Ste. Genevieve, Cape Girardeau, Washington, Wayne, Madison, Ripley, and Shannon.

The writer is acutely aware of how inadequate and incomplete this effort may seem. However, with all its imperfections, if it can inspire someone to do a better book on Reynolds County, then this book will have fulfilled its main purpose.

James E. Bell
May 15, 1986

i

REYNOLDS COUNTY

Reynolds County owes its beginning to two fur trappers, Henry Fry and Andrew Henry. Henry Fry, the first white inhabitant of the county, settled here in 1812. Andrew Henry came in 1816. Other pioneers soon followed and slowly the narrow valleys along the numerous small streams became dotted with picturesque log cabins. Reynolds County, named for Thomas Reynolds, Missouri's 7th governor, was organized Feb. 28, 1845 by the authority of the 13th General Assembly. William C. Love, Landon Copeland, and James Crownover were appointed by Governor Edwards to serve as the first governing body, then known as the Justices of the County Court. He also chose Marvin Munger as sheriff and John Buford as surveyor. These three justices chose Colin C. Campbell as Circuit and County Clerk. Pate Buford, a brother to John, had been elected in 1844 as Shannon County's State Representative and through his diligence, Reynolds became one of 19 counties organized in 1845. Pate Buford was elected in 1846 as the county's first representative. The first county court selected 14 of the best qualified men in the various communities to the important position of Justice of the Peace. Aryes Hudspeth of Washington County, John Miller of Madison County, and Moses Carty of St. Francois County were selected in the Legislative Act of 1845 to locate and lay out a permanent county seat. After due consideration, Centerville was chosen. As specified by the General Assembly, Lesterville and the home of Joseph McNail was used as the first meeting place for the Circuit and County Court until a permanent seat of justice was established. James George of Madison County was given the contract to build the courthouse, which he completed in 1849 or 1850. This brick structure survived until 1863, when Tim Reeves of the 15th Missouri Cavalry surprised Capt. Bartlett's Company "C" of the 3rd Missouri State Militia, took them prisoners, and burned the courthouse with all it's records. A new courthouse was built by John Johnston and James B. Barnes in 1872 at a cost of $8,000. Reynolds County's citizens have met and overcome many adversities in the past. They stand ready and eager to face the challenges of the future.

written by James E. Bell

This stone sits in the court yard at Centerville. The stone was purchased by the county officials and paid for from the county budget. The engraving on the stone was donated by Mr. & Mrs. Charles L. Pewitt of the Pewitt Funeral Home to mark their 35th year of serving the people of Reynolds County.

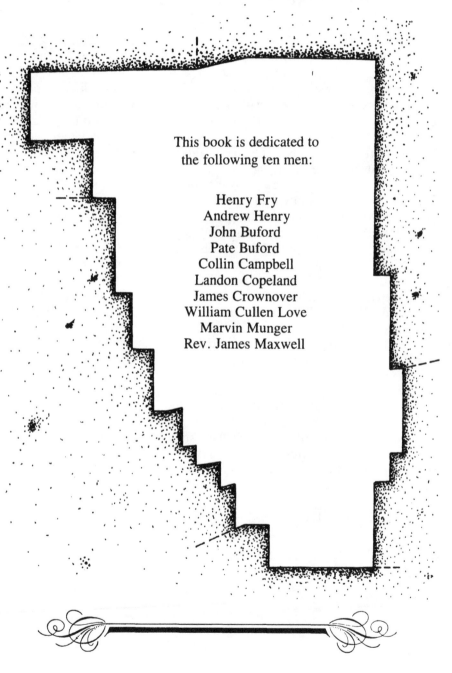

This book is dedicated to
the following ten men:

Henry Fry
Andrew Henry
John Buford
Pate Buford
Collin Campbell
Landon Copeland
James Crownover
William Cullen Love
Marvin Munger
Rev. James Maxwell

ACKNOWLEDGEMENTS

I have endeavored to make this publication as error-free as my limited ability will permit. It is my hope that you will correct me on any mistake you discover with the supporting proof.

Many people have in some way contributed to this book and I have attempted to give credit at the end of each chapter, but without a doubt a number of deserving persons were overlooked due to my poor record keeping.

Althea Copeland Taylor has been my "right hand" and without her professionalism I would not have completed this book. She thought her job was to be my typist, but after receiving the first few pages of my handwritten manuscript, she immediately knew what her duties were. Althea's first thought must have been, "this guy wants to do a book?" She purchased several red pencils and went to work. Spelling, punctuation, awkward phraseology and etc., all became her unsolicited responsibility.

Althea is the co-author of the Copeland book, published in 1980.

When it was decided to dedicate this book to ten men, an effort was made to find a descendant of each that would agree to do their family history and genealogy, but only three were found. Althea Copeland Taylor agreed to do the Copelands. Floyd F. Crownover is the author of the Crownovers. John L. Lillibridge, an enthusiastic researcher, agreed to do the Mungers.

Kathryn McKenzie Vickery agreed to help with the Bufords even though she is not a descendant but had done some research on them during the bicentennial.

These four people have made a lasting contribution to the history of this county and I am indeed grateful for their help.

When this book had progressed to being about half completed, it became obvious that my expertise did not include southern Reynolds County. Glenda Stockton heard my distress signal. Although hampered by a very tight time frame plus serious health problems, she contributed greatly to this publication.

James E. Bell, 1986

HOME IN THE OZARKS

Where brother went I trudged along
Across the Ozark trail
O'er brambling briar and wooded hills
Thru summer's sun and winter's gale

I stubbed my toes on many a stone
Upon that rugged pathway
But I would give a city block
Could I just go back half way

Back to the log hut on the hill
And the spreading elm beside it
Back to the arms of Mother there
It breaks my heart to describe it.

"I think I hear the cooing dove
In the early spring time fair
I think I see the new mown hay
And smell the perfumed air"

The golden wheat in shimmering fields
Waves softly in the breeze
The rustling corn and meadow lark
Are singing with the trees

Then across sweet clover fields
The dinnerbell rings its gong
Calling the men from plow and hoe
And away from the reapers song.

In the quiet peace of even-tide
We play in the twilight glow
That the stars are diamonds we will wear
When we great ladies grow.

Then fathers foot fall on the walk
Coming in by lantern light
The bleating sheep and lowing kine
Are carefully sheltered for the night

We served no dinners in a dining room
Our dresses were cotton, not silk
But I'd give a cocktail banquet
For a bowl of hoe cake and milk

And see the leaves, turning brown and gold
With heaps of snow to fall
And sit before that pine knot fire
That lighted the room for us all

Happy the circle then unbroken
And life was pleasure, no sorrow
If only days could endless be
We'd never known the morrow

But years now find me far away
Still thinking of home and God
And when he calls, please let me rest
'Neath the peaceful Ozark sod.

This poem was written by Adella Robinette Smith, who lived in Bellflower, California, but who grew to young womanhood in Reynolds County. She was the daughter of Jordon Robinette and Nancy E. Jamison; the granddaughter of Steven and Martha Miner Robinette and John C. and Andromache Carty Jamison. This poem was written on August 23, 1933, and was taken from the John Carty book, published in 1979 by Jamison, Cauley, Bell and Jaycox.

TABLE OF CONTENTS

HISTORY OF
REYNOLDS COUNTY, MISSOURI

Reynolds County was formed on February 25, 1845, from land acquired from Shannon County. Shannon County had gained the area from Washington and Ripley Counties and a small portion of Madison County on January 29, 1841. Ripley County had taken the southern portion of the county from Wayne County on January 5, 1833; and the northern half of the county had been a part of Washington County since 1813. Missouri's population was rapidly increasing in the 1840's and new counties were being added often. More Missouri counties were authorized in 1845 than in any other period. Nineteen counties met the requirements imposed by the State Legislature.

Reynolds County, located near the center of the St. Francois Mountains, is today almost entirely covered with forest. Only areas along the various small streams have been converted to agriculture. The main source of revenue for many years was its forest products, but in the last fifteen years, lead has become a very important part of the economy. Less than one-tenth of Reynolds County's 817 square miles are suitable for farming, yet this small region produces a sizeable number of cattle and hogs.

This county had its greatest population about the turn of the twentieth century; then started a slow decline which was only reversed when the lead companies became large employers. For many years, when the native sons and daughters completed their education they had to go elsewhere to find employment. Not so now; a high percentage may find work in this county.

Black River is the principal stream with its many tributaries of crystal clear water fed from numerous springs. These, along with the intense beauty of its rugged terrain, make this county a popular recreation area.

There are only four small towns in the entire county: Lesterville, to the northeast; Bunker to the northwest; Centerville, the county seat, to the north central; and Ellington to the south. Each town has a school with elementary grades through high school — except Centerville, which has only elementary grades. Back in the 1930's the county had 64 schools, but presently there are only four, as improved roads and modern transportation made consolidation possible. Thus fewer schools were needed. But the quality of these modern, up-to-date buildings is much improved and the curriculum of education now offered far surpasses what was offered in 1930.

The assessed valuation of the county has increased dramatically in the last twenty years, producing a "rags to riches" condition for the various county offices of government. These riches have not come without a price; as drugs, crime, arson and divorce have all accelerated.

When Reynolds County was formed in 1845, the average family had about eight or nine members, but today that number had decreased to just over three. Therefore, we may have more families now than at any time in the county's history, but the population is less due to the declining family size.

The country doctor is gone, who once could be found in almost every community. Now the only doctors in the county may only be found in Ellington, where they have the benefit of a Medical Center and a modern 30-bed hospital.

Our forefathers and mothers worked from "daylight til dark" to eke out a meager subsistence as opposed to the 40 hour week we have today. And "mom's" work-load has been reduced proportionately with her automated house, which takes care of the chores while she relaxes with her favorite soap opera.

The "good ole days" often were not so good. Life expectancy once was less than 40 years. This was due in great part to the babies and young mothers lost in childbirth. The country doctor and his black pill bag may have had some physiological value, but very little help for the truly ill. Yet, with all the adversities and hardships that our ancestors faced and often died in their attempt to conquer, we, the researcher, often feel those days had a certain charm . . . leaving us with the feeling that perhaps we got cheated by being born too late in history.

To better understand the present, it is helpful to know something of the past. With that as our criteria, we will return to the period in history when Reynolds County was the hunting ground of several Indian Tribes, including the Osage, Delaware, Kickapoo, Shawnee and perhaps others.

Only the Osage Indians seemed to be native to Missouri and the Ozarks region. All the other aborigines were driven from the east of the Mississippi River as the white man made his gradual advance across the eastern portion of North America.

The American Indians by most accounts had been on this continent for more than 10,000 years. Their coarse black hair, dark eyes and reddish-brown skin led most anthropologists to reason they were Asiatics and had somehow migrated by way of the Bering Strait. There is considerable evidence to support the theory that the red man had been on this continent for a long time. The many tribes differed in many respects. Size, language, and cultural traits that would take many years of separation to develop a distinct difference.

The Osage empire covered roughly a portion of four states: Missouri, Kansas, Oklahoma, and Arkansas. It had been reported by the first Europeans that there were about seventeen Osage villages when they first scouted the area. How many people this represented is not known, but the war-like Osage had the numbers to rule this area preeminently against the other tribes that flanked them on every side.

The Osage Indians had given up their claim to most of the Ozark Plateau in their treaty with the federal government in 1808. They always considered this treaty not to include their right to use the Ozarks for their frequent hunting trips. This often caused many problems for the first white settlers.

Due to their marriage customs, the Osage were tall, physically strong, and possessed unquestionable courage. The smaller, weaker males often were denied marriage and the mightiest warriors got the girl plus all her sisters. In this way they had a form of selective breeding, which undoubtedly accounts for most of the tribe being over six feet tall.

The Kickapoos came out of Wisconsin and Illinois into Missouri where they established a village near Ste. Genevieve and perhaps another village near the vicinity where the Missouri and Mississippi join. In 1812 these villages were moved to the southwestern part of Missouri near Springfield. It has been estimated there were about 20,000 Indians in Missouri in 1810 with the Osage being the greater in number.

When the first white settlers came to Reynolds County, Indians' temporary hunting camps could be found along the many small streams that lazily wind their way toward the southeast.

The Mann family, who came to Missouri in a very early day, according to tradition, encountered Delaware Indians on the Black River in present day Reynolds County. Early maps verify the presence of a village of Delaware In-

3

dians in that general area.

The Indians were mostly friendly and often hunted and traded with the white man. On occasion they would resort to thievery and sometimes would attack the small settlements. The ever increasing white population in conjunction with the various treaties that relocated the many tribes that were common to this area, made it rare to see a red man in this locale after 1830.

———————————·◦◦◦◦◦◦·———————————

REFERENCES

"Indians of the Ozarks Plateau" by Elmo Engelthal
Glenda Stockton, LeMay, Missouri

It is always interesting to learn, or, if the facts cannot be found, to speculate on who was the first white man to see the region you are trying to research. We undoubtedly will never know who was the first white man to tread the "hills and hollows" of Reynolds County.

Hernando de Soto landed in Florida in 1539 with over 6,000 soldiers and started his wandering in the southeastern United States, which eventually lead him to the Mississippi River in May, 1541. He crossed the river near present day Memphis into Arkansas and explored a major portion of the Ozark region, which could have included the St. Francois mountain range and Reynolds County.

The French had established a settlement at Kaskaskia in present day Illinois in 1700; and from there they crossed the Mississippi River and scouted some of the area that is now Missouri. It is known that the French, who were interested in mining, had penetrated deeper into Missouri by 1715 when La Motte Cadillac discovered lead in present day Washington County. Phillips Francis Renout, Sr., a leading foundry owner and operator of several iron mines in France, sent his son in 1720 to Missouri to open new lead mines. Exploratory parties were sent out to locate lead deposits from Fort Chartres, which was near Ste. Genevieve. whether any of these parties penetrated into Reynolds County is not known; however, there is at least an even chance they did.

France made a number of attempts to establish settlements which would enhance their authority in Louisiana and discourage the British, who were actively involved in the fur trade in the area claimed by France. From the time the French explorer La Salle formally took possession of the new land for King Louis XIV in 1682 and called it "Louisiana," until France relinquished its claim to Spain in 1762, only one permanent settlement, Ste. Genevieve, had been established in Missouri.

Spain, after taking control of the territory formally in 1770, attempted to settle the region with emigrants who would be loyal to the Spanish government. They were able to entice but few settlers, and French influence in the territory still prevailed and all the new settlements had definite French characteristics. Mining, fur trading, and salt development started to take on greater importance, which contributed to the establishment and growth of a number of new settlements. St. Louis was founded by Pierre Laclede and Auguste Chouteau in 1764. Other small communities in that locale soon followed: Crondelet in 1767 and St. Charles in 1769. Mine-A-Breton, founded by Francois Azor, also known as "Breton," became the first settlement in Missouri that was not located near a major river. Some historians say the year was 1767, while others believe the year was 1773. Francois Azor's only other apparent claim to fame was his long life, which ended in his 111th year.

New Madrid was settled by a group of Americans who had come from the eastern United States in 1789. Col. George Morgan, trader, public official, Revolutionary soldier, Indian agent, and land speculator, organized a group of 70 men to form a colony in Upper Louisiana. Cape Girardeau became a small frontier settlement in 1793 when a Frenchman by the name of Louis Lorimier arrived from the Ohio Valley, where he, like most Canadians, was a trader and had gained some influence with the Shawnee and Delaware Indians.

In 1800 the Spanish secretly ceded the Louisiana Territory back to France. This disturbed the American government since all exports west of the Appalachians were taken by boat down the various streams that flowed into the Mississippi River and on to New Orleans. Here the American government had made an agreement in 1795 with the Spanish to store their goods, duty free, for export.

The Americans immediately started to negotiate with French to gain control of the Mississippi River. Napoleon had not abandoned his hopes to build an empire in the New World, but he also knew that war with Great Britain was eminent. When war came, the Americans could certainly take control of the river by force while France was engaged in Europe. Faced with these problems, Napoleon decided to sell all of Louisiana to the United States.

In this transaction, the United States bought 827,987 square miles of land for about $15,000,000. This vast area lay between the Mississippi River and the Rocky Mountains, stretching from the Canadian border to the Gulf of Mexico. The United States took possession of Louisiana on December 20, 1803. In 1804 Congress divided the huge territory to make it easier to govern. One part became the Territory of Orleans. The other part, beyond the present northern boundary of the State of Louisiana, became the District of Louisiana. In 1805, the name was changed to the Territory of Louisiana.

Although the Spanish had ruled for almost four decades, they had done little to shape life in Upper Louisiana. Only a few remained of the small number who had immigrated there. For the most part, the new settlers were French until about 1790, when Americans started to move into the territory in greater numbers.

The District of Louisiana was further sub-divided into five smaller districts; St. Louis, St. Charles, Ste. Genevieve, Cape Girardeau and New Madrid. St. Louis was chosen as the new capitol and the District of Louisiana government was run by four appointed officials, a governor and three judges.

Seven years later, in 1812, Congress raised Missouri to the rank of a second-class territory. This was the beginning of a democratic government for the inhabitants of Missouri. Ste. Genevieve, Cape Girardeau, New Madrid, St. Louis and St. Charles, which had been known as districts before 1812, now became counties and were eligible to elect members for the Territorial House of Representatives, as well as for a delegate to Congress.

At the election, Edward Hempstead, a native of New London, Connecticut, before coming to Upper Louisiana, was elected first delegate to Congress. He was born June 3, 1780, and was the son of Stephen Hempstead, a soldier in the Revolution. Edward Hempstead received a liberal education and was admitted to the bar and practiced law in Rhode Island before coming to Louisiana in about 1803.

When the War of 1812 ended, reducing the serious Indian depredations, new settlers coming to the Missouri Territory accelerated dramatically. Almost daily caravans from Virginia, Kentucky, Tennessee and North Carolina were arriving and penetrating deeper into the interior of the territory. As the population grew, the territory legislature created additional counties to govern the newly settled areas. Thus Washington County was created from Ste. Genevieve County in 1813 by the territorial legislature. The northern half of present day Reynolds County would now be a part of Washington, while the southern half would remain the possession of Cape Girardeau County until 1818 when Wayne county was established.

The members of the first Territorial House of Representatives chosen at this first election in 1812 were Richard S. Thomas and Israel McCready from Ste. Genevieve County, and George Fredrick Bollinger and Stephen Byrd from Cape Girardeau County. Andrew Scott from Ste. Genevieve was chosen permanent clerk. Andrew was a brother to John Scott, who was the first congressman from Missouri in 1820. Andrew Scott was appointed Judge of the Superior Court of the Territory of Arkansas in 1818.

An act of Congress provided for the nomination of eighteen persons from the Missouri Territory to be submitted to the President of the United States. He would then select nine for the first Territorial Council. John Scott and Rev. James Maxwell were chosen from Ste. Genevieve County, and Joseph Cavender and William Neely from Cape Girardeau County.

———————

REFERENCES

A History of Missouri, Vol. I, 1673-1830, by William E. Foley
The Heritage of Missouri, by Duane Meyer
Ste. Genevieve, by Gregory M. Franzwa
Kaskaskia Under the French Regime, by Natalia Belting
History of Missouri, by Louis Houck

WASHINGTON COUNTY

Washington County became the sixth county in the Missouri Territory primarily because of its many deposits of minerals that lay close to the surface, which could ideally be mined with the crude tools and techniques used in that period of time. Another important contributing factor was the rich agricultural land along Big River and the scenic and productive land in Bellevue Valley. These stories told back east charmed and thrilled the adventurous spirit of many frontier persons, causing them to pull up roots once again, pack their meager belongings into a wagon — most often pulled by slow-moving oxen — and head for "ole Missouri" and what would become Washington County.

In 1813, when Washington County was cut away from Ste. Genevieve County and started to function on its own, some 300 families lived within its boundaries. At the time of the Louisiana Purchase in 1803, perhaps 40 families would be a high estimate of its total population. This was a very large county, extending from St. Louis County on the north to Cape Girardeau County on the south; and from Ste. Genevieve County on the east to the Kansas boarder on the west.

Washington County was reported to have a white population of 2,769 in 1820. This would seem to indicate the county was growing quite slowly, as there were about 2,200 inhabitants in 1813. We must remember, however, it had lost much of its territory in the formation of other counties. According to the 1830 census, Washington County was sub-divided into ten townships; Harmony, Meramac, Richwood, Liberty, Union, Breton, Potosi, Concord, Belleview and Black River. It supported 6,784 whites and 1,202 blacks.

Black River Township, which would later include the northern portion of Reynolds County, had 369 people. Of that number, 49 were black slaves and five were free blacks.

When Washington County was formed on August 21, 1813, Lionel Brown, Samuel Perry, John Hawkins, Martin Ruggles and John Andrew were chosen as commissioners to select a permanent seat of justice. Mine-A-Breton was chosen as a temporary meeting place for the justices of the county court. The three justices chosen by the Territorial Governor were; Martin Ruggles, William Sloan and John Stanton. They, in turn, chose John Brickey as clerk. Lionel Brown became the first sheriff. Daniel Dunklin was later selected as sheriff by William Clark, territorial governor of the Missouri Territory. Lionel Brown would again be selected to the position of county sheriff, but his tenure in office would be shortened by the infamous John "T" in a duel which cost Brown his life on September 20, 1819. John Smith used the "T" after his name to help identify him from so many other John Smiths. He, as one writer said, "traveled, ate and slept with his guns, including a rifle he called 'Hark from the Tombs.'"

On February 26, 1814, the permanent county seat was established across

Breton Creek from Mine-A-Breton. Moses Austin gave 40 acres of this site and John Rice Jones gave ten acres. This new county seat was called Potosi and remained separate from Mine-A-Breton until 1826, at which time the two towns were incorporated into one with the name Potosi surviving.

John Rice Jones, Samuel Perry and John Hutchings were representatives from Washington County to the constitutional convention which met in St. Louis on June 12, 1820. They came very close in their efforts to have the new state capitol located at Potosi, but lost out to St. Charles.

So many of Reynolds County's pioneers came by way of Washington County that we believe it would be of genealogical value to name some of "the heads of household" who came here before 1816. We shall use many sources, however, the major ones will be Spanish land grants, church records, family records, and the few court records that are available. Often it is difficult to determine where a given person is living as the community names have changed, as well as the county boundaries. It is possible we may have included a few names which would be outside the bounds of Washington County pre-1816.

1. John Alley	27. William Boydston	53. John Gibbons
2. Thomas Alley	28. Francois Breton (Azor)	54. Joseph Gibbons
3. John P. Alexander	29. John Bricky	55. Roberts Gibbons
4. Robert Alexander	30. John R. Broker	56. Samuel Gibbons
5. John Anderson	31. Lionel Brown	57. Andrew Goforth
6. Robert Andrews	32. William Buford	58. Miles Goforth
7. George Ashbrook	33. Robert Cain	59. Zack Goforth
8. William Ashbrook	34. William Campbell	60. Louis Gringa
9. William H. Ashley	35. John Clarkson	61. John Hawkins
10. Moses Austin	36. John Cooper	62. Nicholas Hays
11. Stephen Austin	37. Nehemiah Cravens	63. Samuel Henderson
12. John Baird	38. Benjamine Crow	64. William Henderson
13. Andrew Baker	39. Walter Crow	65. Elizabeth Hewitt
14. Elijah Baker	40. John Davis	66. James Hewitt
15. Elisha Baker	41. Lot Davis	67. John Hughes
16. Reubin Baker	42. Luke Davis	68. Uriah Hull
17. Thomas Baker	43. Soloman Davis	69. William Humphreys
18. J.B. Barnes	44. William Davis	70. Seth Hyatt
19. Elias Bates	45. Daniel Dunklin	71. John James
20. John Bear	46. Abraham Eads	72. Edward Johnson
21. Thomas Bear	47. Williams Eads	73. James Johnson
22. Abraham Beckman	48. Henry Eidson	74. John Johnson
23. Josiah Bell	49. Patrick Estes	75. John Paul Jones
24. John Blair	50. David Gallaher	76. John Rice Jones
25. Thomas Blair	51. Soloman George	77. William Jones
26. William Blanford	52. James Gibbons	78. Thomas Jordon

79. Andrew Joseph	98. John Ottery	117. John Sinclair
80. Lewis Lacroix	99. Henry Padgett	118. Fergus Sloan
81. John Lewis	100. Samuel Perry	119. Robert Sloan
82. Carlton Linsay	101. John Pettigrew	120. Samuel Sloan
83. John Little	102. Daniel Phelps	121. Thomas Sloan
84. Charles Lucas	103. Timothy Phelps	122. William Sloan
85. William McCarty	104. Henry Pinkley	123. Robert M. Stevenson
86. John McClintock	105. Joseph Reed	124. William O. Stevenson
87. James McCormick	106. Thomas Reed	125. John Stewart
88. John McCormick	107. William Reed	126. French Strother
89. Ananias McCoy	108. Abraham Rickman	127. William Strother
90. Mary McCreary	109. John Rickman	128. Frances Tibault
91. Thomas McLaughlin	110. James Robinson	129. Samuel Wakely
92. William McLaughlin	111. John Robinson	130. John Walker
93. John T. McNail	112. Martin Ruggles	131. John T. Webb
94. Curtis Morris	113. Soloman Ruggles	132. William Webb
95. Jacob Neal	114. Moses Russell	133. Joseph Williams
96. John Neal	115. Moses Scott	134. Raul Williams
97. Samuel Neal	116. Anthony Sharpe	135. Thomas Wright

REFERENCES

Bellevue Beautiful View, Bellevue Valley Missouri History 1763-1981, 1983
    by Bellevue Valley Historical Society
History of Washington County, Goodspeed
A Reminiscent History of the Ozark Region, Goodspeed Reprint 1976
The Encyclopedia of the History of Missouri, Vol. VIII, furnished by Glenda
    Stockton, LeMay, Missouri
Spanish Land Grants, Missouri Archives
Presbyterian Church Records as kept by Robert M. Stevenson (1816)
History of Missouri, Houck

SOME MEN WHO ACHIEVED PROMINENCE
IN
STE. GENEVIEVE, CAPE GIRARDEAU AND WASHINGTON COUNTIES

Because Ste. Genevieve, Cape Girardeau and Washington Counties were the parent counties of Reynolds County, we shall briefly mention a few gentlemen who held center stage in the early development of these three counties.

FRANCOIS VALLE, SR.

A very prominent family under the French and Spanish regimes was the Valles of Ste. Genevieve. The emigrant, Francois Valle, came from Reuen, Normany, to Quebec in 1645. His son, Charles, married Genevieve Crebe and one of their sons was Francois Valle, born January 2, 1716, who moved to Kaskaskia, Illinois, where he married Marianne Billeron (1729-1781). She was the daughter of Leonard Billeron, Royal Notary of Kaskaskia, and Marie Claire Catois.

The Valle family was said to be one of the wealthiest families in Ste. Genevieve in the late 1700's, owning large numbers of slaves and, in addition, hiring many white people and keeping all of them constantly employed.

Francois Valle, Sr. served as first civil and military commandant of Ste. Genevieve, holding this position for eighteen years. He supported the American cause during the Revolution — often feeding, housing and supplying the American troops with clothing and other requirements. Two of his sons, Francois Valle, Jr., and Jean Baptiste Valle, would later serve as commandants of Ste. Genevieve.

Francois and Marianne Billeron Valle had five children: Marie, who married Louis Du Brenil Villars; Charles, who married P'elage Carpentier; Joseph, who was killed by the Osage Indians in 1777; Francois, Jr., who married Marie Carpentier, daughter of Henry and Marie Aubuchen Carpentier; and their youngest child, Jean Baptiste, who married Jeanne Barbeau, daughter of Baptiste Barbeau and Marie Jeanne LeGras of Prairie du Rocher.

JOHN SCOTT

John Scott, born in Virginia in 1785, graduated from Princeton College and then studied law in Vincennes, Indiana, where he was admitted to the bar. He came to Ste. Genevieve in 1805, being the first permanent lawyer in the community. Nathaniel Pope, who was born in Louisville, Kentucky, in 1784, and graduated at Transylvania University, then studied law, came to Ste. Genevieve in 1804. He soon moved across the river to Kaskaskia and on to the state capitol, where he had a brilliant career in government.

John Scott and Rev. James Maxwell were appointed by the President of the United States to the territorial council in 1812. Subsequently, Scott was elected delegate from the Missouri Territory to Congress. He became Missouri's first representative to Congress when Missouri came into the Union. He served for four years with distinction. After his defeat in Congress, he served southeastern Missouri for many years as a popular and "much sought after" lawyer. Scott County was named in his honor.

John Scott's first wife died sometime after they came to Ste. Genevieve. Then on September 20, 1824, he married Harriet Jones Brady, widow of Thomas Brady and the daughter of John Rice Jones. This marriage produced three children; Elizabeth Fannie, born June 23, 1825; Emile Josephine, born February 10, 1830; and George, born May 24, 1832. John Scott died in 1865.

His eccentricities, profanity and courage were well known in the area around Ste. Genevieve. He had a nervous, quick and active mind which made him an effective lawyer. When death was near, John Scott was asked to make peace with his Maker. He answered, "I have served the devil all my life and it would not be right to desert him now."

HENRY DODGE

Henry Dodge, born October 12, 1782, in Vincennes, Indiana, was a son of Israel Dodge, a revolutionary soldier. Israel had married Nancy Ann Hunter, a native of Kentucky. After spending a number of years in Kentucky and Illinois, they moved to Ste. Genevieve and became involved in lead mining, farming, brewing, and distilling. Israel Dodge served as sheriff of Ste. Genevieve District in the early 1800's.

Henry Dodge married Christina McDonald in 1800. In 1805, he succeeded his father as sheriff of Ste. Genevieve District and held that office until Missouri gained statehood in 1821. He was a marshall of the Territory of Missouri starting in 1813. While in the Missouri Militia, he rose to the rank of major general.

Dodge had been interested in mines since his early days in Ste. Genevieve; and, in 1827, he migrated to the Territory of Michigan when the fame of the mineral fields of the upper Mississippi River became widely known. While in that territory, he commanded a force of mounted volunteers in the Winnebago War in 1827; and distinguished himself in the Black Hawk War in 1832. His military success came to the attention of President Jackson and other military appointments followed.

When the Territory of Michigan was divided in 1836, Dodge was made governor of the Territory of Wisconsin. This included the present states of Wisconsin, Minnesota, Iowa and parts of the Dakotas. He was later elected to Congress from the territory. When Wisconsin was admitted to the Union in 1848, Henry Dodge became one of the first United States Senators. He retired from public life in 1857 and died ten years later on June 19, 1867.

Henry Dodge's son, Augustine C. Dodge, who was born in Ste. Genevieve in 1812, married Clara Hertick of Ste. Genevieve. They moved to the Wisconsin Territory in 1839, where he served as a delegate to Congress 1841-

1847 and as a United States Senator from Iowa from 1848 to 1855. He died in Burlington, Iowa, in 1883.

WILLIAM HENRY ASHLEY

William Henry Ashley was born 1778 in Powhatan County, Virginia, where he received a limited education. In about 1804, he came to Missouri and settled at Mine-A-Breton (Potosi) where he became engaged in mining and the manufacture of gun powder. Saltpeter, a nitrate used to make gun powder, was found in various caves which lay to the southwest of Potosi. Andrew Henry was also involved with Ashley in this mining and manufacturing venture. Ashley served on the Board of Trustees of Potosi Academy and advanced from captain in the early years of the War of 1812 to general in the Missouri Militia in 1822.

Ashley, in partnership with Andrew Henry, formed the Rock Mountain Fur Company. Here he gained fame and considerable fortune. When Missouri came into the Union in 1821, William Ashley was Missouri's lieutenant governor.

He ran for governor in 1824 and was defeated, then ran for United States Senate in 1829, where he was again defeated. In 1831, success finally came when he was elected to Congress — and was re-elected twice. He retired then to run for state governor once more . . . and again he went down to defeat.

William Henry Ashley married Mary Able on November 17, 1806. She died in 1821. On October 17, 1832, he married Mrs. Elizabeth Moss Wilcox. Ashley died of pneumonia March 26, 1838.

JOHN RICE JONES

John Rice Jones was born in Wales on February 10, 1759, and educated at Oxford. He practiced law in London and then came to America. He settled first in Pennsylvania and, like many Americans, moved in stages toward the west. He served in the closing days of the American Revolution in Kentucky under George Rogers Clark. Jones came to Missouri about the same time as Moses Austin and may have been a member of Austin's group, as they formed a partnership at Mine-A-Breton where lead mining had become important.

Jones served in Missouri Territory Assembly in 1814 and helped found the Potosi Academy. He served as a trustee of this pioneer institution. He was elected delegate from Washington County in 1820 to the first constitutional convention. When Missouri became a state, Jones ran for the United States Senate, but Barton and Benton proved to be very formidable opponents and Jones ran a distant third. Governor McNair, the first chief executive, appointed Jones to the Missouri Supreme Court, where he served until his death on February 1, 1824.

It is not known whom John Rice Jones married, but we do know he had five sons and two daughters who would constitute one of the most intelligent and successful families in American history. John Rice Jones, Sr. was fluent in six languages and had an amazing knowledge of Greek and Roman history, besides being a brilliant jurist. The oldest son, Rice, was a lawyer in Kaskaskia and served in the lower house of the Indian Territory. He was one of the leaders in establishing the State of Illinois from Indian Territory. The second son, John Rice, Jr., grew up in Potosi with Stephen Austin and followed his friend to Texas, where he played center stage along side Austin in Texas independence. He became the first Postmaster General of the Republic of Texas.

Augustus Fisher Jones and Miers Jones also went to Texas. Miers Jones served two terms in the Missouri Assembly before going to Texas. George Wallace Jones, son number five, fought in the Black Hawk War, then served as a congressional delegate in the Territory of Michigan. He had a similar post in the Territory of Wisconsin and became one of the first two United States Senators from Iowa. Harriet Jones married John Scott and Elizabeth Jones married Andrew Scott, two gentlemen who distinguished themselves in Missouri . . . and Andrew Scott later in Arkansas. So the Jones family became well known in Missouri, Arkansas, Texas, Iowa, Michigan, and Wisconsin.

MOSES AUSTIN

Moses Austin was born October 4, 1716 and died June 10, 1821. He was a son of Elias and Eunice Austin, a great-grandson of Anthony and a great-great-grandson of Richard Austin, who came to Boston from England in 1638. Anthony, a son of the emigrant Richard, became the first town clerk of Suffield, Connecticut. Moses Austin had been interested and involved in mines from the time he was a young boy in Middletown, Connecticut, and later in Philadelphia, Pennsylvania . . . then finally in southwestern Virginia before coming to Missouri and the Potosi area.

Austin recorded his observation of the mines he saw at Potosi near the surface, "in great plenty and better quality than I have ever seen either from the mines of England or America." In 1812, he estimated his mining property was worth $150,000. He joined with others in organizing The Bank of St. Louis in 1816 and its failure two years later left him with little resources. He did have his pride left and was not a quitter. He planned to establish three hundred families in Texas. He died before he could carry out his plans and his son, Stephen F. Austin, became renowned for the successful colonization of Texas.

Moses Austin and Marie Brown were married September 29, 1785. Marie Brown was born Jan. 1, 1768 and died January 8, 1824 near Potosi, Missouri. They had five children; Anna Maria, Eliza Fuller, Stephen Fuller, Emily Margaret and James Elijah Brown Austin. Anna and Eliza died very young.

Dr. LEWIS F. LINN

Dr. Lewis F. Linn, a half brother to Henry Dodge, was born in Louisville, Kentucky, on November 5, 1795, to Asael and Nancy Hunter Dodge Linn. He was a grandson of Col. William Linn who served with George Rogers Clark. Lewis Linn came to Ste. Genevieve in 1815 and married Elizabeth Relf in 1818. This marriage produced two children.

He represented the 3rd District in the Missouri Senate in 1830. He was appointed to fill the unexpired term of United States Senator Alexander Buckner, who had died of cholera in 1833. Dr. Linn held this Senate seat until his death on October 3, 1843. He was well known for his knowledge of cholera.

JOHN SMITH T.

John Smith T. was born in 1770 to Francis and Lucy Wilkinson Smith, who lived in Essex County, Virginia. John Smith T.'s grandfather, Col. Francis Smith, served in the Virginia House of Burgesses, representing Essex County. His family was both influential and wealthy and John Smith T. had the benefit of a full education at William and Mary College at Williamsburg, Virginia.

John Smith T. married Nancy Walker, a daughter of Rev. Sanders and Sarah Lamarr Walker of Oglethorpe County, Georgia.

They moved to Tennessee soon after their marriage and he started to engage in land speculation that continued in Missouri a few years later, which brought him wealth and much controversy. He was in direct competition with Moses Austin in lead mining in the Potosi area, which may have contributed to his running feud with Frederick Bates, secretary of the territory. Bates had replaced Dr. Joseph Browne, resulting in two challenges from Smith T. to a duel which Bates wisely chose to disregard, as Smith T. was a deadly marksman.

General Wilkinson and Aaron Burr, two notorious planners who engaged in questionable activities, involved John Smith T. and other men of influence in Missouri. It was generally believed they planned to invade Mexico and then detach part of the American Southwest from the United States for their own empire. John Smith T. probably did not know of their intentions, but regardless of his innocence, his reputation was damaged, which led to his dismissal from the militia, the judgeship of Ste. Genevieve Court of Quarter and Sessions and Commissioner of Rates by Acting Governor Frederick Bates.

Some researchers have written in defense of Smith T. . . . we quote: "It has been said John Smith T. killed as many as thirteen or fifteen men in duels." Miss Valle Higginbotham of Potosi has researched and compiled a vertical file on John Smith T. which is, perhaps, the first real effort to present a true history of this flamboyant personality who contributed much to early Ste. Genevieve and Washington Counties. She feels most of these duels can not be substantiated and only three duels can be proved. The duel that received the most publicity was the duel that killed Lionel Browne, Washington County's representative, on September 20, 1819. Lionel Browne was the son of Dr. Joseph Browne.

John and Nancy Walker Smith T. had only one child, Ann, who was married to David S. Deadrick in Tennessee. After his death in 1823, she married James M. White.

Nancy Walker Smith T. was not enumerated on the 1830 census with her husband in Union Township, Washington County. John Smith T. died in 1836. A headstone has never been found for either of them, although their wealth was quite evident.

DANIEL DUNKLIN

Daniel Dunklin, fifth governor of Missouri, was born in Greenville, South Carolina, on January 14, 1790. The family moved to Mercer County, Kentucky, in about 1806 and then on to Missouri and Potosi in 1810.

He rose through Missouri politics from sheriff of Washington County in 1815, to representative in 1822, lieutenant governor in 1828, and then governor in 1832.

In 1836, before his term as governor had expired, he was appointed surveyor general by President Jackson. When Dunklin County was organized on February 14, 1845, it was named in his honor. Like most politicians, then as well as now, he was a lawyer.

Daniel Dunklin married Pamelia Willis Haley on May 2, 1815, and they became the parents of six children. Daniel Dunklin died August 25, 1844, and was buried in Jefferson County, Missouri.

NATHANIEL COOK

The Cook family came to America from England and settled in Virginia in the early part of the eighteenth century. John Dillard Cook, the son or grandson of the emigrant, moved to Scott County, Kentucky, where he raised his family, which would include three sons who would gain some prominence.

The eldest son, Col. Nathaniel Cook, came to Missouri in 1797. In 1802, he married Honore Madden, daughter of Thomas Madden, Spanish Deputy Surveyor for the Ste. Genevieve District. Madison County was formed in 1818 and Cook lived near Murphy Settlement (Farmington) in the community that was named for him, "Cook," not far from St. Michael (Fredricktown).

Nathaniel Cook was elected a member from Madison County to the constitution convention in 1820. He ran for lieutenant governor against William Ashley and was defeated by a small plurality. He also ran against Thomas H. Benton for United States Senate, but could not match so formidable an opponent.

John B. Cook, a brother, was one of the first judges of the Missouri Supreme Court. Daniel P. Cook was the first representative to Congress from the state of Illinois. Cook County, in which the city of Chicago is located, was named for Daniel P. Cook, the third brother.

LOUIS LORIMIER

Louis Lorimier is recognized as the founder of Cape Girardeau even though Sieur Jean B. Girardot established a trading post there much earlier (1730's) than Lorimier.

Our subject was born in Canada in about 1748, being one of ten children of Claude-Nicolas Lorimier. While still in Canada, Louis married Charlotte Pemanpich Bougainville, a half-blood Indian. His will would indicate he had been married earlier and had one son, Guillaume. This will also implies that Pemanpich was his common-law wife. They were the parents of six children.

Lorimier became well known during the American Revolution as being an opponent of the American cause. He recruited and furnished arms to the Shawnee and Delaware Indians and often led raids on American settlements.

After the war he was forced to abandon the Ohio Valley and take refuge in the Spanish held land west of the Mississippi River. He first came to the Ste. Genevieve area in about 1787, then moved to Cape Girardeau in 1793 where he established a post for himself and his Indian followers. He became a Spanish subject and was given 3,200 arpents of land, which was later increased to 30,000 arpents.

Louis Lorimier died June 26, 1812, and left the following will. We quote: "Natural son, Guillaume, age 27 years, 2 months. Granson, William, illegitimate son of my daughter, Marie Louise. Shawnee woman named Pemanich whom I regard as my wife and mother of my six children: Louis, age 23 years; Augustus Bougaenville, age 18 years and eight months; Marie Louis, 21 1/2 years; Agatha, age 16 years and four months; Verneuel Raphael, age 14 years and seven months; and Victor, age 10 years and eight months."

Guillaume married Hetty Thorn; Louis, Jr., first married Polly Berthieaume, then Margaret Penney; Agatha married Daniel Stewbeck; and Mary (Marie?) married John Logan.

GEORGE FREDERICK BOLLINGER

George Bollinger played an important part in Cape Girardeau County for almost two decades. He was their territorial representative in 1812, 1814, and 1816. He became a member of the legislative council in 1818 and would become Cape Girardeau and New Madrid's first state senator in 1820. George Bollinger would again represent his county in the state legislature in 1826, 1834, and 1838. He was state senator from the 4th Senatorial district in 1828 and 1830.

The emigrant Heinrich Bollinger (1710-1770) came to America in 1738 where he settled in Pennsylvania at first, then moved his family to North

Carolina. He and his wife, Magdalene, were the parents of ten children. Their son, Henry, married Elizabeth Cline in 1764 and they became the parents of our subject.

George Frederick Bollinger (1770-1842) married Elizabeth Hunziker in 1798. This marriage produced only one child, Sarah, who married Joseph Frizel on January 25, 1819. Her second marriage was to Ralph Daughtery on October 13, 1825.

The town of Fredericktown was named for George Frederick Bollinger and the land was donated by Nathaniel Cook.

REFERENCES

Lead King: Moses Austin, by James Alexander Gardner

Missouri's Governors 1820-1964, Published by Warren E. Hearnes, Secretary of State. (Courtesy of Missouri Archives)

A History of Missouri, Vol. I 1673-1830, by Foley

The Heritage of Missouri, by Meyer

Ste. Genevieve, by Franzwa

Kaskaskia Under the French Regime, by Belting

History of Missouri, by Houck

Official Manuel of Missouri 1975-76

The World Book Encyclopedia

Missouri Heritage, by Larkin

Missouri General Assembly, 1812-1976, by James C. Kirkpatrick, Secretary of State (Missouri Archives Division)

Bollinger County 1851-1976, by Mary L. Hann, Editor; Blanche Reilly, Associate Editor

Cape Girardeau County, formed in 1812, when Missouri became a Territory, covered about one fifth of the state, but, for most part, it represented only the people who had settled along the Mississippi River on its eastern boarder. The scattered settlers who were living deep in the interior had little or nothing to do with selecting the officials who had the responsibility for the county's functions.

The settlers who had obtained Spanish land grants on the St. Francois, Lower Black and Castor Rivers and their tributaries wanted a greater voice in what went on in their county. Out of this desire to have more equal representation, in conjunction with the indifference shown by the county's eastern establishment, the vast County of Wayne was created by the Territorial Assembly on December 11, 1818. The "State of Wayne" as it was sometimes called, would become the mother of many counties in the next 40 years, including southern Reynolds County.

The original description of Wayne County's boundary reads: "Beginning at the southeast corner of the County of Madison (also formed in 1818) running southwardly on the ridge which divides the waters of Crooked Creek and Castor River, until it strikes the edge of the Big Swamp between what is called Jenkins Creek and Castor: thence down the main channel of said River Castor until it strikes the New Madrid County line, thence south as far that a due west line will leave the plantation of Edward H. Matthews on the North; thence west to the Osage boundary line; thence north with said line so far that a due east line will intersect the place of beginning; thence east to the beginning is hereby laid off and erected into a separate and distinct county, to be called and know by the name of Wayne County."

The county was named for an American military officer, Gen. Anthony Wayne. General Wayne was born January 1, 1745, in Chester County, Pennsylvania. He attended an academy in Philadelphia and became a surveyor. He served in the colonial assembly before the War for Independence. Wayne joined the Revolutionary War and served with distinction in a number of campaigns; Brandywine, Germantown, Valley Forge and Yorktown. In 1783 he was made a major general. He died in his home state of Pennsylvania in 1796.

Overton Bettis, James Logan, Soloman Bollinger, William Street and Ezekiel Ruebottom were the commissioners chosen to locate a place for public buildings. The commissioners chose what then was known as Cedar Cabin and later renamed Greenville as the county seat.

The state governor appointed justices of the peace from the time the state came into the Union until 1834. Some of the early justices of Wayne County were: Ezekiel Ruebottom, Jacob Kelly, Sr., Jacob Garret, Benjamine Carter, Chesley Payton, Solomon Bolin, James McFadden, Solomon Bollinger, Matthew Allen, Charles Sweazea, James Varner, John Ulrich, Richard Brazel, John Holmes, Samuel Street, John Ashert, John Logan, William Ingram,

John Howard, Louis Cato, James Logan (James Logan could have been living on Logan Creek in what later became Reynolds County when appointed December 20, 1823) Jesse Spencer, James Vernon, John S. More, Alfred Wheeler, Douglas Merrill, James Wilson, John Shoemaker, Jesse Driskill, Isaac E. Kelly, Henry Carter, Andrew Kerr, Peter Harmosen, Michael Cowan, Elijah Lander, William Thomas, Hay T. Helms, George T. Butler, William Johnston, Jacob Catron and Nicodemus Wood.

Ezekiel Ruebottom was Wayne County's state representative in 1820, then Elijah Bettis was elected in 1822-24 and 1826. He also served as state senator in 1828 and 1830. David Logan was Madison-Wayne Counties' first state senator in 1820.

For the most part, the counties grew slowly, but small pockets of pioneers would suddenly settle an area for a number of reasons. By 1840 small communities could be found throughout the county's vast area. One by one the county was sub-divided into many counties. When Wayne County was formed in 1818, it had less than 1400 inhabitants.

REFERENCES
Missouri General Assembly 1812-1976, Archives Division, Office of Secretary of State
Encyclopedia of History of Missouri, Vol. VII
Wayne County by Cramer
The World Book Encyclopedia, 1971 Edition

BLACK RIVER TOWNSHIP 1812-1820

When Washington County was established in 1813, the area that would later become Black River Township had only one family, Henry and Rebecca Baker Fry. Fry was also known as Henry Padgett and Capt. John Padgett. Why the aliases, we cannot determine. He was born Henry Padgett in about 1752 in South Carolina, the son of William and Mary Priestly Padgett. He joined the Revolutionary War under the name of Henry Fry and continued to use the name periodically for the rest of his life; which lasted, according to one source, to his 115th year. We do know he was alive in 1860, living in St. Francois County, Missouri.

Henry Fry was not a man of the soil, but rather a hunter, fur trapper and trader among the transient Indians who passed through the area from time to time. It is believed he settled near the present day community of Black on the Middle Fork of Black River. The reasons for this are apparent, as the East Fork of the Black River was already being hunted and trapped by settlers just to the east in Bellevue Valley. The many small streams near the headwaters of the Middle Fork of the Black River were well suited to the abundant beaver population, which must have existed in this period. Big Brushy, Little Brushy, Ottery, Strother, Clayton and Neals Creeks were ideal streams for North America's largest rodent to build a dam, a lodge, and raise a family with an endless supply of trees for building material and food.

It is believed Henry Fry continued to live in this area until sometime in the 1820's. He seemed to have prospered in his trapping and trading. Beaver pelts were in demand in Europe and Americans could ask for and get a fair price for their furs. Fry's success on the Black River may have influenced Andrew Henry, Reynolds County's second inhabitant, to settle on the Maxwell Reserve near the area where the East, Middle and West Forks of Black River came together.

Andrew Henry, like his predecessor Fry, was a trapper and trader; but he operated on a grander scale, ordinarily, than his counterpart. Henry knew and had the respect of all the important men of his day in upper Louisiana, Missouri Territory and, later, in the state of Missouri. He was a member of the Missouri Fur Company. Later, in partnership with William Henry Ashley, he formed the Rocky Mountain Fur Company.

Andrew Henry, the son of George and Margaret Young Henry, was born August 15, 1775, in York County, Pennsylvania. He came to Ste. Genevieve in 1802. He tried many endeavors — mining, manufacturing of gun powder, soldiering (where he gained the rank of major in the Missouri Militia). He seemed to have some success in all of these undertakings.

It would appear out of character to believe Henry moved to Black River alone in 1816. This man, known for his enterprise, was not married at this time. So we must believe other men were in his party, but we cannot name them. Seth Hyatt may have been one, but we have little proof. The sketchy history of this county always mentions Seth Hyatt and James Logan "in the same breath," but we cannot find a connection. James Logan seems to have come to Reynolds County by way of Cape Girardeau and Wayne County. He was chosen as one of the commissioners to select a seat of justice when Wayne County was formed from Cape Girardeau and Lawrence Counties on December 11, 1818. Seth Hyatt would appear to have lived in Washington County, near Potosi, before coming to Reynolds County. A Seth Hyatt was brought before a jury in Washington County "for an affray" involving James Hewitt and John Cavandor. This was supposed to have been Washington County's first jury case, so we must be discussing the year 1813-1814.

From this altercation, Seth Hyatt would certainly fit the description of a man who would accompany Henry to remote Reynolds County.

In 1822, Andrew Henry formed the Rocky Mountain Fur Company with his long-time friend, William Henry Ashley and, along with some 100 men, once again returned to the western mountains in search of beaver. He spent two, three or more years in this endeavor, finally returning to Harmony Township, Washington County, in about 1826. Here he worked the mines near Palmer until his death in 1833.

Hyatts Creek, just south of Lesterville in Reynolds County, got its name from Seth Hyatt, without doubt. If he did not come with Andrew Henry, he came soon after. His history for the most part is shrouded in obscurity. The 1830 census shows the following: Head of household, Seth Hyatt, age 40-50; one boy under five; one boy 15-20; one girl 5-10; three girls 10-15; and his wife, 40-50.

Hyatts Creek was probably in Wayne County, Benton Township in 1830. Hyatt is found again in Wayne County on the 1840 census. Not far away lived Delilah Logan, believed to be the wife of James Logan.

Seth Hyatt's wife was apparently dead in 1840 and he is gone before the 1850 census is taken, so we lose the chance to learn more about him. Tradition says he was born in North Carolina.

In Washington County we find a Henry "Hight" who died intestate in 1834. Administrator of his estate was Alfred D. "Hight". This only proves there were Hyatts (Hights) in Washington County in an early period.

Ripley County marriage records show the marriage of two daughters of Seth Hyatt. Joshua Morris and Lovey Hyatt were married on February 18, 1838 and Lucian Farris and Nancy Hyatt were married February 15, 1840.

Spanish land grants were common throughout Missouri during the Spanish rule — especially more accessible areas along large streams or those with rich, deep soil. After the Louisiana Purchase in 1803, these grants became a troublesome problem for the land commissioners, who were appointed to decide what should be honored and what should not.

Black River Township had only one such grant, but it was enormous in size and would remain in litigation before the numerous land boards for many years, therefore obscuring progress — as new settlers arrived looking for land avoided building a cabin and clearing land for crops when the possibility of eviction was a definite eventuality. The Reverend James Maxwell had petitioned the Spanish government for 96,000 acres in present day Reynolds County in 1799. The reason he gave the Spanish government was the coming of Catholics from Ireland in great numbers, who would need land for a new settlement. This pleased the Spanish government, as they were encouraging Catholics to settle in Louisiana. Thus the petition was granted.

Not one Roman Catholic from Ireland came and settled on the Maxwell Reserve, yet, the Rev. Maxwell held on to this immense domain — which was four leagues square — until his death in 1814. Then the land came under the control of John P. and Hugh H. Maxwell, nephews of the Catholic priest.

It would be an almost impossible task to document the arrival of most of the pioneer families in the Black River Township. However, it is apparent that the Lesters, Mungers, Capes, Jamisons and Miners came very early — almost assuredly before 1820. The Jamisons, Capes and Lesters probably came here together, as they all came from Cumberland County, Kentucky, by way of Illinois, where they may have resided for a year or more.

Early maps of this area show only two hamlets; Buford, near present day Lesterville, and Munger, near the Reynolds-Iron County line. Marvin Munger, born in Charleston, Montgomery County, New York, in 1792, came and settled on the headwaters of the East Fork of the Black River and started the community of Mungers Mill sometime between 1816 and 1818. On October 28, 1819, he married Salina Lewis, a native of Bellevue Valley, Missouri.

Marvin Munger was a man of multiple talents; teacher, preacher, farmer, grist mill-saw mill entrepreneur, sheriff in Ripley County — and, later, sheriff of Reynolds County in 1845. He was a member of the Black River Baptist Church near present day Black. This church was a long way from Mungers Mill, indicating that Marvin Munger was a devout Christian, as his forefathers had been since coming to America in 1630.

Daniel Lester married Millie Flowers March 16, 1795, in Pittsylvania County, Virginia. They are first found in the records of Cumberland County, Kentucky, in 1800 and are shown on that county's census in 1810 as follows: Head of household, Daniel Lester, 26-45 years old; three boys under 10; two boys 10-16; two girls under ten; and his wife, Millie, 26-45. Also, on the 1810 census are three other Lester families, Abraham, Thomas and William, all shown as being between 26-45 years old. These four Lesters, all living in close proximity, could be brothers or close relatives. None of these Lesters are shown on the 1820 census or Cumberland County and we must believe Daniel Lester was now living in the Black River Township, some three miles north of Lesterville. He was one of the early justices of the peace for this township in the 1820's.

Daniel Lester, for reasons unknown, moved to Wayne County in the late 1830's as did two sons, John and Daniel, Jr. Jesse, probably the oldest son, remained in the Lesterville area. In the late 1840's, Elizabeth Lester Boyd, the wife of John Boyd, came here and lived on the same land that Daniel and, later, Jesse had lived on. We believe she was a daughter of Daniel and Millie Lester. This Lester family undoubtedly gave Lesterville its name. However, we do not believe this was the accepted name until the late 1830's.

Only two marriages for this Lester family have been found in this area — one in Washington County, Isaac Mann and Milley Lester on March 1, 1832, and one in Ripley County, John Lester and Catherine King March 24, 1835. Catherine may have been the daughter of William and Catherine King, who came to this area in the early 1830's. This would indicate the Lesters were still living near Lesterville in 1835.

This is a very confusing period. Just where the Ripley County and Washington County dividing line was after Ripley became a county on January 5, 1833 is not known. Ripley County in the mid 1830's seemed to cover all of Reynolds County except a very narrow band in the Edge Hill area. However, when the 1840 census was taken, the people living on all three forks of Black River — including Lesterville — were listed in Washington County. Boundaries were so poorly defined, leaving us all somewhat confused.

Daniel Lester served in Wayne County as justice of the peace in the late 1830's and was elected justice of the county court August 22, 1838. He was shown on the 1840 census of that county as being 60-70 years old and owning six slaves. He did not live another ten years — or the census enumerator failed to find his cabin. He was not shown on the 1850 census.

Two John Capes are found on Cumberland County, Kentucky's 1810 census; a John Capes, Sr., and a John Cape Jr., as follows:

John Cape, Sr.: one male 45 or over; two males under 10; one male 10-16; one female 16-26; and one female 45 or over. John Cape, Jr.: two males 26-45; one male under 10; one male 10-16; two females under 10; one female 16-26; and one female 45 or over.

This John Cape, Jr. came to Washington County in 1819 and settled on the East Fork of Black River. We can be almost certain that Maston, William P., Susanna and John, who married after coming to Washington County, were children of John Cape, Jr. Maston married Rebecca Whaley, a daughter of James Whaley; William P. married Amy Ann Carty, a daughter of James and Sarah Copeland Carty; John married Sucky Cole; Susanna married James McCoy.

William P. Cape served as a justice of the peace in Washington, Madison and Shannon Counties.

John Jamison, a brother-in-law of John Cape, Jr., undoubtedly came to Missouri with the Capes. He had married Susanna Cape March 26, 1809, and was probably living in the same household as John Cape, Jr. in 1810, as we have two males listed as being 26-45 years old.

Martha Jamison lived very near to the Capes in Cumberland County and is probably the mother of John Jamison. Patsy Jamison, who married William Watkins October 25, 1812, is almost certainly a daughter of Martha Jamison.

We find an Alexander Jamison in survey records in 1807, who may be Martha's son, or possibly her husband. However, he is not shown on the 1810 census of Cumberland County, indicating he is dead, unmarried, or gone from Cumberland County.

John and Susanna Cape Jamison lived in the Black River Township until the 1830's, when they moved to Searcy County, Arkansas.

William and Laban Miner were both born in Virginia — William in about 1783 and Laban in about 1791. They moved to Kentucky, where they grew to manhood and married. William married Lydia McGinnes in Mercer County, Kentucky, June 23, 1811. Laban married Elizabeth Moran. Some records indicate these two brothers and their family moved to Reynolds County in 1818; however, the ages and places of birth of their children shown on the census would suggest "before 1820" would be a less risky position to take on when they arrived in this locale.

Our subjects moved on the Middle Fork of Black River near present day Black and probably were the first close neighbors of Henry Fry.

William and Lydia Miner were the parents of nine children. Laban and Elizabeth Miner had eight children. Many descendants of these two families still live in Reynolds and adjoining counties.

Researchers are often disturbed when they cannot find records of land purchases from the federal government in the 1812 to 1820 period. The United States government had surveyed very little land in the Missouri Territory before 1813, but with the appointment of William Rector in 1813 as surveyor-general for Illinois and Missouri Territories, some progress was soon evident as townships and range lines in the more populace areas were established. The fifth principle Meridian, the basis for future public surveys, was run and recorded in 1815. Some land was finally ready to be sold by the government in 1818. Land in Reynolds County being bought from the federal government before 1830 was rare, if non-existent.

REFERENCES
History of Jefferson County, Missouri, by Goodspeed
History of the Ozark Region, by Goodspeed
Munger Book and other data sent by Calphurnia Munger Merrifield
John Carty and 4,000 Descendants, by Jamison, Cauley, Bell and Jaycox
Federal Census of Cumberland County, Kentucky, Records
Washington County, Missouri Records (State Archives)
Ste. Genevieve County, Missouri Records
Glenda Stockton, LeMay, Missouri (Lester)
Many other "bits and pieces" furnished by interested people

PRE-REYNOLDS COUNTY'S
GROWTH AND DEVELOPMENT

The panic of 1819 back east in conjunction with land being offered in Missouri to veterans of the War of 1812 and the publicity generated by the discussions going on all over the established states east of the Mississippi River on when and how Missouri would become a state, encouraged settlers from the hills of Kentucky and Tennessee to cross the "Mighty Mississippi" and head slowly but steadily toward the Ozark region, which until then had few inhabitants. In many instances, these same families had moved from Virginia or North Carolina only a few years before looking for the same thing they were hoping to find in Missouri — a more productive and rewarding life. Man has always had this dream, and it is amazing the risk, hardship, and sacrifice he will endure to search for this elusive aspiration.

Researchers do not have the benefit of an 1820 census of Missouri, and often it cannot be determined if a family came to Missouri before or after 1820. We often depend on when a child was born for an indication of when a family came to what later became Reynolds County, when in fact, they may have been born in some other area in Missouri.

As the new decade began, one of the first families to arrive was William C. and Sarah Bryan Love with their two small children, James H. and Mary Ann. William Cullen Love, born in Wilkes County, North Carolina, was a veteran of the War of 1812. He returned to Wilkes County in 1816, after the war, and married Sarah Bryan. James Harrison Love, their first child, was born in that county on July 13, 1817. Soon after this, William and Sarah Love moved to Cumberland County, Kentucky, where their second child, Mary Ann, was born November 19, 1819. The decision was made the next spring to move to Missouri to what later became Reynolds County.

In 1817, President Monroe had 500,000 acres in Missouri set aside for veterans of the War of 1812. However, there is no evidence that William Love received any free government land. He chose to settle on land near the mouth of Ottery Creek near what would later be known as Edge Hill.

The Copelands and Cartys arrived from Cumberland County, Kentucky, perhaps 1821 with their rather large families and found land in the Black-Edgehill area. These two families had intermarried in Surry County, North Carolina, when James Carty married Sarah "Sally" Copeland, sister of Lot Copeland. They migrated to Cumberland County, Kentucky, about 1803, where their families grew to maturity. Lot Copeland's entire family moved with him to Missouri, including his one married daughter, Pricilla, who had married Morgan Bailey. James Carty left two daughters in Cumberland County, Elizabeth and Nancy. Moses Carty, a younger brother to James, also came and put down roots in this area.

Jacob Stout, who was born May 18, 1782 in North Carolina to Samuel and Rachel Chaney Stout, came to Missouri in a very early day. Just when he arrived has not been determined, but we do know he sold the land to John Smith T. which contained the site of Missouri's first iron furnace to operate west of the Mississippi River — known as Ashebran's Furnace — in 1819. This furnace was established in 1815 on Stouts Creek about two miles south of Ironton.

Jacob's older brother, Ephraim Stout, was one of the first settlers in Arcadia Valley, arriving there in about 1805.

Exactly when Jacob Stout moved to the East Fork of Black River is in question, but it could have been soon after selling his land on Stouts Creek. His first marriage was to Sarah Long and this marriage produced several children. He moved his family to Tennessee in the early 1830's and Sarah may have died there. He returned to the East Fork of the Black River and married Cynthia Fortinberry on August 25, 1839.

A very early settler to Missouri and the East Fork of Black River was James Edmond (Edmunds), the son of William and Sarah Edmonds of Nelson County, Virginia. William Edmonds left a will dated March 1, 1826, and named his wife, Sarah, and seven children; James, Nancy, Andrew, Lavender, Willis, Moses, Rebecca and Charles.

Letters shown as unclaimed in the post office at Jackson, Missouri, on September 30, 1819, listed a James Edmond. All the early pioneers normally lived a long way from a post office, and James Edmond may have been living on the East Fork of the Black River at this time — some 75 miles from Jackson. The only other places in the Missouri Territory where the government had established post offices were: St. Louis, 1804; New Madrid, 1805; Ste. Genevieve, 1805; Cape Girardeau, 1806; St. Charles, 1806, Mine-A-Breton (Potosi), 1811; and Caledonia, 1819.

All the children of William and Sarah Edmonds came to Missouri with their mother and settled in Washington County, where they married the children of neighbors, for the most part. Willis married Abigail Stricklin November 20, 1831; Moses married Moriah Thomas February 11, 1832; Lavender first married Elizabeth Hughes September 27, 1832, and later married Amanda McCabe November 1, 1836; Charles also married twice, first to Permela Harris March 22, 1846, then to Minerva Fitchpatrick September 4, 1849. Nancy Edmonds probably married Robert Andrew in Virginia then moved to the Emboden Branch of the East Fork of the Black River.

Mary Andrew, who lived near Robert Andrew, was most likely his sister-in-law. She married Samuel Irvin October 13, 1836, and the ceremony was performed by Marvin Munger.

John L. Robinson lived in Madison County, Missouri, when he married Sarah Bryan June 29, 1824. Sarah was the daughter of Dr. Jesse Bryan, who came to Ste. Genevieve near the turn of the century. John and Sarah soon moved on the East Fork in the area of Johnson Shut-Ins, where John Robinson died before 1840. When their son, James, married Sarah Cape on August 13, 1840, his mother had to give her consent as James was under age. A Margaret

Jane Bryan married Samuel Alexander Rayburn March 14, 1844. She could be a daughter. They are shown in the 1850 census of Washington County.

Sarah Bryan Robinson does not show on the 1850 census of Reynolds County. She must have died in the 1840's, as we find a George W. Robinson shown on the census as being 27 years old, living on the old home place. Besides his wife and two small children, a John age 22, Andrew age 20, and Jane age 16 were also members of this household. This would suggest these last three named are children of John and Sarah Robinson.

John L. Robinson is believed to be the son of Jeremiah and Drucilla Robinson. Jeremiah Robinson died and left a will dated August 28, 1833, which mentions John L. Robinson, Elizabeth Terry, Drucilla Tong, Milly Hedspeth, Margery Triffs, Joana Hedspeth, Emily Campbell, Hethy Holbert and Harriet Robinson as his children.

A man who may have come to Missouri with Moses Austin in about 1799 could be John T. McNail. He worked in Austin's lead mines at Mine-A-Breton and appeared many times before the various land boards in efforts to resolve disputes erupting over the Spanish land grants. He probably knew this part of Missouri (Washington County) as well as any man who lived in the region in this early period. He lost a grant that was located in the Bellevue Valley in 1818. It is a matter of conjecture as to when he moved to the Emboden area in Black River Township, but we believe it was in the early or mid 1820's.

John and Mary McNail were the parents of at least four children: Joseph, who became well known in Reynolds County; Benjamine, who married Savannah Stout September 12, 1837, and became a renowned Methodist minister; Allan and Mary. We also find a Daniel McNail (McNeal), age 30, on the 1850 census, St. Francois County, living near this McNail family. He could be another son of John and Mary.

John Buford, who became one of the best known and most influential men in pre- and post-Reynolds County, settled on land just south of Lesterville in 1825. His father, William Buford, had bought this land from the Maxwells in 1819. John married Mrs. Elizabeth Davis Irvin January 2, 1827 and this marriage produced several children. He was appointed as one of the commissioners to select a county seat for Oregon County, and again for Texas County when it was formed. He helped survey much of the land in Ripley, Shannon and Reynolds Counties.

A close neighbor to John Buford was George Hawk, who had married Anna Clark April 11, 1826, and settled near Lesterville. In the 1830's he moved to Strother Creek near the present Reynolds-Iron County line, where we find today a community called Hawk Lane for this early pioneer or for one of his sons.

The 1850 census of Washington County reveals the following: George Hawk, age 56, born Virginia; Anna, age 56, born South Carolina; Elijah, age 21, born Missouri; and Nelson, age 18, born Missouri. Nelson Hawk became a Baptist minister and served in several local churches.

In the late 1820's, a number of families came to what later became northern Reynolds County from Cumberland County, Kentucky. No doubt the Capes, Lesters, Jamisons, Loves, Cartys and Copelands who came to the East and Middle Forks of the Black River from Cumberland County before or soon after 1820 had kept in touch with their relatives and friends back east. Other factors were at work. The fear of Indians was no longer a threat. Cumberland County was becoming a little crowded by pioneer standards. Normally, the oldest son took control of his father's estate, and, out of necessity, the other children had to find their own land.

For a family to make such a move required planning, courage and determination. A pioneer had to know what to take on a long trip for survival and what to discard or sell. He needed to take a number of things to support himself on the trip, as well as supplies necessary to start a new life on the frontier. When a family was planning their trip west, two items were indispensable; a rifle and an axe.

The Goggins, Rayfields and Radfords all came from Cumberland County and all came near the same time, so we must believe they moved westward together. Other families may have been with them on the trip.

William and John Rayfield, two brothers born in North Carolina, came to Cumberland County with their parents before 1807. Their father has not been proven, but we believe him to be Isaac Rayfield, Sr. William married Sarah _____. John married Nancy King, daughter of William and Catherine King, who followed the Rayfields to Reynolds County soon after 1830. A nephew of John and William Rayfield also came, and, in later years, moved to the southern part of the county, married, and became the progenitor of the southern Reynolds County Rayfields. This younger John Rayfield probably was either the son of Isaac, Jr. or James Rayfield, who died in Cumberland County before 1820. This Isaac Rayfield, Jr. married Betsy Stopp October 8, 1816 in Cumberland County.

Milton and Green Berry Goggin, sons of William and Drucilla Jackman Goggin, had married Nancy and Elizabeth Carty, daughters of James and Sarah Copeland Carty, in Cumberland County, Kentucky, then followed the Cartys to Reynolds County — some eight years after the Cartys and Copelands arrived.

The ancestors on the maternal side of the family of Milton and Green Berry Goggin can be traced to John Neville and the first permanent settlement in Maryland on March 25, 1634, when two sailing ships, one a 400 ton vessel, the Ark, and its pinnace companion, the Dove, displacing only forty to fifty tons, sailed up the Potomac River and dropped anchor off St. Clements Island.

Elizabeth and Nancy Carty's lineage is traceable to John Copeland, born ca. 1616 in Dolphin Leigh, England, who came to Virginia in 1635.

Riley, Milner and Charles Radford seem to have migrated from Virginia via Cumberland County and came to this county with their Cumberland

County neighbors. Their father could be Milner Radford, who is shown in the court records of Cumberland County, but is not on the census.

Riley, the oldest of the three brothers, had apparently married before leaving Kentucky to Catherine _____. Riley Radford and James Ferrel are both shown on the 1830 census, Black River Township, and moved to Wayne County in the 1830's, as did Daniel Lester and Cary Copeland — indicating some family connection. All lived close together. James Ferrel, almost without doubt, came to Reynolds County with the Goggins, Rayfields and Radfords.

Milner Radford married a neighbor girl, Lovey Parker, July 22, 1830, a daughter of Joseph Parker. Charles Radford married Polly Stilwell on November 1, 1838. In Franklin County, Missouri, marriages, we find the marriage of Joseph Bay and Emily Parker, who may be a daughter of Joseph Parker.

Joseph Parker had a very large family and many of his descendants still live in Reynolds County. Yet we know very little about him. The 1830 census of Black River Township shows him with five boys and four girls. The 1840 census of Black River Township shows him living on the West Fork of the Black River with four boys and one girl. The 1850 census shows him as 80 years old, born in North Carolina; his wife (or daughter) listed as 50 years old, also born in North Carolina.

John Parker, who married Sarah Rayfield January 2, 1832, is the only son we can be sure about. They were married by William C. Love and he shows them both to be living on Black River, which makes Sarah the daughter of William and Sarah Rayfield. William Rayfield died in 1831 without a will and his brother, John, was appointed administrator February 1, 1832.

A family which may have more descendants living in Reynolds and the adjacent counties today than any other family who came here, could be Able and Jane Goforth Stricklin. They came to Black River in 1829 from Fish Rock Creek, Virginia. They has six boys and three girls in their family when they came to Black River. Only six of the children's marriages are known. John Stricklin married Nancy Blackwell May 6, 1830; Abigail married Willis Edmonds November 20, 1831; William married Rachel Stout December 5, 1833; Abial married Isabella Henderson March 27, 1834; Henry married Jane Hurt December 31, 1835; and Rachel married Henry Cable January 24, 1839. We know that Thomas Stricklin was another son, born March 31, 1806, and the census shows his wife to be Cynthia _____.

Nimrod Mason was still single in 1830, as shown on the 1830 census Black River Township. He married Latty Baldwin in Ripley County on February 23, 1835. On the 1850 census of Reynolds County, his wife is shown as Arlotta. We do not know if this is another wife or just a variation given for the first wife's name by the census enumerator. Nimrod Mason served as a justice of the peace after Reynolds County was formed.

Robert Johnston settled in the Shut-Ins area of the East Fork undoubtedly to develop its ideal water power for a mill that was needed for a growing population. His family had operated a mill near the head-waters of Big River in the early 1820's. He was born December 25, 1796, in Virginia and came to Missouri as a very young lad with his parents, John and Frances Johnston. The Shut-Ins got its name from Robert Johnston, and over a period of time, the name became Johnson.

Robert Johnston's known sisters and brothers were: Elizabeth, who married Landon Copeland; Celinda, who married Dale Copeland — Landon's brother; Reuben, who first married Ruthy Hicks November 10, 1836, then on the 1850 census of St. Francois County his wife is shown as Curincy, perhaps indicating a second marriage; Emmeline, the youngest sister, married George Washington Mills April 28, 1836.

In 1830 Robert King Love moved his family to Edge Hill where his younger brother, William, had moved ten years before. Robert, the son of John and Margaret King Love of Wilkes County, North Carolina, had gone to Lincoln County, Tennessee, where he married Margaret C. Davis in 1821. Margaret died in 1838 and Robert died in 1843, leaving six children, some of whom were very young. They soon moved to what later became Iron and Dent Counties.

Mark Hughes, who is shown on the 1830 census of Black River Township, had married Ellen Campbell, the daughter of William and Nancy Robinson Campbell, October 12, 1826. Mark, born June 19, 1808, was the son of John and Susanna Hayes Hughes. He did not remain long in Reynolds County, but moved on land in Washington County near Irondale when his parents gave him 243 acres in 1833. He sold his land on East Fork to John Robinson, his wife's uncle.

Thomas Thorp would be anonymous if we did not have the benefit of data obtained from the census. He lived in the Emboden area in 1830. On the 1840 census of Ripley county, we find a Thomas Thorp, age 40-50; one male, 20-30; one male 5-10; one female 15-20; and one female 30-40.

On the 1860 census of Reynolds County, a John Wadlow is shown as follows: John Wadlow, age 35, born in Tennessee; Cintha, age 37, born in Missouri; Sarah, age 15; Nancy, age 11; William, age 8; Thomas, age 7; John, age 5; James, age 2; and a Sarah Thorp, age 58, born in Tennessee. Sarah may be the wife of Thomas Thorp and Cintha his daughter.

Another man we know little about is Jacob Eliott, even though he lived to be an old man and can be found on Washington and Reynolds County censuses from 1830-1870. We shall only give here the data as shown on the 1850 census of Reynolds County: Jacob Elliott, age 48, born in North Carolina; Jane, age 45, born in Kentucky; Joseph, age 20; Unity, age 18; Sarah, age 16; Arlotta, age 12; Samuel, age 10; Cassia, age 8; and Thomas T., age 5.

Moses Ashbrook is shown on the 1830 census of Black River Township, but we cannot be sure this would be in what later became Reynolds County. Also, we cannot be certain if he is the son of George or of William Ashbrook, who came to Bellevue Valley in a very early period. George and William Ashbrook were born in Hampshire County, Virginia. They came to Missouri about the time of the Louisiana Purchase and settled near Caledonia. We find the following information in Washington County marriages: Elizabeth Ashbrook to James Hickman, June 7, 1827; Rosanah Ashbrook to John Orchard, April 13, 1828; and William Ashbrook to Elizabeth Kirby April 13, 1843. These may be sisters and brother of Moses, but we can only surmise.

Thomas Ross, according to the 1830 census of Black River Township, lived near Edge Hill. He is shown with a wife and two daughters. One daughter, Amy Ann, married Moses Copeland March 13, 1831. No other information has been found on Thomas Ross or his family.

Clayton Creek got its name from Beverly Clayton or his son, Elbridge H., who married Mary Ann Adams on January 29, 1838. She was the daughter of David and Rachel Koonce Adams. Beverly Clayton, son of Henry Clayton, married Sally Rion (Sarah Ryan) on June 28, 1814, in Cumberland County, Kentucky, and most likely came with the Cartys and Copelands to pre-Reynolds County in 1821. Beverly is shown in the 1830 census living with his children in what later may have become Iron County. His wife did not appear on the census and we would presume she is dead. The populace, as a rule, seldom separated or divorced. In the Ripley County marriages, we find a Beverly W. Clayton marriage to Elizabeth Oxford dated May 31, 1835. William Love, who lived only a few miles away at Edge Hill, performed the marriage — adding substance to the belief that this was the same Beverly Clayton.

The next pioneer we will discuss has caused some confusion because of his middle initial. Andrew L. Dickey is listed in the 1830 census, but all other records we have found use the name Andrew S. Dickey; therefore, we cannot be sure they are the same person. The 1850 census of Washington County shows the following: A.S. Dickey, age 51, born in Virginia; Elizabeth, age 56, born in Virginia; Joseph, age 26, born in Tennessee; Robert, age 21, born in Missouri; and Andrew S. Dickey, age 12.

In Washington County marriages, we find the marriage of Caroline Dickey and Robert Henry Scott, June 4, 1846, and Jane Dickey's marriage to William Hawkins, June 18, 1835. Jane Dickey Hawkins is shown as 28 years old on the 1850 census of Washington County, living near the household of Andrew S. Dickey. We believe this is a daughter, although she was only 13 years old when she married. Adeline Dickey married George William Scott on July 1, 1847. We cannot say with certainty if Andrew Stewart Dickey and Andrew L. Dickey are the same — some things fit and some do not.

Jesse Thomas lived near the Johnson Shut-Ins, as shown by the 1830 census, with a wife and five boys. He died in 1833 without a will. The administrator appointed was his brother, John Thomas, the well-known Methodist minister whose parents came to Bellevue Valley about 1820. John Thomas founded the Thomas Chapel in the 1830's.

Edward Thomas, Jesse's father, died in 1840 and his will names the following children; William H., Edward, Jr., Jesse, John, James, Moses, Reuben, Elizabeth Fitzpatrick, and Jane Fisher. All of these children were born in Virginia.

Benjamine and Elias Neal, found on the 1830 census living near the headwaters of the Middle Fork of the Black River, have left no visible trail to the researcher. We would have to believe Benjamine was the forefather of all the Neals who lived on the creek that got its name from Benjamine or his descendants. We find in Washington County land records that Jesse and Elizabeth Neal sold land to Milton Goggin April 28, 1835. This consisted of 40 acres and the price was stated as $100. The land lay on Strother Creek. The marriage of Valentine Neal to Polly Sumpter on February 21, 1835, is found in Washington County marriages.

Gradually, the East and Middle Forks of the Black River in the 1820's got new settlers looking for a new life, a new beginning in an often hostile environment. Slowly, tiny openings were carved in the vast forests and small cabins came into view, dotting the landscape along the streams. The "Virginia rail fence" was evident around or near each cabin. Orchards, gardens and fields were planted and started to produce a portion of the subsistence needed for the frontier to survive. A variety of game abounded in the forests.

The pioneer life had a romantic setting for readers of American history, but hardship and deprivation was a daily reality for most of the early settlers. This hardy pioneer stock was equal to the task as they fought and conquered a wilderness that might have defeated a less determined people. Soon the fruits of their struggle were evident. They found time to socialize with their distant neighbors, to meet together to worship and give thanks to their God.

The West Fork of the Black River had not begun to attract settlers until after 1830, partly because the Maxwell Reserve covered the West Fork well beyond what is now Centerville. Jesse Lester, son of Daniel and Milly Lester, seems to have been the only family to take up land on the West Fork. John Jones, still single, lived near Jesse — as indicated on the 1830 census. Jesse Lester moved to his father's farm on the Middle Fork before 1840.

Along with the increase in the population came the need for someone to perform marriages, settle quarrels and administer justice. That responsibility fell on the justice of the peace. His duties were similar to a magistrate court today. William Cullen Love seems to have been the first justice of the Peace in the Black River Township, being appointed by Governor Miller in 1828. Others soon followed.

The southern part of the county was slower to get settlers in what later became Reynolds County. We do not have an explanation for this. The southern part of the county was generally better suited for agriculture. After 1830, some of the pioneers who had settled in the northern portion of the county resettled in the southern part along Logan and Webb Creeks.

The western edge of Madison County became a part of Ripley County in 1833, then eventually became Reynolds County. This would be the area north of Clearwater Lake on Black River. The Clearwater area was a part of Wayne County in 1830 when the census was taken.

The Mann family would seem to be one of the first, if not the first, to come to the southern part of present day Reynolds County. Jacob, Thomas, John, Andrew and George Mann are all found in Lincoln County, Kentucky in the late 1780's. Their relationship is not known, but they certainly could all be brothers, as Jacob would use these same names for his sons that are found in the 1830 census of Wayne County, Missouri.

Jacob Mann married Mary Arnold on February 27, 1788. George Mann married Mary Mansfile on April 14, 1791. Andrew Mann married Rachel Tucker on May 12, 1793. John Mann married Susanna Roundtree on June 1, 1794. Thomas Mann married Elizabeth Jones on August 29, 1785.

In the 1800 census of Christian County, Kentucky, we find Jacob, Andrew and George Mann. Jacob apparently was the only Mann to come to Wayne County, Missouri, and therefore become the forefather of the large family of Manns found in early Reynolds County. Three marriages are found, one in Washington and two in Madison County, of early Manns: Jacob Mann to Elizabeth Cavit on September 4, 1828; Issac Mann to Milley Lester on March 1, 1832; and Finas Mann to Deanna Duncan on March 25, 1835. Arnold, James, Andrew and George must also be sons of Jacob.

Another family that came very early to pre-Reynolds County and settled in the same area as the Manns was Absolem Randolph's young family. He had married Matilda Gorden in Kentucky in 1826. This was his second marriage. He moved to pre-Reynolds County before 1830.

In the 1850 census of Reynolds County, Absolem was shown as age 49; Matilda, age 45; Jennette, age 16; Sophronia, age 14; Andrew Jackson, age 11; and James Polk Randolph, age five.

James Logan has been credited with being an early settler on Logan Creek in southern Reynolds County and the date given was about 1825. We know he lived on Black River much earlier than that, but where on Black River we cannot be sure. On July 3, 1820, "James Logan on Black River" advertises, "he has taken up a stray horse" in a Jackson, Missouri, paper. He was shown as a justice of the peace in Wayne County on December 20, 1823, and was census enumerator for that county in 1830. The Logans came to the St. Francois River area early in the century, including John Logan, Sr., who might have been James' father. They all seem to be natives of North Carolina.

James Logan died in the 1830's. leaving a wife, Delilah, and 10 children, according to the 1840 census of Wayne County. A Delila R. Logan was married to Jacob Woolford on November 14, 1844, in Washington County. She could be a daughter of James and Delilah Logan, being named "Delilah" for her mother. Jacob Woolford is shown on the census of Washington County in 1850 as follows: Jacob Woolford, age 30, born in Missouri; Lila, age 30, born in Virginia; John C., age four, born in Missouri; and Lucy J., age three, born in Missouri.

Delila Logan being 30 years old and born in Virginia does not fit in our James Logan research. She may have been a sister of John V. Logan, who served in many government positions in Washington, Reynolds, and Iron Counties, including being state representative of Iron County.

A well-written and interesting article presented by Dolly Seal and submitted by Irene Hampton to the Reynolds County Genealogical Society on James Hampton and John Smith certainly warrants mentioning as possible families who came to pre-Reynolds County before 1830, although we could not find them on the Wayne County census of 1830. We quote here from that article:

"One such James Hampton can be found about the year 1820 with his recently married wife, Elizabeth, and accompanied by John Smith and his wife, Nancy, stopped to camp at a spring near the mouth of Sinkin' Creek. The time was late autumn and they were anxious to select a homestead and build some sort of shelter before winter. They must have land cleared by planting time in the spring and a good log cabin built as soon as possible. Leaving their young wives at camp by the spring, Hampton and Smith set out to scout the area for a few days and select a site for a permanent settlement.

"While the men were gone, Elizabeth Hampton and Nancy Smith did some scouting for themselves near the camp. They found Sinkin' Creek Valley wide and fertile, with a creek full of fish and much game abundant in the surrounding forest. A nearby cave and spring made an ideal refuge from storms and possible Indian attacks. It was a near perfect natural cold-storage vault for meat and other perishable foods. On the second day of the men's absence, the women stepped into a clearing. At one edge of the clearing stood a number of Indian wigwams. The place looked abandoned, but the women did not investigate further but hurried back to camp."

This story goes on to narrate the Hamptons' spending the winter in the wigwams and the Smiths' moving on to Pine Valley near the Current River. James Hampton is shown on the 1840 census of Ripley County and again on the 1850 census of Reynolds County, but we failed to find a John Smith.

Undoubtedly, the southern part of what later became Reynolds County had other settlers before 1830, but we cannot identify them with a high degree of certainty. The Reynolds County Genealogical Society, founded two years ago, will probably help fill this void. They plan a publication sometime in the future.

REFERENCES
John Carty and 4000 Descendants, 1979 by Jamison, Cauley, Bell and Jaycox
Genealogy of the Families of Copeland-Morris Baker-Barnes and Related
    Families, 1980 by Guess and Taylor

Bellevue Beautiful View, Bellevue Valley Missouri History 1763-1981, 1983,
    by Bellevue Valley Historical Society
Delsa Lesh, Ellington, Missouri (Stout)
Connie Stretch, Dittmer, Missouri (McNail)
Mary Ann Thornton (Rayfield-Goggin)
Clara Holland, Elvins, Missouri (Stricklin)
Glenda Stockton, LeMay, Missouri (Mann)
"Reynolds County Heavily Populated by Descendants of Pioneer Hamptons"
    by J. Loyd Huett
Faye Gish, Manhattan, Kansas (Johnston)
Juanita Randolph Daniels, Fresno, California (Randolph)

Wayne County grew slowly during the early 1820's, but settlers coming into this area soon increased noticeably in the later part of the decade. The path of migration to Missouri normally followed rivers and overland trails established by the earlier settlers. The Westward Movement almost always followed a direct east to west pattern as pioneers stayed on the same latitude as the state they had left. Kentucky and Tennessee mountaineers were in a big majority as the origin of southern Missouri's new settlers.

Some of these newcomers would find land and build a home a long way from Greenville, the county seat of Wayne County. Pressure would soon build to form a new county to meet the needs of the populace which had penetrated deeper into southwestern Wayne County. Ripley County, which was formed in 1833, would meet that need for the inhabitants of Black, Current and Eleven Point Rivers.

The area which would later become Reynolds County was getting an ever increasing population, as the West Fork of the Black River was opened to settlers when the Maxwell Reserve was finally disallowed by the second land board. The southern part of the county was also starting to attract a number of pioneers.

Marshall and Mary Williams Parks moved to the Lesterville area in 1830 from Britton Township, Washington County, Missouri. Marshall Parks was born in Georgia on August 5, 1794, and came to Washington County in a very early period, where he married Mary Williams March 17, 1822. Mary was a daughter of Theophilus and Margaret Williams. Their first born, Andrew Jackson Parks, was born near Potosi, Missouri, on November 13, 1823.

Eli and Mary Elizabeth Smith Shy also came and settled near Lesterville in 1831. Eli was born in Sumner County, Tennessee, on January 3, 1802, and Mary was born June 20, 1807, in Kentucky. They were the parents of Martha Jane, Alfred H., Sarah Ann, John W., Robert M., Elmina, William F., Mary E. and Minerva.

Most of the families who moved to the area which later would become Reynolds County were Baptists in their religious belief and a few were of the Methodist faith. Church services were held from time to time in the homes of the believers. Occasionally a traveling minister of the gospel would conduct services in the area.

The Franklin Association was organized in 1832. This association embraced the counties of Washington, Franklin, Gasconade, Crawford, St. Francois, and the southern part of Jefferson. One of their main objectives was to create new churches in this sparsely populated region. Elder Hezekiah Laseter's job, without a doubt, was to further this missionary endeavor.

The populace for the most part were humble, God-fearing people, who worshiped a higher form not only when a tragedy occurred, but sought divine guidance daily. So it would seem reasonable and logical to believe that when Elder Laseter started his efforts to organize a church at Black in 1833 that he received enthusiastic support from the settlers. We can only surmise why the community of Black, or Black River, as it was first called, was chosen for the county's first church. A number of its early members were from the East Fork of the Black River — a long way from this Baptist Church, which was recognized by the Franklin Association as a sister member in October of 1833.

Elder Hezekiah Laseter came from Tennessee to Missouri in the late 1820's. The name "Laseter" in its various spellings is found many times in the records of Tennessee, especially Wilson County — suggesting that might be the county of his birth.

Laseter's first marriage has not been found, but his marriage to Mary Holt on August 27, 1835 is recorded in St. Francois County, Missouri.

Elder Hezekiah left a will dated February 17, 1847, which names his wife Polly and children, Reuben, Jonathan David, Rebecca Simpson, Elizabeth Harris, John Daniel, Hezekiah, Jr., and Edward Laseter.

Hezekiah, Jr., married Lavena Harris on June 7, 1836. Elizabeth married Issac Harris on June 26, 1836. Rueben married Eliza Govero on June 15, 1848.

Elder Laseter performed a number of marriages in Washington, Madison, St. Francois and Ste. Genevieve Counties from 1831 until the 1840's. He was shown on the 1840 census of Berry County, Missouri. The first evidence we have of him being in the Black River community was when he performed the marriage of Redmond Black and Sarah Carty on December 24, 1832.

No record has been found of the Black River Baptist Church's first members. Not until 1850, when a new record book was started, do we find a list of the church's membership. Some of these members in 1850, no doubt, were organizers and supporters in 1833.

We quote from page one of History of Black River Baptist Church, compiled in 1969 by Mrs. Flora Angel Estep: "There were twelve charter members. The names of two charter members have been handed down through family tradition. One name was Mrs. Lydia Miner. The other was Mrs. Nancy Baker Miner. The importance of the association is often underestimated. Frequently, the associational records are the only records to be had of some of the churches that were established in pioneer days. For example, the statistics of Black River Church, as found in the records of the Franklin Association, are all we have of our church from 1833 to 1850."

No doubt the first house of worship was built of logs. Pate Buford, often called the "Father of Reynolds County," donated the ground for the site of the church house. Black River Church was often spoken of as the "Camp Ground Church" because a spring, issuing from the base of a hill, is located on the church property. We quote again from Mrs. Estep's book: "In the early days of the settlement of this county, travelers used the vicinity of the spring as a rest stop on their journeys to and fro. Religious gatherings, known as 'camp meetings,' were held during hot weather under the trees near the spring. Later, Civil War soldiers used the area for a camping ground."

Minutes of the Franklin Association name the pastor of Black River Church starting in 1838. Rev. Jesse Richardson Pratte was pastor from 1838 to 1841, and again in 1851 through 1854, probably in 1855, then 1856 to 1858, indicating he was well liked by his constituency.

Rev. Pratte was born in Tennessee January 13, 1804. He spent a number of years in Illinois and some records indicate he may have lived in Randolph County before coming to Missouri in 1837. His first marriage is unknown, but he married Elizabeth Gibson in Washington County, Missouri, on February 6, 1844.

When the Black River Baptist Church was formed most of its membership were not sure if they lived in the newly-formed Ripley County or still lived in Washington County, as the description dividing the two counties was vague and confusing. When the 1840 census was taken, the entire Black River Township was recorded as still part of Washington County — much the same as it had been since 1813. Ripley County was organized on January 12, 1831, but could not entirely meet the requirements dictated by the general assembly until 1833. According to the records:

"Be it enacted by the General Assembly of the State of Missouri (as follows) 1. "The County of Ripley, heretofore attached by law to the County of Wayne, for all Civil and Military purposes, be and the same is hereby declared to be erected into a separate and distinct county; and that all rights and privileges guaranteed by law to separate and distinct counties be and the same are hereby extended to said County of Ripley. 2. "The line heretofore established between the County of Washington and Ripley be so altered as to run from the southwest corner of Washington with the original southern boundary of said County, to the western boundary of Madison County: thence with said line to Black River: thence down said river river to the main channel thereof, to a point due west of the Cedar Cabin, as was heretofore established by law. 3. "John Howard and John Greggs, of the County of Wayne and Allen Dunkin of the County of Madison, be, and they are hereby Appointed Commissioners for the purpose of selecting the Seat of Justice for the said County of Ripley; and the said Commissioners are hereby vested with all the power granted to the Commissions under the law entitled 'an Act to provide for organizing counties hereafter established.' Approved January fourteenth, one thousand eight hundred and twenty-five. 4. "The Court to be held in said County, shall be held at the house now occupied by Isaac Kelley, until the County Court of said County shall fix on a temporary Seat of Justice for said County: and the Courts to be holden in said County, shall be holden on the second Monday in February, May, August, and November. 5. "All taxes now due and owing to the County of Wayne, shall be collected as though this Act had not passed. This Act to take effect and be in force from and after the passage thereof. January 5, 1833.

A historical sketch was found in the Missouri Archives on General Eleazor W. Ripley, for whom the county was named. We shall quote here from that sketch: "Ripley County, organized January 5, 1833, under the Authority of an Act of the General Assembly, was named in honor of General Eleazor W. Ripley. This American officer had no part in the history of Missouri; and, as far as is known, never visited the State nor the Territory before it became a State. Ripley was born at Hanover, New Hampshire, April 15, 1782; and died at West Feliciana, Louisiana, March 2, 1839. He was graduated from Dartmouth College in 1800, engaged in the Practice of Law, and in 1811 settled in Portland, Maine. He was a member of the Massachusetts Legislature 1810-11, served as Speaker in 1811, and in 1812 was elected State Senator. Ripley entered the Army at the outbreak of the War of 1812, and became Brigadier General in 1813. He was voted a Gold Medal by Congress for his services at Niagara, Chippewa and Erie. Ripley remained in the Army until 1820, when he removed to Louisiana and resumed the Practice of Law. He served in the Louisiana Senate and was a member of Congress from 1835 until his death."

The governor appointed Isaac E. Kelly, John. W. George and Silas M. Sininore as the first justices of the county court of Ripley County. He also chose Zimri A. Carter as sheriff. The three justices chose Andrew Lewis George county clerk.

John William George and Andrew Lewis George were born in Virginia and came to Washington County with their mother, Catherine Bryan George, in about 1819. Their father, John George, died in Botetourt County, Virginia, in about 1809. John William George married Sarah Peppers and Andrew George married Mary Jane Eidson while they were living in Washington County, Missouri. John and Andrew moved often and it is hard to determine where they were living when Ripley County was formed — perhaps in the area which would later become Carter County. Andrew George was elected county clerk in 1836.

Daniel Lester, who lived near Lesterville, was elected a justice of the county court on August 29, 1834, for a four-year term.

In August of 1838, the following men were elected to become justices of the peace: Landen Copeland, Thomas Armstrong, Charles Huddleston, Thomas Susk, Arthur McFarland, Abraham Laveale, William Lawson, Washington Harris, David Saurince, John Burris, William Capps, Thomas Burns, Whiley B. Green, West Maulding, Lewis S. O'Neal, Samuel Nesbit, and William Johnston.

John Brawley was elected in 1836 as Ripley County's representative to the state legislature. In 1838, Alfred Deatherage was the voters' choice for representative.

John Brawley, born July 16, 1789, in North Carolina, came to Ripley County along with other related families about the year the county was organized. He had married Easter Dickey — probably in Tennessee. She was born February 20, 1790. John had held county offices in Illinois and had gained the knowledge and experience necessary to represent Ripley County in the general assembly.

Researchers generally agree that James Crownover and his young family were with the Brawleys on their trek to Missouri. James had married Sally Jordon in Shelby County, Illinois, on December 16, 1830. Rueben and William Jordon, brothers of Sally Crownover, also came. They are shown in Washington County, Black River Township, on the 1840 census. John Brawley lived in what later became southern Reynolds County. Reuben Westley Jordon was born August 21, 1791, in Franklin County, Tennessee. He married Mary Ann Brawley on December 22, 1833, after coming to Ripley County.

Leanold P. Piles also came to southern Reynolds County from Illinois about the same time as the Jordons, Crownovers and Brawleys, lending credence to the conjecture that he and others of the Piles family found on the 1840 census of Ripley County may have come in this Illinois caravan. James D., John S., Josiah, Richard and Leanold Piles were living in close proximity as shown by the 1840 census. Leanold is the oldest member of the Piles clan and could be the father of John and Josiah.

In Ripley County marriages, we find the marriage of Leanold P. Piles and Margaret Roach on February 2, 1840. The 1840 census shows him between 50 and 60 years old and a female 20-30 years old. Ripley County marriages also shows a Margaret Piles marriage to Thomas Douglass on February 1, 1838 and a John Piles to Polly Douglass on December 25, 1838.

Living near Leanold Piles in Ripley County is Jesse and Matilda Fort Allen. They were married in Orange County, Indiana, on January 12, 1821. Allen had died apparently before the 1850 census of Reynolds County was taken. The 1850 census reveals the following: Matilda Allen, age 49, born in Tennessee; Lewis, age 18, born in Indiana; Charles, age 17, born in Illinois; John, age 15, born in Illinois; Soloman, age 12, born in Missouri; Jasper, age 10, born in Missouri; and Martha, age eight, born in Missouri. So we find a number of families living in southern Reynolds County who came there in the mid 1830's from Illinois.

James and Sina Huff Ellington came to Madison County, Missouri, about 1828 and may have settled in the area that later became Reynolds County in the very early 1830's. They were shown on the 1830 census of Madison County living near John Sutton, Sr., John Sutton, Jr., Joseph Huff and Nimrod Brewer. Nimrod Brewer was the forefather of all the Brewers in Reynolds and Iron Counties.

James and Sina Ellington were the parents of five children: Mary, who married William Copeland; Elizabeth, who married Lott Copeland; Harriett, who died young with tuberculosis; Artimissa, who married Patrick Reed; and John, who married Helen Thompson — their daughter, Sina, married James "Jim" Copeland, only son of Lewis and a grandson of Landon.

The town of Ellington, Missouri, got its name from Sina Ellington. In fact, Ellington was the third name it had.

When Thomas Barnes, Sr., brought his young family to the settlement on Logan Creek in 1835, he bought some land and engaged in farming. He built a water wheel and used water from Dry Valley Branch to operate the over shot mill that ran the wheel for milling. He also erected a small distillery where he made corn whiskey. The village was then called "Barnesville" for Thomas Barnes.

For some years the village was known by both Barnesville and Logan Creek. Thomas Barnes lived out his life there and died in 1857. When the first post office was built, it was called "Logan Creek." The mail was carried through Ironton to Van Buren once a week on horseback.

William Copeland, oldest son of Landon, owned a store there and marketed with businesses in Ste. Genevieve an St. Louis. Goods were hauled by wagon and ox teams and it took three weeks to make a round trip. The wagons going out would carry a cargo of deer pelts, other hides and furs, and, sometimes, tobacco. They returned loaded with brown sugar, sole leather, weaving cards, cloth, etc.

The village was destroyed in the Civil War. All houses were burned with the exception of one. After the war, in 1868, William Copeland brought his family back from Pilot Knob, built a crude store, and encouraged other settlers to return and take up their lives again. He erected a good grist mill and saw mill in 1870, which proved to be a paying project as was the only one in the country.

Soon after this William died, leaving the business in the hands of his sons, M.L. and W.A. Copeland. They cleaned up farms for a new town site, cutting timber and hauling it to their saw mill and making it into lumber. They took the initiative in seeing that the new town was properly laid out — and they changed the name of the town to Ellington in honor of their grandmother, Sina Huff Ellington.

William Wadlow, shown on the 1840 census of Ripley County as being 30 to 40 years old, was the first Wadlow to settle in Reynolds County. He and John Brawley, Sr., owned adjoining farms. Elijah Wadlow, who married Nancy Brawley in Ripley County on February 11, 1841, would appear to be a brother of William. There was also a brother Elish, who married _____ Mann and moved to Illinois and became the progenitor of the "Alton Giant," the world's tallest man.

Edward Sutterfield came from White County, Tennessee, to the West Fork of the Black River in 1839. About one year later, his son, William, followed him to the same area. William Sutterfield had married Dovie Tappley in Tennessee. The Sutterfields had lived in South Carolina before moving to Tennessee. The West Fork of the Black River was very slow to be settled and by 1840 only five or six families lived on the creek upstream from present day Centerville. James Sutterfield, who married Jane Campbell on August 8,

1846, and Thomas Sutterfield are shown on the census of Black River Township. We would venture to guess they were also sons of Edward.

Moses Latham apparently came directly to Missouri and Ripley County from Virginia — not stopping in Tennessee or Kentucky like most families did on their westward movement. The 1840 census shows Moses, his wife and nine other household members, supposedly his children, six boys and three girls. We can name only seven: Edward, who married Angeline Hillen; David, who married Emeline Hillen (a sister to Angeline); Nancy, who married William Vinyard on December 19, 1847; Robert, who married Hannah _____; Mariola, Thomas, and Moses, Jr.

Thomas Newton Bell and his brother Milton, sons of James and Sarah Newton Bell, according to family tradition ran away from home when they were in their early teens and joined the westward migration. Eventually, they came to Bellevue Valley in Missouri in about 1820. Milton married Jane Warner and stayed in Bellevue Valley. Thomas Bell married Mahala Cain, the daughter of Robert and Catherine Cain, in 1834. They moved to Black River soon after, where they lived for over fifty years. Mahala Cain Bell was born January 1, 1815 in Bellevue Valley, Missouri, and died March 30, 1893. Thomas Newton Bell was born about 1807 in Tennessee — probably Green County — and he died October 18, 1887 at Black, Missouri. They are believed to be buried in the Black River Cemetery.

The Reynolds County Gallahers descend from David and Lydia Warner Gallaher, who came from Tennessee to Bellevue Valley in about 1810. Like most families in this early period, they became parents of a large family of children. Only two of their children came to Reynolds County; George, who married Serena Miner on October 21, 1830, and Eliza, who married Samuel Trollinger. According to family tradition, David Gallaher was born in Ireland and came to Harrison County, Virginia, in about 1750. If this is true, he was much older than his wife, Lydia, who was born about 1784.

George Adams, born on September 13, 1805, and his brother William, born August 8, 1807, came with their parents, David and Rachel Koonce Adams to Missouri in 1833 and settled in what later (1857) became Iron County. There were seven children in this family, but only George and William moved to Reynolds County after their marriages. George married Charlotte Carty on March 9, 1835. William married Mary Radford. (Some records indicate Mary Parker.)

By the end of the decade of the 1830's, frontier life in this area of Missouri became somewhat easier. However, many hardships were still evident. Neighbors did live closer together. Wagon roads were found along most streams that were suitable for habitation. Two post offices had been authorized by the Postal Service. Lesterville was the first community to get a post office in 1838. Mungers Mill soon followed in 1840.

Before this, the families living in what would become Reynolds County had to get their mail from Harmony in Washington County, Farmington in St. Francois County, or Fredericktown in Madison County.

Starting in 1832, land was being surveyed and the early settlers who had been "squatters" could now buy the land they had improved for $1.25 per acre. Man had challenged the rugged Ozark wilderness and, after 20 years, the wilderness was slowly, begrudgingly, retreating to man's unrelenting onslaught.

REFERENCES

John L. Lillibridge, Hialeah, Florida (Parks)
John Carty and 4000 Descendants, 1979, by Jamison, Cauley, Bell and Jaycox
Black River Baptist Church History, 1969, by Flora Angel Estep
Missouri Archives (Ripley County)
Paul Reeves, Arcadia, Missouri (George)
Missouri General Assembly, 1812-1976, Missouri Archives
Sarah Fisher, Tulsa, Oklahoma (Brawley-Jordon-Piles)
Lois Buckner Sewell, North Bend, Oregon (Brawley-Crownover)
Jackie Parks, Burkburnett, Texas (Crownover)
Floyd Crownover, Florissant, Missouri (Crownover)
Glenda Stockton, LeMay, Missouri (Allen)
Old Reynolds, Reynolds County Courier, Ellington, Missouri
Althea Copeland Taylor, Temple, Texas (Barnes-Morris-Baker)
A Reminiscent History of the Ozark Region, Goodspeed, Reprint 1976
Robert Wadlow, Flat River, Missouri (Wadlow)
Mary Ann Thornton, Sedalia, Colorado (Bell)
Bellevue Beautiful View, Bellevue Valley Missouri History, 1763-1981, 1983 by Bellevue Historical Society
Billie H. Smith, Missouri Archives
Hazel Lesh, Ironton, Missouri (Latham)
Nora Reed, Poplar Bluff, Missouri (Laseter)
Jeannine Preston, Manchester, Missouri (Bell)

Pioneer families from back east were heading for Missouri in great numbers by 1840. The area which would soon become Reynolds County was getting a fair number of these new settlers. The wide, more fertile valleys along the major streams in the county were almost all taken. The families now arriving were forced to look for land in the narrow valleys and hollows where the soil was thin, rocky, and less productive than the richer alluvial soil found on the larger streams.

As the area grew, the need for a government more accessible to the people became a paramount consideration once again for the state government. Van Buren, the county seat of Ripley County, was near the center of the county, but a long way from the people who lived near the outer perimeter. Travel by wagon was slow and the roads were bad to impassible during the rainy seasons.

Shannon County was named for George Shannon of Lewis and Clark fame. He was only a lad of 17 when the Northwest expedition set out from St. Louis on May 14, 1804, in a party of 45 men. He was a trusted member, but became best known for the many times he lost his way, as he seemed to have a poor sense of direction.

He later became a lawyer and subsequently a judge, then a state senator in Kentucky. George Shannon died in 1836, being 49 years old.

Shannon County would alleviate time spent traveling to the county seat for the people living on the headwaters of Current and Jack Fork Rivers, but was not much help to the settlements along the upper Black River and its tributaries.

The official records show the following about Shannon County's formation: 44. John L. Pettit of Wayne County, Richard Britton of Madison County, and David Hanger of Washington County are hereby Appointed Commissioners to select the permanent seat of justice for Said County; and Said Selection shall be made as near the centre of Said County as may be practicable, having regard to the convenience of the majority of the population of the Said County. 45. "The Circuit and County Courts for Said County shall be holden at the house of Andrew McCane, on Jack's Fork of Current River, until the permanent Seat of Justice for Said County is established, or the County Court shall otherwise direct. 47. "The Commissioners shall each receive two dollars per pay for every day they may be necessarily employed in the discharge of their duties, to be paid by the county for which the service is rendered. 48. "The Governor is hereby authorized and required to Appoint and Commission three persons as Justices of the County Court, and one person as sheriff; and the persons Appointed and Commissioned, as aforesaid, shall hold their offices until the next General Election, and until their Successors are duly elected and qualified."

The governor, as authorized and required by the state legislature, appointed William C. Love, Landon Copeland and Alfred Deatherage as justices of the county court on February 13, 1841. He also appointed Arthur McFarland as sheriff.

Alfred Deatherage lived in the area that remained Shannon County and the 1850 census shows the following: Alfred Deatherage, age 44, born in North Carolina; Amanda, age 24, born in Tennessee; Newton, age 15, born in Missouri; Telitha A., age five, born in Missouri; and Jasper A.R., age 10 months, born in Missouri.

The three judges apparently could not agree on a county seat. No doubt, William Cullen Love, who lived at Edge Hill, was interested in a county seat that would best represent his district. Alfred Deatherage was trying to represent his best interests. Perhaps Landon Copeland, was somewhat caught in the middle, since he lived on Logan Creek. The records are not clear on this event, but we do know that on January 26, 1843, the general assembly appointed Samuel Hyer of Crawford County, Joseph M. Stephenson of Madison County, and West Maulding of Ripley County commissioners to locate a permanent seat of justice for Shannon County.

The first justices of the peace were: William Thornton, William Guilliam, Larneer Thorp, Ira Munger, John Gordon, John Brawley, Edward McMullen, Nimrod Bay, William I. Davis, James Crownover, Moses Brooks, Alfred S. Rider, William B. Cape, Samuel Nesbit, John V. Logan, William Hughes, and James B. Campbell. The justices of the peace were about equally divided, as about one half lived in what became Reynolds County and the other half lived in what would remain Shannon County.

When the elections were held in 1842, James Crownover and Isaac Bracher were elected and William Thornton was appointed justices of the county court. Samuel B. Wingo apparently was elected sheriff in 1842, but was killed on June 28, 1843. Marvin Munger was appointed sheriff on October 8, 1843. John Buford had been appointed surveyor in August of 1842.

Pate Buford, who lived on Black River and had married Arlotte Carty, daughter of James and Sarah Copeland Carty, was elected Shannon County's representative in 1844. He began immediately to push for a new county to be formed which would better meet the needs of the people who lived to the east and north of Current River. He was successful in the endeavor in 1845 and became known as the "father of Reynolds County." He served as Reynolds County's first representative in 1846.

REFERENCES

Missouri State Archives

Deep resentment and dissatisfaction were evident when Shannon County was formed and Eminence was finally, after a long struggle, selected as the county seat. The area that would soon become Reynolds County had as many or perhaps slightly more officials in the county government than did the area that would remain Shannon County. The 1850 census shows Reynolds County with 293 households and Shannon County with only 204 households. So one must believe this resentment had some merit.

The division would not last for long, however, as an effort was soon instigated to reduce Shannon County's size by forming a new county from its eastern section. This would appease the population who had felt betrayed when they lost in their efforts to have the county seat located more to the east.

Alfred Deatherage was likely the most influential man in western Shannon County. He had served as state representative for Ripley County and was appointed by the governor as a justice of the first county court when Shannon County was formed. The Chiltons were also early settlers who exerted considerable influence in the county as well as the state. John, Joshua and their father, Thomas Chilton, were all active in county politics as were other Chilton clan members.

Thomas C. Rogers had been elected in 1842 as Shannon County's state representative. Pate Buford of Black River would become the next representative in 1844; thus, the catalyst was finally added that would apply the necessary pressure to get the 13th General Assembly to create the following act: 1. "All that portion of territory included within the following limits to wit: beginning at the Southeast corner of township 28 North, range 2 East: thence due West with said township line until the same strikes the dividing ridge, dividing the waters of Black River and Current River: then Northwardly with the main divide of said ridge until the same strikes the Northern boundary line of Shannon County: then East with said line until it intersects the Northwest corner line of Madison County; then due South with the direction of said line until it strikes the beginning corner, is hereby created a separate and distinct county, to be called the County of Reynolds. 2. "Ayres Hudspeth, of Washington County, John Miller, of Madison County, and Moses Carty, of St. Francois County, are hereby appointed Commissioners, whose duty it shall be to lay out the permanent seat of justice for said county. 3. "The Circuit and County Courts shall be held at the dwelling house of Joseph McNails, until the permanent seat of justice be located or the County Court otherwise order.

"This Act to take effect and be in force from and after its passage. Approved Feb. 25, 1845."

The three Commissioners appointed were men who had gained some degree of respect and status in their respective counties.

Ayres Hudspeth had a long and successful career in state government. He was elected as Washington County's representative in 1834, 1838, and 1840, then became state senator in 1842 and served in that legislative body until his death in 1853. He was president pro tem of the senate from 1846 until 1852 and may have continued in that capacity until his death.

His father, George Hudspeth, married Sarah Harris and their known children were: William; Ayres; Ahijah; Malinda (Nathaniel Highley); Nancy (William Brittain Gage); and Lewis Calvin Hudspeth. George Hudspeth was Washington County's first state representative in 1820.

Ayres Hudspeth married Nancy Ann Highley and the 1850 census of Washington County reveals the following: Ayres Hudspeth, age 49, born in Kentucky; John, age 70, born in Virginia (this is believed to be an uncle of Ayres); Nancy, age 44, born in Virginia; George, age 20, born in Missouri; Susan C., age 14, born in Missouri; and James H., age two, born in Missouri.

Some records indicate that the Hudspeths came from Jefferson County, Virginia, to Warren County, Kentucky, before moving to Washington County, Missouri, prior to 1820.

John Miller is shown often in the records of Madison County with the prestigious title "Esquire" after his name. It is not clear how he earned this title. We do know when Iron County was formed a special election was held and John W. Miller was elected judge of the county court. The other two judges were John V. Logan and Moses Edmonds.

The Millers came to Missouri most likely between 1810 and 1820. John was born in Virginia about 1793 and died on October 29, 1882. His first marriage was to Sarah D. Harrison and this marriage produced seven known children. Sarah Harrison Miller died about 1832. John then married Margaret Matthews on January 24, 1836, and sired ten or eleven more children.

We have not researched all the records of Madison County, but there must be records that would indicate John W. Miller held political positions in that county in its early period. He was appointed and elected justice of the peace many times in Madison County, starting in the 1820's.

Moses Carty was born about 1794 in Surry County, North Carolina, the youngest of six children of John Carty, who was born prior to 1755 of Irish or Scotch-Irish ancestry. The Carty family moved to Cumberland County, Kentucky, in about 1803. While in Cumberland County, Moses learned surveying and served his apprenticeship beginning as chain carrier for surveyors and deputy surveyors. He married Elizabeth _____ probably in Cumberland County in 1812 or 1813. In 1821, four Carty brothers, James, Morris, William and Moses all moved to Missouri.

Moses Carty settled on the Middle Fork of the Black River and his farm bordered on Reynolds County's northern line. His children have been difficult to impossible to document. Sarah, Greenberry, William, James, Pricilla, Martha, Amy Ann, John and Nancy are believed to be his children. Charlotte Carty, born April 25, 1816, in Kentucky, who married George Adams on

March 9, 1835, would certainly appear to be a daughter as the Cartys and Adams lived on adjoining farms. John Carty, who married Martha Clayton on October 27, 1836, would also appear to be a son, as Martha would also be a close neighbor — she was a daughter of Beverly Clayton. The 1850 census of St. Francois County shows a John, age 16, living in the Moses Carty household. It would seem unusual to have two sons named John.

Joseph P. McNail was born in July of 1810 in Bellevue Valley, Missouri. He was the son of John T. and Mary McNail. His father moved to what would eventually become Reynolds County in the 1820's.

Joseph remained active in Reynolds County politics for many years, serving as justice of the peace and justice of the county court.

He was married four times. His first marriage was to Rachael Long on September 1, 1835. His second marriage was to Sarah Carty Black. The third was to Jane Strothers and the fourth was to Elizabeth _____. Joseph died August 18, 1885.

Reynolds County got its name from Thomas Reynolds, who was governor of Missouri from 1840 to 1844. He was born in Brecken County, Kentucky, on March 12, 1796, to Nathaniel and Catherine Vernon Reynolds. Thomas received his law degree and was admitted to the Kentucky bar. He soon moved to Illinois and rose rapidly through Illinois politics to chief justice of the state supreme court on August 31, 1822. He was married to Eliza Ann Young in Fayette County, Kentucky, on September 2, 1823. They became parents of only one child, Ambrose Dudley Reynolds.

Thomas Reynolds came to Missouri and Howard County in 1829, and would again distinguish himself as a very gifted man. He held many responsible positions before being elected Missouri's seventh governor.

Brilliance and success do not always bring happiness and, on February 9, 1944, he took his own life. He was 48.

Governor Edwards, as instructed by the 13th General Assembly, chose three men to serve as justices of the court. Landon Copeland, James Crownover and William C. Love were the recipients of this appointment. The governor chose Marvin Munger for sheriff and John Buford for surveyor. The three justices selected Colin C. Campbell to be their clerk. These six men, plus Pate Buford, who was Shannon County's state representative, would constitute the first county government of Reynolds County.

The three justices almost immediately began to carry out their designated mandate. This was no easy task, as the population had not been enumerated, townships were non-existent, and the geographical center of the new county was not known. The population was still somewhat more heavily concentrated in the northern portion of the county, and the commission had to take this into account.

After all the information was gathered, weighed, and evaluated, 80 acres was bought from John Buford for $100 and the county seat was to be called Centreville (Centerville) — even though no one lived on the entire 80 acres.

The going rate for government land had been $1.25 per acre and perhaps John Buford sold the land for the same price he had given the government after the land had been wrestled away from the Maxwells.

The book, Old Reynolds, in an article submitted to the Reynolds County Courier by Reva Gilmer for the Bicentennial Series, gives the best account of early Reynolds County history available, although some mistakes are apparent. We will quote their description of the county seat in its infancy:

"The third term of the county court was held at the new county capitol under the spreading boughs of a mighty oak which stood near the big spring. No house had, at that time, been erected at or near the new town. Hazel and underbrush covered the ground and the deer and bear could be seen at every turn in the trail that had been cut through the forest to the new county seat. Soon thereafter, however, a few lots were sold and two log houses were erected in the town, one on the north and one on the south side of the public square. A temporary clerk's office was erected near the spring and here the county and circuit courts were held."

(This article was taken from a newspaper dated 1901, so some of the places and names may have been changed by now. The article is one of four found in a family Bible of the late Henry Carter, Mrs. Gilmer's husband's grandfather, who at one time was collector in Reynolds County. Old Reynolds, pages 22-24.)

The first county government was temporarily located at Lesterville until the designated county seat, Centerville, could be prepared to provide the public building needed for the government to function.

The three members of the county court selected 14 men to serve in their respective communities in the important position of justice of the peace. These men were: John Brawley, Landon Copeland, Issac M. Cotton, Andrew L. George, William C. Love, John V. Logan, Charles C. Gatewood, James Crownover, Alexander Cox, Ira Munger, Edward McMullen, John Gordon, David Moore and William Gilliland. The date of their appointment was August of 1845.

The new county had progressed under the guidance of the governor-appointed justices of the county court to the extent that they were prepared to hold a county wide election in the fall of 1846 — certainly no small accomplishment.

When the election was held in August of 1846, James D. Morris, Landon Copeland and John Brawley were the voters' choice to be justices of the county court. Others elected were: Marvin Munger, for sheriff; Colin C. Campbell, circuit and county clerk; Elijah Wadlow, assessor; and Nimrod Newman, coroner.

The records show these justices of the peace were elected in August of 1846 for a four-year term: Jacob Copeland, William Sexton, John V. Logan, Phillips Mallow, Landon Copeland, Joseph McNail, Calvin S. Bowens, John

Brawley, Reuben N. Gordon, Edward McMullin, Jesse Conway, and David Moore.

The county court had the authority to fill any vacancy as justice of the peace that might occur. Nimrod Mason and Abiel Stricklin were appointed November 17, 1847 as justices of the peace. Marshall Parks and R. Pennington were appointed justices of the peace on August 10, 1849.

Other changes in county officials were Marshall Parks' appointment to justice of the county court on November 30, 1847 to replace James Morris, who was living in Wayne County. Joseph Ketcherside was elected as coroner. Gamblin Weeks became sheriff and Thomas Pile became assessor in August of 1848.

It was certainly appropriate and proper that Pate Buford would be elected as Reynolds County's first state representative in 1846. William Edmonston was elected in 1848.

Edmonston is shown on the 1850 census of Reynolds County as follows: William Edmonston, age 54, born in North Carolina; Elizabeth, age 51, born in Indiana; Argyle, age 26, born in Indiana; Elizabeth, age 14, born in Indiana; William, age 10, born in Illinois; and Thomas, age six, born in Illinois. Unfortunately, we know nothing more about this man.

We quote again from Mrs. Reva Gilmer's article in Old Reynolds (page 24):

"During 1849 the new county began the erection of a brick courthouse on the public square at the new county seat. James George, who at the time lived at "Log Town", now in Iron County, was the contractor. A man by the name of Stinger got out the rock and laid the foundation, the same foundation on which the present courthouse now stands. The house was completed and the county officers moved into the same during the spring of 1850."

James B. George, son of John and Catherine Bryan George, was born in Montgomery or Rotetourte County, Virginia, on March 21, 1798. His father died in Virginia and his mother moved her family to Bellevue Valley in about 1819. His two brothers, Andrew Lewis and John William George, were appointed to the first county government when Ripley County was formed in 1833.

James George first married Elizabeth Eidson, daughter of Henry and Mary Buford Eidson. His second marriage was to Lucinda Arnett, daughter of John and Elizabeth Arnett. James then married Mrs. Nancy Powell.

James George had built a number of public and private buildings in Madison and Iron Counties, some being constructed of brick. He died on May 11, 1871, at Logtown in Iron County and was buried on Marble Creek.

We quote further from Old Reynolds (page 24):

"In 1849 Collin C. Campbell, the County and Circuit Clerk of the County, resigned and moved away and a special election was ordered to fill the vacancy. James Crownover and James A. Slade were candidates for the position. The election was held on the 27th day of November 1849, a day long remembered by the people who lived there then; not so much on account of it being election day, as on account of the violent hurricane that passed over this county on that day. The trees and timber were twisted and torn up by the roots, blocking all passways and roads: houses were blown down and stock killed; also many people crippled. At this election James Crownover was elected. He qualified and at once entered upon the discharge of duties of this office. He continued in office until his death, which occurred about 1869."

A letter written by John H. Love to his family at Edge Hill in 1851 also mentions this hurricane. He was living in Johnson County, Arkansas, near the Arkansas River. We quote from that letter:

"That dreadful hurricane that passed Black River started at a large pond or lake on Pettagou about 20 miles from this place. In passed this place where I live and turned a frame house about half way round."

James Adkins Slade was born in Richmond, Virginia, on November 2, 1814, the son of John Westly Slade. James married Ellen K. Smith on December 10, 1839, in Sparta, Illinois. Ellen, who was the daughter of Dr. John and Martha Brown Smith, was born December 28, 1825. This marriage produced 13 children. A number of these children did not live to maturity.

James Slade lost in his political contest with James Crownover, but would later hold county office as justice of the county court. His son, John Westly Slade, would also hold county office. James Adkins Slade died on December 15, 1869, of typhoid fever. He was one of the early school teachers in this new county and was also postmaster at Lesterville for sometime.

The post office at Lesterville was established April 6, 1838, with John Amonett as the first postmaster. John Amonett is shown on the 1840 census of Washington County, living in the Bellevue Township. The post office was discontinued on March 22, 1839, then re-established September 14, 1842.

Munger Mill followed Lesterville with a post office on March 24, 1840, and — as would be expected — Marvin Munger was appointed the postmaster. This post office would continue until November 18, 1872, when the name was changed to "Munger." Two of Marvin's sons are known to have also been postmasters; Ira at Centerville and Moses at Munger.

Logan Creek's post office was established on December 29, 1845, with Thomas Barnes being appointed postmaster. The post office was re-named "Ellington" on February 12, 1895.

Centerville and Alamode got post offices in 1846. Alamode, a name that has disappeared from modern maps, was located in the Corridon-Reynolds area. The post office was established on June 13, 1846, and Henry L. Ligate was destined to be first postmaster.

Centerville's getting a post office in 1846 would indicate a population was growing in the area and perhaps the county seat was not completely void of people when the three commissioners selected it as the county seat.

We quote again from the Bicentennial Series, Old Reynolds, page 26:

"During those years John R. Middleton, who lived near the junction of the three forks of Black River, was elected constable, and for some years was the only constable in the county and frequently acted as deputy sheriff. He was a man who thought processes of courts should be served with a great deal of ceremony in order to make them impressive. He had a large bull that he always rode when serving papers, and, with his coon skin cap with a long bill, his bottle of ink made from barks, and his goose-quill pen sticking up in his cap, he went forth to conquer and command."

The records do not show constables being elected, so we would assume Mr. Middleton was appointed. He is shown on the 1850 census of Reynolds County: John Middleton, age 57, born in Tennessee; Agness, age 35, born in Tennessee; John R. age 14; Ephe J., age 13; Rachel, age 11; Wesley, age nine; Rhebecca, age seven; Allen, age six; and Mary, age four, all born in Tennessee. Catherine, age two, was born in Missouri.

Reynolds County had gotten a number of new settlers in the decade of the 1840's. A goodly number of these new families were German. They were especially adept at getting the most from the poor hillside slopes in the narrow valleys and hollows. All the government land had been bought in the wider, more fertile valleys. The families now arriving had to either buy from an individual or take marginal government land.

Many new names show on the 1850 census that were not enumerated in 1840. Some families came, stayed a few years, then moved on. Apparently they had not yet found their utopia. Reynolds County did not then nor now have the resources to support a big population.

John Barton came to Reynolds County in about 1845. He was born about 1786 in Kentucky or Virginia. He married Mary Earles in Pendleton County, Kentucky, in 1816. They lived in Clark County, Illinois, before coming to Missouri. Some of their children were: Rhode Barton, Sarah Blankenship, James, John, George, Joel and Squire Barton, and Nancy Lands.

William Copeland, born July 12, 1783 in North Carolina, married Margery Carmac in 1805 and spent a number of years in Overton County, Tennessee, before coming to Reynolds County in about 1846. His son, Jacob, who was born January 28, 1822, was elected as justice of the peace in August of 1846. Jacob married Sarah Barry on April 5, 1846.

Another new family was Jesse Andrew and Susan Weeks Pinkley. Jesse was born about 1828 in Madison County, Missouri, to William and Louisa Pinkley. His grandfather may have been Henry Pinkley, who came to Missouri very early and whose name is found in records of Ste. Genevieve and Washington Counties. Henry Pinkley is shown on the 1850 census of Washington County as 69 years old, born in North Carolina.

Some of the Weeks family came to this area in the 1830's and others came in the mid-1840's. Gideon, Garret, and Gamblin Weeks probably were brothers. Gamblin, who became sheriff in 1848, married Julia Jamison Carty, widow of Joseph Carty.

John Boyd and his wife Elizabeth Lester Boyd came to the county and put down roots north of Lesterville in an area still known to local people as "Boyd Hill." They had a large family of girls and only one son, John, Jr. Lucy married William Rayfield, Lettice married William Goggin, Martha first married Jube Goggin then George Bell, Sarah married James Mann, Milly Jane married Zimri Mann, Mary married Andrew Carter, Catherine married William King, Elizabeth — a twin to Lettice — married William Baxter, and John, Jr., married Drucilla Goggin.

About the time Reynolds County was formed, Joel and Anna Dennison moved their growing family to Little Brushy Creek from Cross Road, Kentucky. Joel was killed during the Civil War, as was his oldest son, James. The other children survived the conflict to perpetuate the Dennison name. Joel had two brother, James and Daniel, who settled on Ottery Creek near Edge Hill. James married Elizabeth Bell December 29, 1837. She was the daughter of John and Elizabeth Harbison Bell, who came to Ottery Creek, in St. Francis County ca. 1835. The 1870 census of Reynolds County shows Daniel age 48, Nancy age 47, Martha age 15, and Charles age 12.

Charles Ford was born February 14, 1807, in Buckingham County, Virginia, the son of Elisha Ford. In 1810, Elisha Ford's family in company with his brother Joseph's family moved to Knox County, Tennessee. Charles Ford moved to Alabama about 1826, where he married Iphey Grizzle in 1827. She was born in Virginia on August 19, 1810. They moved to Kentucky in 1847 and on to Reynolds County in 1849. Fifteen children were born to this marriage. Charles Ford was elected as justice of the county court in Reynolds County in 1857.

John V. Logan and Phillip Mallow, who were elected justices of the peace in 1846, were brothers-in-law. John V. Logan had married Elizabeth Hariat Mallow on December 13, 1832. Phillip had married Martha Miner, the daughter of William and Lydia McGinnes Miner, who came to pre-Reynolds County in a very early day. Catherine Charlotte Mallow, born June 20, 1808, was a sister to Elizabeth and Phillip. They were children of Jacob and Catherine Gortner Mallow, who came to Washington County, Missouri, in the 1820's. Catherine Charlotte Mallow married Joshua Carty on December 22, 1829.

We do not know the parents of John V. Logan, but, in Kentucky research, we found a John Venable Logan, which leads us to believe there might be a connection.

Recanny Pennington, with the unusual first name, was found in Campbell County, Tennessee, in the 1830's. He was appointed by the county justices as justice of the peace in 1849. He moved his family to Reynolds County in the early 1840's.

The Chitwoods are apparently all related, but they did not all come to Reynolds County at the same time. William Chitwood, who had married Cecilia Cotton, came first with his father-in-law, Aaron Cotton, in the late 1830's. Andrew Chitwood, who had married Elizabeth, another daughter of Aaron and Nancy Cotton, seems to have arrived about 1850. Hugh Chitwood arrived a few years later. He, too, came from Scott County, Tennessee, where he married Jane Nichols.

One of Hugh Chitwood's daughters, Cintha, married William Black. Another daughter, Delila, became Pate Buford's second wife. Their son, Henderson Chitwood, became well known and served four terms in the Missouri House as Reynolds County's representative. He was born June 28, 1845, in Scott County, Tennessee. Henderson Chitwood married Elizabeth Robinson.

Pleasant Chitwood is believed to be the father of William, Andrew and Hugh.

Another family arriving from Illinois was Caswell Warren, born in January of 1811. He married Mary Ann McKee and came to Reynolds County about 1845 from Fayette County, Illinois. He was a Baptist minister.

Tolbert Hackworth came to Reynolds County early enough to be enumerated in the 1850 census, but his son, Thomas, was shown as old three months old and born in Kentucky. Tolbert married Lettie Front on August 21, 1826, in Pike County, Kentucky.

Another family who may have come to Reynolds County from Pike County, Kentucky, was Jacob Helvey and his wife, Barbara. There are only two of his children we can be reasonable certain about: Barbara, who married Turner Hampton on May 28, 1840; and John, who married Serethy Bailey. Serethy was the daughter of Morgan and Pricilla Copeland Bailey, who came from Cumberland County, Kentucky, to pre-Reynolds County in 1821.

Jacob Helvey, found on the 1850 census of Reynolds County, certainly would be a likely son of Jacob and Barbara. He married Mary Hampton before leaving Tennessee.

The 1850 census would also suggest that Selina Hampton, who had married Jacob Brooks in May of 1832 in Clay County, Illinois, would also be a daughter of James and Elizabeth Hampton.

The Brooks genealogy has almost completely defied our efforts to prove their relationships. The 1850 census of Reynolds County shows Jacob to be 39 years old, born in Georgia. William, who must be a brother, was 40 years old and born in Kentucky. Elijah, 50 years old, was born in Georgia. This could be a census error on Jacob or William. It would be unlikely they moved to Kentucky, then back to Georgia, then, almost immediately, back to Kentucky. The Lear jet had not yet come of age.

Another problem encountered in this family: living in the household of Elijah, we find Micajah, age 96, born in North Carolina, and Rachel, age 100, born in Pennsylvania. The logical reasoning would be to think this was the parents of Elijah, William and Jacob, but Rachel is about 60 years older than William and Jacob. These families lived in southern Reynolds County and in the same neighborhood.

We also find a Moses Brooks living in the Black-Edge Hill area, born in North Carolina and shown on the 1850 census as 63 years old. Certainly he could be a son of Micajah and Rachel. Moses Brook's son, William, married Martha Rayfield, daughter of John and Nancy King Rayfield. He was born on January 20, 1831, and would represent Reynolds County in the Missouri House just before the turn of the century.

Tennessee was the home of John and Nancy Cotton Smith until 1843, when, according to A Reminiscent History of the Ozarks Region, published first in 1894 by Goodspeed and reprinted in 1976 by BNL Library Service of Independence, Missouri, they hitched up their ox team and came to Reynolds County, settling on Webb Creek. Then, one year later, they moved to Pine Valley, where they would remain. John was a son of Isaac Smith and Nancy was a daughter of Aaron Cotton. Nancy Cotton Smith was born February 13, 1821.

Isaac Cotton, who was one of the original 14 justices of the peace when Reynolds County was formed, and later, in 1858, became sheriff, somehow fits into the "Cotton clan," but we cannot be sure whether he is the son of Aaron or, perhaps, of Isaac, Sr., whom we find in Hickman County, Tennessee, in 1840. His wife, Christine, is most likely a Jeffrey.

We had indicated in this chapter that Henry L. Ligate was the first postmaster at Alamode, but a more careful check of the records would indicate John Gordon was appointed January 5, 1846, and Ligate June 12, 1846. In about the same time frame, Ira Munger was appointed postmaster at Centerville on February 2, 1846. George W. Robinson replaced him in April of 1846. Collin C. Campbell was appointed postmaster at Lesterville on September 14, 1842, when the post office was re-established.

The Mexican War (1846-1848) was followed with much interest by most Missourians, and many young men were eager to join in the fight. But Mexico proved to be a weak opponent, poorly equipped and with poor leadership. Americans readily overwhelmed their neighbor with only a few thousand troops, so many of those eager to fight had to sit out the encounter.

A limited search was made by Glenda Stockton to find Reynolds Countians who served. Even though a number of names familiar to the county have been found, positive proof of their service was not found.

Daniel Lester, from the Lesterville area, was completely documented as having served in the Mexican War. He was born April 1, 1822 near Lesterville, Missouri, to Jesse and _____ Brown Lester and died February 10, 1890. He was enrolled May 8, 1847, at Potosi, Missouri, by Capt. Augustus Jones and mustered in St. Louis, Missouri, May 28, 1847, in the 3rd Regt., Missouri Mounted Volunteers, commanded by Col. John Ralls. This regiment saw action at El Paso, Texas, Chihuahua, Mexico, and Santa Cruz de Rosales. At the latter place, a hard-fought battle took place on March 10, 1848. About

650 American troops were engaged in battle. After an all-day siege, the Mexicans were force to surrender with heavy losses, some 350 men killed.

Seven Companies of the 3rd Regiment were stationed at Santa Cruz de Rosales until July, when they were ordered back to Independence, Missouri, and discharged in October. Daniel Lester was discharged on October 19, 1848.

Daniel Lester's first marriage was to Susan Weeks. Then he married Martha Weeks Ledbetter on March 10, 1870.

We quote from A Genealogy of the Families of Copeland-Morris Baker-Barnes and Related Families, published in 1980 by Eula Venita Copeland Guess and Althea Copeland Taylor, page 397:

"We have the services records of Isaac Baker from General Services Administration, National Archives & Records Service, Washington, D.C., showing that Isaac Baker enlisted April 19, 1847, to serve during the War with Mexico. He was honorably discharged from the Army of the United States on July 22, 1848, by reason of expiration of service.

"Isaac Baker is said to have been wounded in the War with Mexico, and was in a hospital in New Orleans in 1847.

"A letter of Thomas Keeling to Nathaniel Baker, headed State of Arkansas, Madison County, dated June the 29th, 1848, informs Nathaniel, 'I received your letter on this day and Clark rote a letter here and said your son was ded and I can tell you nothing for sertin about it but Plesent M. Philips received a letter from Capt. A. Wood on the 9th of May and it said your son was well and was a brave soldier.' This report of death was erroneous.

"Washington Clark writes to Nathaniel and Hettie from Dade County, Missouri, dated October 12, 1849: 'When father went to Arkansas he saw Capt. A. Woods and he got Cirtificats for John R. Clark & Isaac Bakers Extery pay. father, Rufus & My Self went on to Bolliver the other day and Got lawyer Awter to make them all out and Father will send your affidavid and the directions How to get it.'

"John R. Clark penned this message to Isaac Baker on the back of his letter to Nathaniel (Baker), dated February 25, 1850: 'I shall now tell you some thing about My extra pay and yours also. When father was out in Arkansas he got Captten woods affidavid for me and you all so and I sold mine for eighteen dollars and lawyers said that he woould Giv you the same but you wood have to Come and assign your affidavid and I think that you had better come out.'"

Isaac Baker was a son of Nathaniel and Hettie Morris Baker, very early settlers in pre-Reynolds County. In fact, Nathaniel Baker, a 13-year-old runaway from his family in Maryland, came to the Bellevue Valley ca. 1813 with some immigrants. He married Hettie Morris about 1823 in Missouri and they reared nine children. They were in the Wayne County census in 1830, in the Ripley County census in 1840, and living at Logan Creek, Missouri, when he contacted his Maryland family in 1846.

Isaac Baker, born ca. 1827, is listed as "head of household" in the 1850 census of Reynolds County as 23 years old, born in Missouri. His wife, Sarah was 18 years old, born in Tennessee. Isaac died after December 5, 1861 — we have land records as late as this date.

Although we have no service records of John R. (Rufus) Clark, we believe these letters from which we have quoted (letters in possession of Althea Copeland Taylor) are proof that John R. Clark did serve with Isaac Baker in the Mexican War.

We quote again from the aforementioned book, page 375: "George Washington Clark came with his parents to Missouri about 1846. They were en route to the Lone Star State. His father was John Clark of Indiana. There were two other brothers in the family, John Rufus Clark and McAuther Clark. A daughter, Nancy Jane Clark, married Samuel Brooks on November 11, 1847, in Bentonville, Arkansas.

REFERENCES

Missouri Archives
Old Reynolds, Reynolds County Courier, Ellington, Missouri
Clara Moore Jacobs, Sacramento, California (Hudspeth)
Paul Reeves, Arcadia, Missouri (Miller-George)
United States Post Office, Washington, D.C.
Connie Stretch, Dittmer, Missouri (McNail)
Althea Copeland Taylor, Temple, Texas (Copeland-Baker-Clark)
Muriel Goggin, Evansville, Illinois (Boyd)
Mary Ford Southwort, Garden Grove, California (Ford)
Betty Tyre, St. Louis, Missouri (Slade)
Tom Caulley, O'Fallon, Missouri (Barton)
Riva Gilmer, Ellington, Missouri (Articles submitted from the Archives for the Bicentennial Series. They served as a nucleus for early Reynolds County history.)
Glenda Stockton, LeMay, Missouri (Boyd, Warren, Hackworth, Brooks, the Mexican War, and bits and pieces on many families.)
Barbara Smith, St. Louis, Missouri (Smith)
John Carty and 4,000 Descendants by Jamison, Cauley, Bell and Jaycox, 1979
Genealogy of the Families of Copeland-Morris, Baker-Barnes and Related Families, by Guess and Taylor, 1980
Marie Edgar, Potosi, Missouri (Hudspeth)

As Reynolds County passes from the decade of the 1840's to the 1850's, we find about 293 log cabins dotting the landscape. There were approximately 2.8 homes for each section of land — still plenty of "elbow room" even by pioneer standards, but not nearly as inaccessible and isolated as it had been on a few years before.

The 1850 federal census of Reynolds County discloses the county had 1,815 inhabitants, or an average of just under 6.2 persons per household. This census also reveals more heads of households were born in Tennessee than in any other state. The state at large would show Kentucky as the leading state. Reynolds County had 72 heads of household born in Tennessee, 53 born in Kentucky, 40 born in Missouri, 34 born in Virginia, 34 born in North Carolina, 21 born in South Carolina, and, somewhat surprisingly, only nine who were born in Illinois.

The average county size for the state is 611 square miles; We have 114 counties with a total of 69, 686 square miles. Reynolds County, with 817 square miles, ranks in the top ten in size. The "rule of thumb" criterion for county size was that every family should be within a day's horseback ride of the county seat.

John Buford was elected as the county's representative in 1850, 1852, and 1854. Thomas B. Harrison would take over the county's number one political office in 1856; Lucien N. Farris in 1858, then Pate Buford would again represent Reynolds County in the state legislature in 1860.

Pate and John Buford have been well documented, but the histories and genealogies of Lucien N. Farris and Thomas B. Harrison still remain lost for the most part. We do know Lucien married Nancy Hyatt on February 15, 1840. She was a daughter of Seth Hyatt, one of Reynolds County's earliest settlers. Nancy died in the 1850's and Lucien married again — perhaps to Anne Piles, but we cannot be sure. Anne is thought to have been the daughter of Leonard Piles.

Thomas B. Harrison married Minerva Dobbins after coming to Reynolds County. Both Thomas and Minerva had previous marriages. James Dobbins, Minerva's son by her first marriage, would later become the founder of The Reynolds County Savings Bank and one of the largest land holders in the county. He married Amy Ann Carty, the daughter of Moses Carty, on March 5, 1857. Thomas B. Harrison apparently sired only one child, Elvis, who married Mary Elizabeth Pratt, the daughter of Rev. Jesse Richardson Pratt, on October 20, 1853. Elvis would later serve Reynolds County as sheriff and collector.

The county officials elected in 1850 were: John Brawley, Joseph P. McNail, and Dale Copeland as justices of the county court; Gamblin Weeks was elected sheriff; James Crownover, who had been appointed by the county court to circuit and county clerk when Collin C. Campbell moved to Jefferson County, defeated James A. Slade for the office and would continue to hold the office until his death in 1869. Joseph Ketcherside was elected as coroner and Thomas Piles was elected assessor in 1848, both for a two-year term. Preston M. Speck replaced Piles as assessor in the 1850 election.

When the election was held in 1854, Dale Copeland and Joseph McNail held on to their positions as justices of the county court, but John Brawley was replaced by Joseph T. Mallory. Joseph Ketcherside was appointed surveyor until the 1855 elections.

The records are confusing. Many times only a part of the officers were mentioned when an election was held. This was the case in 1856 when only Charles Ford is shown as being elected as justice of the county court. Andrew Jackson Parks had been appointed by the governor as justice in 1855. The governor also appointed Aaron Rogers surveyor in 1856 and John Buford surveyor in 1857 before Marcellus Cozine was elected in 1859 to that position. Marcellus Cozine had a son, Benjamin Franklin, who later would hold office for many years. Benjamin F. married Margaret Bell, the daughter of Thomas Newton and Mahala Cain Bell.

In the election of 1858, Isaac Cotton was elected sheriff and Elijah D. Brawley, Andrew J. Parks and William Reese were elected justices of the county court. Here, for the first time, each justice was elected for a different term. Reese was elected for a six-year term, Brawley for a four-year term, and Parks for a two-year term. Now, justices would be elected for six-year terms, but staggered so only one would be elected every two years. This improved system certainly made for a more orderly transfer of county business.

Nine men were elected in 1850 as justices of the peace: James Brooks, William Reese, James Crownover, John C. Stricklin, John Brawley, William Copeland, Samuel Ligate, David Moore, and Morgan Bailey. The county court appointed Vance Callahan and Joseph Bay.

Robert Finn was elected justice in 1860, but resigned in 1861.

By 1850, Reynolds County had a post office at Lesterville, Centerville, Munger Mill, Logan Creek, and Alamode. James A. Slade was appointed postmaster at Lesterville in January of 1850. Marshall Parks would take that position in January of 1851. At Centerville, William Bowles was postmaster in December of 1852. James Crownover was appointed in May of 1854.

Looking at the post office records, we find only one new post office being created in the 1850's. Robert Edward Bryan Love was appointed postmaster at Edge Hill on June 10, 1854. This office was discontinued in 1863 and reorganized in 1870 with William Cullen Love as postmaster. Robert was now deceased and his father would be the recipient of the appointment.

The great potato famine which took place in Ireland in the late 1840's seemed to have little effect on Reynolds County's growth, but the county almost doubled in population from 1850 to 1860. Perhaps the Irish settling in the eastern United States would, in turn, influence citizenry of the established east to migrate westward for a new life, a new beginning. Other people from Europe, especially Germans, were coming to America in great numbers, which must have had some effect on the county's growth.

For almost 17 years, Black River Baptist Church seems to have been the only permanent church in the county. One would find this difficult to believe, so perhaps some records are missing. We do know that membership of Black River Baptist Church included people from East Fork, Lesterville, and Centerville well into the 1850's.

A number of the members of Black River Baptist Church, lead by Nelson Adams, broke away in 1849 and formed the Mt. Plesant Church, but the church survived.

When members were asked to come forward and sign the registry as being members, 29 responded. Undoubtedly, some members were absent. Those signing the church registry as members of Black River Baptist Church at that time were: James and Sally Copeland Carty, Jacob and Cynthia Fortinberry Stout, Marshall and Mary Williams Parks, Milton and Nancy Carty Goggin, Eli and Mary Smith Shy, John and Nancy King Rayfield, Green Berry and Elizabeth Carty Goggin, James Crownover, William J. and Margaret Caroline Love Goggin, Milton and Nancy Baker Miner, Sarah M. Bryan Love (wife of William Cullen Love), Lydia McGuinnes Miner (wife of William Miner), Catherine King (wife of William King), Charlotte Mallow Carty (wife of Joshua Carty), Lucinda Rayfield Parks (wife of Andrew Jackson Parks), Calphurnia Carty Buford (wife of Thomas Buford), Nancy Ketcherside, Arlotta Carty Buford (wife of Pate Buford), Cyrenia Miner Gallaher (wife of George Gallaher), and Abram, a black man.

Perhaps one reason churches were slow to develop was meetings were held in homes of individual members. Records of the Black River Baptist Church show church services were held in the homes of John Buford, Eli Shy, and William Love. Undoubtedly, services were held on the East Fork and West Fork in individual homes, too, since church members lived in those areas.

The population of Reynolds County grew from about 1,815 in 1850 to over 3,100 by 1860. Some of this growth could be accounted for by families coming to Reynolds County from back east, but a large portion was from population growth of the settlers who were already here.

One new family who came here in the 1850's was Joel, Jr., and Elizabeth De Gaston Buffington. Joel, Jr., was born in 1807 and Elizabeth in 1813. Both came from the area near Centralia, Illinois, and settled in the Webb Creek area.

William Dickson was born in North Carolina and remained in that state until he was grown and married Frances Cross. They later moved to Scott County, Tennessee, and then to Reynolds County, Missouri. This marriage produced 12 children: Hiram C., Nancy E., Temperance A., Thomas M., Mary A., William D., John W., Sarah J., Malinda C., Rebecca E., John C., and Amanda J. So William and Frances Dickson were certainly contributors to the population growth of Reynolds County.

Samuel Trollinger, the son of Joseph and Susan Plummer Trollinger, was born in Bedford County, Tennessee, ca. 1822. He apparently moved to Arkansas before coming to Missouri, as his second child, Harriet, was born there on November 29, 1845. Samuel's first marriage was to Adline Trott. They soon moved to Iron County, Missouri, where Adline died and Samuel married Eliza Gallaher. They are shown on the 1850 census in Washington County, Kaolin Township. By 1860, Samuel had moved his family to Reynolds County.

The Wilsons, three brothers and two sisters, came to Reynolds County in about 1856. Jacob, who had married Jemima Burgess, James Hasty, who had married Nancy Arnett Kindle, Jemima, who had married Elijah Forehand, and Mary "Polly", who had married Oliver P. Hill, all apparently came from Wayne County, Tennessee.

According to the 1900 census of Reynolds County, James H. Wilson was born in April of 1824 in Tennessee and Nancy was born in July of 1827 in that state.

Riley Wilson is shown on the 1900 census as born in Tennessee in March of 1830 and his wife, Elizabeth, was born in May of 1848. He had married Elizabeth "Lizzie" Copeland, without a doubt the granddaughter of William Copeland, who came to Reynolds County in the late 1840's. Riley was the third brother, but he may not have come to Missouri in 1856 unless his name was Riley Green and he was living in the household of James Wilson in the 1860 census.

Moses Matison Botkins married Elizabeth Gastineau on March 2, 1854, in Pulaski County, Kentucky, and four years later moved his family to Reynolds County, settling on the West Fork of the Black River. Moses was the son of William H. and Catherine Warner Botkins.

Very early pioneers to Bellevue Valley, Missouri, include: Rev. Robert and Jane Kirkpatrick Proffit, who arrived in about 1820. Not until much later did any member of the family come to Reynolds County. Two sons, James and Patrick, moved into the area known as Taum Sauk Creek in the 1850's. James had married Martha Ann Kelley on March 12, 1840. Patrick had married Elizabeth Ann Pullock on September 14, 1848.

William Moore, the son of Alexander and Patsy Barmer Moore, was born in North Carolina, probably in Stokes County. He married Mary Westmoreland and they came to Reynolds County in the mid-1850's. His brother, Creed Moore, followed him to Reynolds County. Creed Moore had married Nancy Kiser.

Slavery was a problem this young nation had faced long before Missouri became a state. The problem was not about to go away as most people wishfully, but not realistically, had hoped.

There never were many slaves in Reynolds County and the number had gradually decreased from 1830, when the area which would become Reynolds County had, perhaps, 80 slaves. The slave census in 1850, which surely in not complete, shows only 25 and the 1860 census show 39.

James Edmond was the largest slave owner in 1830, with ten slaves. John Buford had nine slaves and James Logan, if he was still living in what would later become Reynolds County, had seven slaves. William Street, Sr., had 18 slaves, but we did not include him as we do not have any proof that he ever lived inside the boundaries of Reynolds County, even though some of the people who appear to have been his neighbors later lived in Reynolds County.

Another somewhat large slave owner who lived close to Reynolds County, if not within its confines, was James McFadden, with 12 slaves. The Manns and McFaddens had some kind of family ties, as they migrated to Kentucky, where they were neighbors, then on to Missouri very early.

The largest slave owner in 1850, according to the slave census, was Jane Goforth Stricklin, the widow of Abel Stricklin. She had nine slaves. James Carty has seven slaves and William Carter had five slaves. John Buford is missing from this census, but we know he had a number of slaves.

In the 1860 census, William Carter had increased his slave total to nine. John Buford had five slaves. Richard Johnson had five. William Love and W.B. Brown with three slaves each, and a number of families had two slaves or less.

This hilly county did not lend itself to slavery, and, even though almost all its inhabitants were products of the southern states, slavery was never an important issue in this county. In view of that fact, it was a sad trick of fate that the citizenry had no say, no choice, as this nation gradually edged closer and closer to a internal war that would devastate the county.

REFERENCES

1850 Census of Reynolds County, Missouri
Missouri Archives Records
Old Reynolds, Published by the Reynolds County Courier
United States Post Office
Black River Baptist Church Records
Kathryn Vickery, Ellington, Missouri (Buffington)
Tom Caulley, O'FALLON, Missouri (Proffit)
Buford Family in America, by Mildred Buford Minter, LaBelle, Missouri, 1924
Glenda Stockton, LeMay, Missouri (Dickson)
Ozark Heritage, Published by Dent County Genealogical Society (Botkin)
June Wilson, Lesterville, Missouri (Wilson)
Lurena Volner Sheppard, Boss Missouri (Trollinger)

THE CIVIL WAR

Reynolds County began the 1860's with just over 3,100 inhabitants and 585 households. This would indicate there were a large number of young people who had been married for only a short time. Of those, 167 heads of household were under 30 years old. Another 117 were 35 or under. Tennessee still had produced more heads of household than another state, with 169. Missouri was second with 125. Kentucky was third with 74. North Carolina, Virginia, and Illinois followed with 51, 49 and 28 respectively.

In the next five years many of these young men's graves would dot the county's landscape with the recently disturbed soil that had not yet replenished its sod. A native field stone placed there by a friend or relative would be his only memorial. Many of the older men would also be doomed for a similar fate. Women and children would be left to struggle for subsistence on land that was so deprived of any food by the pilferage of opposing armies that starvation was a constant reality.

During the 1850's, the question of slavery became increasingly bitter and it became more difficult for the federal government to meet the demands of the special sections of the country. Cotton accounted for 57 percent of all exports. And of the 2.5 million black slaves, about 1.8 million were engaged in producing cotton in the South.

During this same period of time, immigrants were arriving on the eastern seaboard in great numbers, a source of seemingly inexhaustible cheap labor. When one worker was gone by death or disability, ten more were standing in line for his job — at almost any wage. Why buy slaves at $500 or more each when labor was so plentiful and cheap? This was the position of the industrial North. It could have eventually been carried out in the South, had not the radical element of the Abolitionists constantly stirred the emotions of the people.

Anti-slavery movements were active in almost every section of the country. The more composed individuals favored gradual emancipation with compensation for the slave owners.

The United States was composed of 18 free states and fifteen slave states in 1860. "A house divided, half slave, half free" were the words President Lincoln used to describe our nation's predicament.

South Carolina seceded from the Union in March of 1861. Six other states soon followed. Fort Sumpter was taken by the Confederates on April 13, 1861. Four more states joined the secession and the war had begun.

Governor Clairbore Jackson of Missouri fully intended to stay neutral and dispatched the following communique to both the North and the South: "Stay out of Missouri and leave us alone." The governor established a brigade for each congressional district and put a brigadier general in charge of each one.

The regular army under Capt. Nathaniel Lyon was upset to say the least at the governor's action and demanded a meeting with him. The meeting took place at the Planters Hotel in St. Louis, Missouri. Governor Jackson was not able to persuade Lyon of his intent. Capt. Lyon ordered the governor to disband the Home Guard or federal troops would drive them from Missouri soil.

Capt. Lyon having the authority and responsibility to make a decision of this magnitude in incomprehensible, so we must believe someone in the army hierarchy had received erroneous reports on Missouri's intentions to have allowed Capt. Lyon and Francis Preston Blair, Jr. — two well-known fanatical abolitionists — to control the destiny of Missouri.

When Governor Jackson refused to disband the regiments, Capt. Lyon ordered General Frost's command at St. Louis to be taken, which was done without a shot being fired, substantiating the intention of Missouri to remain neutral. As the Regular Army of the United States was returning to their barracks, shots were fired from civilians who were indignant at what had happened. The federal troops returned their fire, killing several civilians.

War had come to Missouri.

The federal government set up military control and undertook to drive the Home Guard out of Missouri into Arkansas. Calvary loyal to the Union were rushed to Missouri from Illinois, Wisconsin and Iowa and placed at most county seats to booster up the untrained Missouri Militia.

With the Home Guard stationed throughout Missouri, some atrocities were perpetuated without doubt to those loyal to the Union, but the revenge sought and rendered by the Union forces after the Home Guard retreated into Arkansas can never be excused. Men of southern birth and sympathy had to stay in hiding. Livestock were appropriated without compensation. Homes and barns were burned to the ground. The list goes on.

These stories reached the Home Guard in Arkansas and small raids were planned and held in southern Missouri to "get even."

We have chosen a report made by 1st Lt. John Boyd, 6th Provisional Regiment, Enrolled Missouri Militia, to illustrate a typical scouting exercise. This did not take place in Reynolds County, but not far away in Shannon and Oregon Counties. We quote from the record:

"Sir, In compliance with Special Orders No. 42, issued from your headquarters November 3, 1863, on the morning of the 4th instant, I started on Scout with fifteen men of my Company, five men of Company B and five of Company G, Fifth Missouri State Militia, in the direction of Spring Valley. Marched that day 25 miles, without discovering any thing worthy of note. Visited the residence of Benjamin Carter and Wilson Barrow, who were engaged in burning Huston; they were gone. Burned Carter's house. November 5, divided the Scouts. Sent 10 men under Orderly Sergeant Basket Company 1 to march by way of Bay Creek to Jacks Fork. I proceeded with the balance of the Command by way of Leatherwood or Wollsey's Trail; found fresh trail of horses; followed them on Jack's Fork to the residence of Miles

Stephens and brother Jack Stephens, whom I was satisfied were bushwhackers. Burned the house. Heard that Fed Taylor had been at Stephens last week with 25 men. Proceeded down Jack's Fork 10 miles, having marched 30 miles that day. Camped at Widow McCormick's Had positive evidence that the widow had kept a general rendezvous for Freeman and Cotemans guerrillas. On the morning of the 6th, burned the buildings. Learned from the widow's son, a young lad, that on the previous evening James Mahan had got him to give news of our approach. Sent back and took Mahan prisoner. Went down Jack's Fork to mouth of Mahan's Creek: turned up said creek on Thomasville road. Prisoner Mahan attempted to escape, and was shot by the guard. Camped at William Mahan's that night, (having) marched 24 miles. On the morning of the 9th marched up Mahan's Creek. About 9 o'clock discovered about 20 of the enemy on the bluff above us; fired a few shots at them, when they fell back. I took 20 men up the hill and reconnoitered, expecting to find them in force to give us battle, but they had fled into the rocky ravines and hills, where it is impossible to pursue to advantage, mounted; returned to the road and had gone about one mile, and met 3 men, who started to escape on seeing us; killed 2 of them, whom I ascertained from papers found on their persons to be William Chandler, supposed to live in Dent County, and a man named Hackley, who had in his pocket a discharge as Lieutenant from Company F, Mitchell's Regiment, rebel army. He also had several packages of letters from persons in the rebel army and citizens in Arkansas, directed to persons in Dent and Phelps Counties, all of which are submitted for your disposal. Two miles farther on we captured William Story on a United States horse. He was recognized and well known as a notorious horse thief and house robber. He attempted to escape and was killed. Camped that night at Morgan Dean's, on Birch Prairie. November 8 started in the direction of Houstin. Marched 5 miles, and captured William Hulsey, James Hulsey, William McCuan, and Sam Jones at the house of James Harris, all well provided and packed, going to Freeman. One of them had a horse that was stolen some time since from one of our men; also goods of different kinds. The first three, viz, the Hulseys and McCuan were killed. Jones, on account of his extreme youth and apparent innocence, I had brought in Prisoner. Five miles farther, at the house of John Nicholson, a known rebel and bushwhacker, we captured the said John Nicholson, Robert B. Richards, alias Bruce Russell and Jesse Story, all of who were killed. We then marched by way of McCubbins Mill to Spring Valley and camped at Wiley Purcels. November 9, started direct for this post, sending a few men by way of Upper Jack's Fork, and all arriving here in the evening, all in good health having been out six days, marched 145 miles, killed 10 men, returned 1 prisoner, burned 23 houses, recaptured 9 horses that had previously been stolen, and took 6 contraband horses and mules. All of which is respectfully submitted."

John Boyd. First Lieut. Co. 2 Sixth Prov. Regt. E.M.M. Comdg. Scout Captain Murphy, Commanding Post Huston

Lt. Boyd was raised on Jack's Fork in Shannon County, the son of James and Mary Boyd. He knew all the people in the area and he, no doubt, requested this scouting trip for revenge. As he stated, when asked to give a more detailed report, the following:

"In conclusion I take the liberty to say that these things were done by my sanction and order, and that I have acted throughout as I felt it my duty to do under the circumstances, being an officer of the United States, and knowing, as I do, that these men (with others) have murdered loyal citizens at their own homes, viz, Wilson Smith, of Spring Valley; that they captured N.P. Hackwith and Graham, while Scouting for this post, carried them to Jack's Fork, and murdered them, where they are now buried; that they have stolen and burned Government property, and also that whilst I was endeavoring to live a peaceable citizen of the Country, they have hunted me like a wild beast and tried to kill me for my principles, and that, were I again placed in similar circumstances, I would do as I have done."

Word of atrocities similar to those Lt. Boyd described would soon reach relatives and friends who were in Arkansas supporting the southern cause, causing emotions to reach a fervid hatred. Retaliation would be planned and normally carried out to "get even," to teach them a lesson. And so it was a constant struggle for the civilian populations of Reynolds County and southern Missouri just to stay alive.

Company C, 3rd Missouri State Militia Cavalry was stationed at Centerville, Missouri, where they used the courthouse for a fort. Their stated purpose for being there was to protect the citizens of the surrounding area, but the populace who had southern leanings were often victims of the military who were supposed to protect them. Company C was commanded by Capt. A.C. Bartlett from March 28, 1862, until May 13, 1864, whose home was in Louisiana, Missouri. John W. Hendrick was first lieutenant from June 2, 1862, until May 27, 1864.

Timothy Reeves, born April 28, 1821, in North Carolina, was a major in the 15th Missouri Cavalry (Confederate). He and his brother, William, had lived in Ripley County for a number of years before the war, where both were Baptist ministers. Tim Reeves' first marriage was to Mary Thomas, and his second to Ingealo Hickson on January 31, 1853.

Company N of the 15th Missouri Calvary was lead by another Baptist minister, Capt. Jesse Richardson Pratt. Jesse Pratt had been a minister in Reynolds County for more than 20 years, had children living in the county and knew the people and the county's terrain as well or better than any other man. So it would be logical and reasonable to believe, though we have not been able to prove, that Major Reeves made the daring raid on the Reynolds County Courthouse on December 22, 1863, with some 200 men — a number of whom were from Company N.

Reeves was so well informed of the daily habits and routines of the federal troops that he caught them completely by surprise as they worked building stables. Some accounts of this encounter say only one man was able to escape. All of Company C became prisoners of Major Reeves, apparently without any loss of lives under his command.

They immediately started their retreat toward Patterson, so as to get as much distance as possible before the news of the Centerville fiasco reached Pilot Knob.

Major James S. Wilson, stationed at Pilot Knob under Col. R.G. Woodson, was dispatched almost immediately to pursue the 15th Missouri Cavalry, believed to be retreating toward their Arkansas sanctuary.

Major Wilson, 3rd Missouri State Militia Cavalry, was born May 3, 1834, in Prince George County, Maryland. He married Margaret C. Bomer on May 25, 1856, and soon after his marriage migrated to Missouri and Lincoln County. When the first shots were fired at Camp Jackson on May 10, 1861, James Wilson wasted little time offering his services for the Union cause enlisting the next day. Major Wilson's report reads as follows:

"Pilot Knob, Missouri, December 30, 1863, Col. R.G. Woodson, Commanding Post, Pilot Knob, Missouri. Sir: In compliance with your orders of the 23rd instant, I left Pilot Knob, in command of 200 men, about 10 a.m. December 23, 1863, arriving at Patterson at 9 p.m. Left there at daylight on the 24th and encamped at Long's at 9 p.m., having traveled 35 miles. Marched again at 3 a.m. 25th instant; passed through Doniphan, taking a southwesterly direction toward the Arkansas line. Eight miles from Doniphan, I captured 2 pickets; 2 miles farther I captured one other post, and still 2 miles farther we came upon a rolling picket on patrol and ran them off the road, capturing 1 and compelling him to lead us to the camp of Reeves. Arriving at the Camp, I divided my men into two columns and charged upon them with my whole force. The enemy fired, turned, and threw down their arms and fled, with the exception of 30 or 35, and they were riddled with bullets or pierced through with the saber almost instantly. The enemy lost and killed about 30; wounded mortally, 3; slightly 2; total killed and wounded, 35. Prisoners captured, 112; horses, besides those of Company C, 75; also their arms, ammunition and Camp equipage. On the morning of the 26th, I started for Pilot Knob, arriving here about 4 p.m. on the 29th of December, 1863.

"I cannot speak in too high terms of praise of the officers and men under my Command. There was no loss on our side in killed or wounded. James Wilson, Commanding, Third State Militia Cavalry."

The Daily Missouri Democrat on page one December 29, 1863, quotes the report of Col. R.G. Woodson to Gen. Fisk: "Official dispatches from Major Wilson inform me that he attacked Reeves seventeen miles southwest of Doniphan, Ripley County, Missouri, about three o'clock Christmas Day; killed and wounded 35 of the enemy, captured 115 prisoners, including 13 Commissioned Officers, with all their equipment, ammunition and c, and 125 horses; also recaptured every man of Company C, captured at Centerville with their arms and c. Wilson says that the 3rd behaved splendidly, officers

68

and men."

The saga of Tim Reeves and James Wilson does not end at this disastrous and humiliating defeat of the 15th Missouri Calvary (C.S.A.) near Doniphan.

General Sterling Price, born September 11, 1809, in Prince Edward County, Virginia, to Puch and Elizabeth Williamson Price, was a worshiped hero to many in southern Missouri. Their hopes and aspirations rested heavily on his shoulders.

Sterling Price was educated at Hampden-Sydney College. He then studied law under Creed Taylor, one of Virginia's eminent jurists. He married Martha Head on May 14, 1839.

He had gained some military experience during the Mexican War, and, with the publicity gained from that encounter, he was soon able to move into Missouri's political arena. He became governor of Missouri in 1852.

The summer of 1864 found the Confederacy in total disarray. The ultimate collapse was near unless some grand strategy could be implemented quickly. The invasion of Missouri seemed to be one of the few choices available that had any chance for success. General Price's "Army of Missouri" was composed of three cavalry divisions. Each division was named for its commander; Gen. James F. Fagan, John S. Marmaduke, and Joseph O. Shelby. These three divisions crossed the Arkansas-Missouri state line on September 19, 1864, and the long awaited assault to wrestle Missouri away from the Union had begun.

Major James Wilson was still with the 3rd Missouri State Militia Cavalry, stationed at Pilot Knob. Col. Timothy Reeves was with Maj. Gen. James F. Fagan's Division, Col. Thomas H. McCaray's Brigade, heading up the 15th Missouri Cavalry, when Price made his assault on Missouri and Pilot Knob.

Major Wilson was taken prisoner in this encounter on September 27, 1864, and was executed along with six enlisted men of the 3rd Missouri State Militia Cavalry on October 3rd. Col. Reeves was, no doubt, the perpetrator of this cold-blooded execution. This vendetta between Wilson and Reeves would typify how bitter and emotional this conflict had become. Major Wilson had allowed, if not encouraged, many acts of brutality in Reynolds County, knowing that the county as a whole was pro-South.

Major Wilson normally had an officer of higher rank, most often a colonel, over him at Pilot Knob and cannot be held completely accountable for all the murders, plunderings and harassments that went on in the area controlled by the 3rd Missouri State Militia. However, some of these evils had to have come to his attention.

David Adams, the son of William and Mary Gooding Adams, was born in Jones County, North Carolina, in 1783. He married Rachel Koonce and they soon moved to Tennessee, then on to Missouri and St. Francois County (later Iron County) in about 1833. David and Mary had seven children who came with them to Missouri: George, William, Nelson, Daniel, Julie Ann, Zenas, and Mary.

Nelson Adams, born September 28, 1809 in Roane County, Tennessee, married Rebecca Stevens. This marriage produced 14 children and seven boys would serve in the Union cause. Most would serve in the 3rd Missouri State Militia Cavalry.

Nelson Adams and his wife Rebecca had been members of the Black River Baptist Church until 1849 when the Pleasant Baptist Church was established at Goodland, which was nearer their home. He had been a Baptist minister for some 45 years when he died on June 19, 1892.

With this background, father and mother born in North Carolina, he was born and raised in Tennessee, a faithful elder of the Baptist church for 45 years, we must ask what happened to make him dislike the southern cause with such all-consuming, burning hatred. This hatred was passed on to his sons and they, in turn, would carry on this crusade with an unrelenting vengeance.

The book, Bellevue Beautiful View, published by the Bellevue Valley Historical Society in 1983, states on page 361: "Uncle Morris Adams during the Civil War had the reputation of killing many men. It is said he killed two men on Black River and cut their heads off."

Morris M. Adams, born December 27, 1843, joined Company M, 3rd Missouri State Militia Cavalry on July 28, 1863 as a private — age 19, height 5'5". This was Capt. Hunter's company. Zenas, Daniel and Francis all served in Company M.

From the book, Ozark Heritage: "It was while they were returning from a Scouting assignment during the Civil War in 1865. After stopping to get a drink of water from the George Stricklin Spring on Neals Creek, that the 'Adams Gang' killed Samuel Trolinger and James E. Barton."

In the book, John Carty and 4000 Descendants, published by John H. Jamison, Helen Baker Cauley, James E. Bell, and June Jamison Jaycox in 1979, on page 35, a story is told about William and Milton Goggin being captured as they worked on their farm. No names are mentioned, but it is known fact that Morris Adams and a brother were the captors. On page 216 of the same book, tradition has been passed down that "Adams" was involved in Joel Dennison's death.

Some of these acts may have had some justification, as often family stories are biased and only tell one side. The point we hope to make is that the 3rd Missouri State Militia Cavalry and the 15th Missouri Cavalry (C.S.A.) made it impossible for the citizens of Reynolds County to remain neutral during the Civil War.

After Price's raid into Missouri faltered, recruitment for the Union became easy, even in Reynolds County. All resistance against the North was non-existent and the populace flocked to the North. This was not because they had experienced a change of conscience, but because survival was foremost in their thoughts.

After the war, Timothy Reeves seemed to have kept a low key "out of sight, out of mind" approach in Ripley and the surrounding counties. He had helped organize the Crane Creek and Butler Association in 1857. After the war, he returned to the area and served the association as minister and organizer of new churches. He died March 10, 1885. His brother, William H. Reeves, had died December 8, 1866, in the 53rd year of his life.

Reynolds County to this day has never elected a Republican candidate, even though the county is moderately conservative. The struggle was so bitter that, even after 120 years, emotions and resentment have not completely dissipated from that devastation conflict.

———————————

REFERENCES

Frank R. Hoggard, Southwest Missouri State College, Springfield, Missouri
Jack F. Mayes, Ironton, Missouri
Missouri National Guard Armory, Jefferson City, Missouri
Borderland Rebellion, Elmo Ingethron, Branson, Missouri
The Ozark Mountaineer
Sgt. Ronald E. Warren, U.S. Marine Corps (Pratt)
History of the Baptists of Missouri, R.S. Duncan
The Battle of Pilot Knob, Missouri Civil War Centennial Commission
Gen. Sterling Price and the Civil War in the West, Albert Castel
Dr. Don L. Margreiter, D.O., Chesterfield, Missouri
William Hogan, Ironton, Missouri

Henry Padgett, son of William and Mary Priestly Padgett, was born about 1752 in South Carolina.

Padgett, for reasons unknown to the researchers of this book, joined military service during the Revolutionary War under the name of Henry Fry. He enlisted with the 1st South Carolina Regiment, commanded by Colonel C. Pinckney, on November 4, 1775 as a private. It is believed he attained the rank of captain, but by what means we have not been able to ascertain.

After the war, Henry Padgett joined the western movement, first stopping in Kentucky before moving on to Big River in present day Washington or St. Francois County, Missouri. He, with eight or ten families, started the small community of Alley Mills (or Mines) in 1796. John, Andrew and Elisha Baker were a part of this settlement, as were Thomas and John Alley.

While living on Big River, Padgett won the admiration of Andrew and Margaret Vendler Baker's young daughter, Rebecca, and they planned a wedding trip to Ste. Genevieve to be married in the Catholic church where James Maxwell was the priest.

A number of stories have been recorded concerning the problems the wedding party encountered on their way to Ste. Genevieve. Each account remembers the incident a little differently, but we must remember this event was not recorded until years later. One description of this novel event is given here:

"Among the early settlers of the Territory of Washington County, Missouri, was one Henry Padgett, better known, however, as Henry Fry, who had settled at Big River Mills, near the eastern line of the county as it was originally organized. Miss Elizabeth Baker (name should have been Rebecca) was also among the first settlers of that neighborhood. These persons contracted to marry and, there being no Minister of the Gospel nor Magistrate then in that vicinity, it was planned to include a party of attendants and go to Ste. Genevieve and there have the marriage solemnized by the Catholic Priest. It was also designed to take provisions along for a good supper; and, after supper, have a dance.

"Accordingly, at the appointed time the wedding party, consisting of the bride and the bridegroom, five or six young ladies, and an equal number of young men, all on horseback with two wagons loaded with peltry, bear meat, venison, maple syrup, wild honey, etc. set out for Ste. Genevieve. All moved along merrily until they were near their destination, when they were halted by a band of about sixty Kickapoo Indians, who took from them the wagons and their contents and stripped all the horseback riders naked, except the bride on whom they left her undergarments. The Indians then bade them mount their steeds and proceed on their way, doing them no other harm. Thus the wedding party advanced, gentlemen in front and ladies in the rear. They halted in the timber near the village of Ste. Genevieve, where the bridegroom advanced to within hearing distance of the dwelling of a Frenchman in the suburbs. Loud calling brought out the Frenchman and to him a signal of distress was given. Being a kind-hearted man, he went to the relief of the intended husband. After hearing explanations, he returned into the village to make a quick canvass for clothing and soon gathered an entire outfit for the parties in distress.

"Being reclothed in borrowed garments, the wedding party entered the village and went to the church, found the Priest and the contracting parties were married as though nothing had happened; but the supper from their own provisions was not prepared, and, as the clothing did not exactly fit each individual, the dance was postponed.

"It is said that Padgett lived to a great age, considerably over a hundred. The truth of this narrative is vouched for by the old citizens who learned the facts from the early settlers living when the incident occurred." Henry Fry and Rebecca Baker were married March 12, 1797.

Another account of this story says Rebecca's two sisters and a brother were in the party. The horses, rifles, furs and other items worth over $1,500 were taken. The story also added that Fry lived to be 115 years old.

Henry and Rebecca Fry had two proven children, Abraham, born October 26, 1799, and Marie Marguerita, born January 15, 1802. It is believed that Tarlton Fry, living close to Abraham Fry in Liberty Township, St. Francois County, as shown on the 1830 federal census, is a son. The 1830 census reveals the following: Abraham Fry, age 30-40; two sons under five; one daughter under five; and his wife, 20-30 years old;

Tarlton Fry, age 20-30; one girl under five; and his wife, 20-30 years old.

Tarlton Fry is again found on the 1840 census living in Wayne County.

Henry Fry is also living in St. Francois County, but in Perry Township in the 1830 census. Henry Fry, age 70-80; 1 son, 15-20; and one woman, 30-40 years old. This cannot be Rebecca who Henry married in 1797, so we must assume he has remarried.

James Johnson, Sr., of Washington County, died and left a will dated June 7, 1833. He names a daughter, Nancy Johnson Fry. James Johnson lived in the Big River area, leading us to believe Nancy was the wife of Henry Fry, or of one of his sons, Abraham or Tarlton.

On the 1840 census we located Henry Fry living in Washington County, Concord Township. He is listed as being over 80 and under 90 years old, his wife 50 to 60 years old. Living nearby is William and Anna Hodges. Anna is almost certainly a daughter.

Henry Fry is again located in Washington County, Missouri, on the 1850 census. He stated his age as 98 and his wife, Sally, as being 62 years old.

On that 1850 census of Washington County, we find another Henry Fry, which almost certainly would be Henry, Sr.'s, youngest son. Henry Fry, Jr., is shown as 40 years old and his wife, Sally, as 35. They have three daughters: Polly, age 6; Rhoda, age 5; and Nancy Jane, age 2.

We now believe we have accounted for five children: three sons, Abraham, Tarlton, and Henry, Jr.; and two girls, Marie and Anna.

In marriage records in Washington County, we find Emeline E. Fry's marriage to George Sampson on September 18, 1832. In Ste. Genevieve County we find the marriages of Mary Fry and Henry Hampton on July 19, 1827. This could be two more daughters, but we have little proof. The "coffee" story we will tell later suggests that Henry Fry may have had other daughters.

Henry Padgett (alias Henry Fry) continued to defy what is supposed to be every man's fate. He is found again on the 1860 census of St. Francois County, living with his son-in-law and daughter William and Anna Fry Hodges. The census taker gives his age as 105, but if we are to believe the 1850 census, he would now be 108.

When present day Reynolds County got its first settler in 1812, certainly his motivation was hunting, trapping and trading with the transient Indians who came to that locale on hunting expeditions. Henry seemed to have made this his main subsistence since his early days in Kentucky. This remote, uninhabited river basin must have had a great number of fur-bearing animals.

It has generally been assumed that he, being a trapper and Indian trader, did not remain long in this one area, but a story appeared in the book, Old Reynolds, that would suggest he remained on Black River for a number of years, perhaps into the 1820's.

The researcher of this article does not believe that when Henry Fry moved to the Middle Fork of the Black River in 1812 there was another white settler within the boundary of present day Reynolds County. Andrew Henry, also a trapper, trader and adventurer, has been credited with being this county's second pioneer when he established his residence on the Maxwell Reserve near Lesterville in 1816. So the following story must indicate a period later than 1816:

"Capt. John Padgett (the name 'John' we cannot account for, but we are certain they are speaking of Henry Padgett, or, as he was better known, Henry Fry), who settled on the Middle Fork of the Black River, had been very successful in his hunting and trapping; and, as his girls were getting near grown, concluded to put up a large house. The logs were hewn in the forest and snaked to the place with oxen. The neighbors were invited for twenty miles around and, while the men assisted in erecting the house, the women broke flax under the shade of a tree and the girls were detailed to cook dinner. There were a score or more of bright blooming daughters, healthy lasses of sixteen to eighteen, plump as partridges and rosy-cheeked as the peaches that grew in their father's orchards, all priding themselves on their culinary knowledge. The bear-bacon, the turkey, the squirrel and deer, the cabbage, the turnips, the onions so dear, were soon prepared, but when they came to preparing the coffee, they 'balked'.

"Coffee in those days was a luxury, unknown to the younger inhabitants, as this was the first coffee that had been brought into the new territory. Mr. Padgett wished to give his friends an extraordinary entertainment and had sent up to Ste. Genevieve by one of four ox teams and had swapped some poultry for a few pounds of coffee. After a consultation among themselves, they finally agreed that it should be stewed with bear-bacon. So the first cup of coffee ever used in the new territory was cooked as served with bear-bacon."

This story would seem to indicate a period sometime between 1820 and 1825.

Unfortunately, we have not been able to locate a descendant of Henry Fry. And, without family records and traditions, we cannot honor Reynolds County's first settler properly. We do know that he had physical endurance few people in history have possessed. He was a fearless frontiersman, who always ventured beyond where other settlers hesitated to go.

REFERENCES

1830 Census St. Francois County, Missouri
1840 Census Washington County, Missouri
1850 Census Washington County, Missouri
1860 Census St. Francois County, Missouri
Goodspeeds History of Southeast Missouri
Lucille Basler, Ste. Genevieve, Missouri
National Archives, researched by Thomas Halloway, Fall Church, Virginia
History of Southeast Missouri, by Douglass
Missouri History, by Houck
Old Reynolds, Reynolds County Courier

# ANDREW HENRY

Andrew Henry, the son of George and Margaret Young Henry, was born on August 15, 1775, in York County, Pennsylvania. After leaving Pennsylvania, Henry stopped in Tennessee before coming on to Upper Louisiana in April of 1800. He apparently had some connection in Tennessee, as he returned there in 1802, but returned to Ste. Genevieve the following year.

James Maxwell, the Catholic priest at Ste. Genevieve, performed the marriage for Henry and Marie Villars on December 16, 1805. Marie was the daughter of Louis Dubriel Villars and Marie Louise Valle. Marie Valle's father and mother were prominent natives of Opalussa, Louisiana, where her father, Frances Valle, the Elder, was first commandant of Louisiana. William H. Ashley, whom Andrew Henry would be closely associated with later in the fur trade, was a witness to this marriage. Marie was Catholic and Andrew was Protestant. Whether this was a factor in the separation and divorce that followed we can on surmise, but they were separated on January 3, 1806 and divorced on October 15, 1807.

At the time of the acquisition of the Louisiana Territory in 1803, the only Masonic organizations therein were two lodges in New Orleans. Soon, a lodge was established at Ste. Genevieve. A number of French merchants in that place, while visiting in Philadelphia, had taken the Masonic degrees and, on their return, called a meeting to organize a lodge. Otho Strader presided. As a result of this meeting, Louisiana Lodge No. 109 was chartered on July 17, 1807, by the Grand Lodge of Pennsylvania. Aaron Elliot was worshipful master. Andrew Henry was senior warden and George Bullit was junior warden.

In the summer of 1809, Andrew Henry, a member of the Missouri Fur Company, was commander of an expedition up the Missouri River. Other partners of this company were: Benjamin Wilkinson; Pierre Chouteau, Jr.; Auguste Chouteau, Jr.; Reubin Lewis, a brother of Meriweather Lewis; William Clark, who would later be governor of Missouri Territory; Sylvester Labadie of St. Louis; Pierre Menard, afterward lieutenant governor of Illinois; William Morrison of Kaskaskia, Illinois; and Dennis Fitzpatrick of Louisville, Kentucky.

This company was well financed and all the partners agreed to make the expedition along with 150 men they hired. They left St. Louis and headed up the Missouri River with a large supply of arms and other necessities that were imperative if this endeavor was to be successful.

The party reached the upper waters of the Missouri River without any serious problem or delay. Beaver and other fur-bearing animals were found in abundance, and at first the Blackfeet Indians seemed friendly. For reasons unknown, the Blackfeet soon opened a relentless war that made it almost impossible to trap or to kill game the party needed for food.

Soon, as difficulties increased, the other partners and most of the men returned to St. Louis, leaving Henry with only fifteen or twenty men. They eventually crossed the continental divide to get away from the attacking Blackfeet. There they built a post on the Snake River in Idaho, which since has been known as "Henrys Fort." They thus became the first American traders to operate on the western side of the Rocky Mountains. Andrew Henry returned to St. Louis in 1811.

The War of 1812 soon turned men's thoughts and energies toward the British threat. The English government was encouraging the Indians to harass and generally to apply pressure in a number of areas in the Missouri Territory. Under this threat, the settlers living in the territory started to form combat units to protect themselves and their property.

Capt. Martin Ruggles of Washington County, Missouri, formed a company of mounted volunteers and Henry was mustered in as a private on September 8, 1813, and was mustered out September 17, 1813. The day after receiving his release, he was appointed quartermaster in field staff officers of the western army belonging to the Mounted Militia (and Rangers) of Missouri and Illinois Territories. The archive record shows his monthly pay as a private was eight dollars. As an officer, his pay was forty dollars.

In 1814, Andrew Henry served as major in the Washington County regiment of which William H. Ashley was Lieutenant Colonel Commanding. Also in 1814, Henry was selected juror on the first Washington County grand jury. The court sat in January and Henry was delegated foreman. Washington County had been created in 1813 from a part of Ste. Genevieve District, which had become a part of Ste. Genevieve County by a proclamation of Governor Howard.

Henry was still in Washington County on July 30, 1815, as he signed a bond for Daniel Dunklin for $10,000 when he was appointed sheriff by William Clark. He often signed bonds and counter-signed loans for friends. These sometimes proved to be mistakes. No doubt this at least partially accounted for his lack of money or property at his death.

It was about this time that Andrew Henry moved onto the Maxwell Reserve in present day Reynolds County, in vicinity where the three forks of the Black River connected. Undoubtedly, the fur-bearing animals that were found in abundance in this remote area were the motivation for his move to Black River.

This extraordinary man, who never received the recognition he so deserved, who seldom planted roots for long in any one place, married Mary Fleming in 1819. Mary was the daughter of Patrick Fleming of Ste. Genevieve.

How long Henry remained on the Maxwell Reserve is difficult to determine. He had bought two lots in May of 1818 in the town of Caledonia, when Alexander Craighead had the town divided into lots. We have no information that Henry ever used these lots to build a house. He may have remained in present day Reynolds County until the spring of 1822, when he again would head a party to the northwest.

Henry and his long-time friend William Ashley would form their own fur enterprise. Henry, with about 100 men under his command, again headed up the Missouri River in April of 1822. His partner, Ashley, was also in the party. They spent their first winter near the mouth of the Yellowstone. With the arrival of spring, Henry, with a portion of the men, pressed on westward, but was forced by his old antagonists, the Blackfeet, to return to the post where he has spent the winter. While at this post, word was received that Ashley had been badly defeated by the Arikarus. Henry immediately made preparations to go to the aid of Ashley. He joined his old friend in July of 1823.

Colonel Leavenworth was sent to this area in August to silence the Arikarus uprising, but his expedition fell short of accomplishing its objective. Leavenworth soon retired and Henry, with about 80 men, proceeded to the mouth of the Big Horn River. It was in this general area to the southwest that a group sent from the main party under the command of Provost had discovered the South Pass. In 1824, Henry returned to St. Louis, his keel boats laden with beaver fur. Even with all the adversities this party had encountered in the northwest, the expedition seemed to be profitable.

After a time lapse, we again find Henry back in Washington County. He may have returned to the northwest in 1824, as his partner, William Ashley, apparently had not yet returned.

Family tradition says that Ashley and Henry were successful in their joint venture, yet Henry spent his remaining years working the shallow mines of Harmony Township, Washington County.

Major Andrew Henry was a man much respected for his honesty, intelligence and enterprise, but loyalty to his friends apparently cost him the material benefit of his labor and he died intestate in Harmony Township, Washington County, Missouri, on June 10, 1833, with little money or property.

The 1830 census locates Henry living in Harmony Township. The census reports: Henry, Andrew, age 40-50; one boy, under five; one girl 10-15; and wife 20-30.

The 1840 census of Washington County reveals: Mrs. Mary Henry, age 40-50; one boy under five; one boy, five to 10; one boy 10-15; on girl 10-15; and one girl 20-30 (cannot account for boy under five).

Jane, the oldest daughter, who was born on February 19, 1820, married Robert Cain, Jr., on January 13, 1842. Robert was the son of Robert and Catherine Cain, who came to Bellevue Valley about 1814, probably from Hayward County, North Carolina. Robert and Jane Henry Cain had three known children; Mary C., Andrew, and Patrick B. Jane Henry Cain died July 10, 1868, and was buried in the Methodist Cemetery at Caledonia, Missouri.

George B. Henry, born February 3, 1830, married Angeline Harris. Angeline, born January 19, 1831, was a daughter of Ranklin and Vicy Breckenridge Harris. George and Angeline Henry had five daughters: Georganna, Lucetta, Nevada, Carrie and Grace. George Henry died February 20, 1867 while working in the mines near Palmer, Missouri, and was buried in the Bellevue Presbyterian Cemetery, as were his wife and three of his daughters.

Mary Henry, born about 1832, married John A. Harris, a son of Ranklin Harris. She died very young, leaving two small children, Firman and Ava.

We have no data on Patrick Henry, and Missouri Henry died as an infant.

———————————

REFERENCES

Adelle Breckenridge Moore's research was furnished by her daughter Clara Moore Jacobs of Sacramento, California. Adella was "the authority" on Washington County before her death in 1957.

Missouri Day by Day, State Historical Society of Missouri

American Fur Traders of Far West, H.M. Chittenden

Three Years Among the Indians and Mexicans, Thomas James

Historical Society of York, Pennsylvania

United States Archives, researched by Thomas Holloway, Falls Church, Virginia

1830 and 1840 Federal Census, Washington County, Missouri

Methodist and Presbyterian Cemeteries, Caledonia, Missouri

Iron County Register Newspaper (1939)

History of Missouri, Houck

Lucill Basler, Ste. Genevieve, Missouri

LANDON COPELAND

Landon Copeland was a pioneer to Washington County, Missouri, who was later appointed by the governor of Missouri to serve on the first county court of the newly formed Reynolds County, which was formed by an act of the Missouri General Assembly on February 25, 1845. He was one of "three discreet persons" appointed as justices of the county court to further advance the development of the new county. Seven pioneers were appointed at this time and they formed the first government of Reynolds County. The county progressed as expected under their guidance. When the first election was held on August 17, 1846, Landon Copeland was one of the elected justices of the county court, for a four-year term.

Landon Copeland, born April 3, 1796, in Winston Salem, Surry County, North Carolina, was a son of Lot (Lott) and Amy Ann Copeland, natives of North Carolina. As far as our research has revealed, Lot Copeland was a pioneer to Washington County, Missouri, in about 1820. He descended from John (Jo.) Copeland born 1616 in Dolphin Leigh, England, who came as a missionary of the Quakers to Plymouth Colony, Massachusetts, on the "Speedwell" in 1656, who was whipped and driven from the colony for his religion.

He and others of the Copeland family later settled in Isle of Wight County, Virginia, which lies in the extreme southeastern portion of the state, between the James River and the present day North Carolina line. The Copelands later moved into North Carolina, many of them in Chatham and Surry Counties.

John Copeland is found in the 1800 Census of Surry County, with a wife, one male under 10, one male 10-16 years old, two males 16-26, two females under 10, and two females 10-16 in his household. These eight children would have been his youngest. His son, Lot, was listed with three males under ten. Two of these would have been Landon, born in 1796, and Cary, born in 1800. John's daughter, Sarah (Sally), had married James Carty in 1797 in Surry County.

It seems likely the John Copeland family and the John Carty family were neighbors and friends in Surry County, North Carolina. It has been said that John Copeland was born about 1748, a son of William Copeland, and raised in North Carolina, married young and settled before 1800 in Surry County. It is known that John Carty was in Surry County on August 11, 1774, for the birth of his eldest son, James Carty.

Landon Copeland was still a young lad in the early 1800's when his parents, with other relatives, moved into the new territory of Cumberland County, Kentucky, where they are found in that county's land records for some fifteen years. These land records of Copeland and Carty Deeds show them all together there on the Cumberland River. The Carty family information reveals they left there about 1820-21 and came to Washington County, Missouri, settling in the Black-Edge Hill area.

Landon was the oldest of the ten children believed to have been born to Lot and Amy Ann Copeland. Eight boys are listed in some research information, but we have names for only four: Landon, Cary, Dale and Moses are usually found in the Copeland-Carty family information. Landon, Cary and Dale, born in 1796, 1800, and 1805 respectively, were born in Surry County, North Carolina. (The birthplace of Cary is shown as North Carolina in the 1850 census of Wayne County, Benton Township.) Moses was born in Kentucky about 1810. The fifth and sixth children were the only daughters, Pricilla and Sarah.

Pricilla Copeland, born in 1804 in Kentucky, married Morgan D. Bailey, born ca. 1792 in Virginia. He was probably a son of William Bailey, who was shown in the 1810 census of Cumberland County, Kentucky, with one male under 10, one male 10-16, one male 16-26, one male 26-45, and one male over 45. William Bailey was found in survey records several times in the 1815-1818 period. Morgan and Pricilla Baily named their first son William. He was born about 1821 in Kentucky and the family accompanied the Copelands and Cartys to Washington County, Missouri. They were in Missouri in 1825 when their second child, Serenthy, was born. Their other five children were: Mogan D., born ca. 1832; Moses and Merret, twin sons, born ca. 1834; James, born ca. 1841, and Pincknig, born ca. 1846. All were born in Missouri.

Sarah Copeland, born in 1810 in Kentucky, married James "Jim" Webb, born 1803 in Tennessee. Family #261 in the 1850 census of Reynolds County lists: Webb, James, 47, born in Tennessee; Sarah, 40, born in Kentucky; Lott, 22, born in Missouri; Pricilla, 17, born in Missouri; Cary, 13, born in Missouri; Richard, 11, born in Missouri; Amy Ann, eight, born in Missouri; and Polly, two months, born in Missouri. Family #260 lists: Webb, John P., 24, born in Missouri; Sarah, 21, born in Missouri; James, two, born in Missouri; and William, one month, born in Missouri. Family #262 lists: Webb, John W., 24, born in Missouri; Elizabeth, 22, born in Missouri; Lucy Jane, three, born in Missouri; and Sarah E., six months, born in Missouri. It is probable that John P. and John W. are twin sons of James and Sarah Webb.

Cary James Webb, 1837-1865, married Ruth McNeal, daughter of Joseph John McNeal, and they farmed in Logan Township. They had two sons: John T., 1864-1930, who married Lou Pennington; and they had Floyd L., 1902-1950, who married Anna May Castile. Della, 1905-1975, married Dwight Louisda; and Joseph Andrew, 1865-1945, married Lucy Frances Morton. Cary James Webb was taken prisoner in the Civil War and died of measles. His widow married William McCarty eleven years after Cary died.

Landon Copeland married Elizabeth Johnston in the early 1820's. The exact date is not known, but their oldest son, William, was born March 1, 1825. Elizabeth's parentage has not been ascertained, but we believe her parents were John and Frances Johnston, who brought their family to Missouri about 1800 and their son Reubin was born in eastern Missouri in 1806. By family tradition, they had come from Georgia and were in the St. Louis District of Missouri before coming to Washington County. From family records they are known to have been in Washington County near the Johnston Mountain in the early 1820's. John Johnston died in 1827, but Frances Johnston, age 74, was listed with the family of Dale and Celinda Copeland on the 1850 census of Reynolds County. It is believed she was Celinda's mother. Dale was Landon Copeland's brother.

Elizabeth Johnston Copeland, born ca. 1800, and her sister Emaline, born ca. 1817, and married to George Washington Mills, would certainly appear to be daughters of John and Frances Johnston. Yet they are not found in family Bible records kept by later generations of the John Johnston family.

The Copelands moved into what is known today as southern Reynolds County in about 1830 when land on Logan Creek was being settled by home seekers. No records are found of Lot Copeland taking land. It is not known whether Amy Ann was still living. The land that Landon homesteaded was a large and fertile farm where he raised his large family, many of whom are buried in the family cemetery near the home site. It is impossible to tell how many graves are there, as stones are moved about. In October of 1977, there were only three professionally-made tombstones there. Those were at the graves of William Copeland, Landon's eldest son, William's second wife, Margaret Elizabeth Tubbs Copeland, and their son, Harry F. Copeland. Those three were buried there in in 1877 and the inscriptions were still readable enough to photograph well. Landon and Elizabeth are buried there, as is his father, Lot, who died in 1850. Also, the second son, Lot, born in 1827, and Lewis, last child of the first marriage, who was killed by bushwhackers during the Civil War.

The farm Landon Copeland homesteaded was in the Mills Settlement just east of present day Ellington. Rough sketches of this settlement show some early families who homesteaded down Logan Creek from Barnesville and Ellington were: Thorntons, Bowers, John Mills, Lafe Mills, Bascom Mills, George Morris, Dallas Johnson, Landon Copeland, and Jake Goodson. Hamp Angel, father of Mrs. Flora Angel Estep, did not homestead, but brought his family to the settlement about 1894. Mrs. Estep attended the Mills School and knew these families. She wrote A Reminiscent History of Mills School, Reynolds County, Missouri in 1972. It is well worth reading!

George Washington and Emaline Johnston Mills, who were married April 28, 1836, in Washington County by Andrew Goforth, J.P., deeded the land to the school directors of Point Pleasant School, District No. 2, for the school on September 14, 1878. It was called the "Mills School."

The Mills family is said to have been one of the first to homestead land on Logan Creek. The farm of G.W. and Emaline Johnston Mills on Logan Creek was patented in 1839, but most of the homesteaded land there was patented on

September 10, 1859. "When it was opened for patent, many neighbors went together to claim land. Some of them had lived on the land and had cabins," according to Delsa Lesh's files. "It is said that almost every piece of land here was watered by a clear spring, hence the reason for choosing home sites."

Another cemetery is located in the Mills Settlement. The Morris Cemetery near the sites of the George Morris and Jake Goodson farms and adjoining the Mills properties. Mrs. Hannah Morris Thornton Copeland, second wife of Landon, is thought by some to have been buried there, near her son, William "Billy" Thornton.

Elizabeth Johnston Copeland died February 19, 1837, at the birth of their sixth child. Their children were: William, born on March 1, 1825; Lot, born on June 7, 1827; Mary, born on July 9, 1830; James, born on August 21, 1831; Sarah Ann, born on May 21, 1836 (married Lafayette Carty on January 18, 1857); and Lewis, born February 17 or 19, 1837. All were born in Missouri.

Landon Copeland married again on September 24, 1837, in Ripley County. He married Mrs. Hannah Morris Thornton, born May 22, 1801, in Kentucky, widow of _____ Thornton (His Christian name may have been William), who had five Thornton children: Allen, born on March 1, 1820; William "Billy", born on April 12, 1823, in Indiana; July Mirien, born on May 10, 1825 (married Isiah Daniels on March 15, 1840); Jane, born ca. 1832 in Missouri, according to the 1850 Reynolds County census (married Samuel Hanger, born in 1822 in Virginia, ca. 1850); and Van B., born ca. 1834 in Ripley County. This information is found in the family Bible of Samuel Copeland, which may have originally belonged to his mother, Hannah Morris Thornton Copeland.

Caleb, George and Joshua Morris were brothers who migrated from Kentucky to southeastern Missouri in the early 1800's. Census records show they were in Missouri by about 1830, earliest birth records and that they came from Kentucky. We did not pursue research on Caleb Morris, who is said to have gone to Salem, Missouri. We have record that Joshua Morris was married in Ripley County in 1838.

George Morris, born about 1803 in Kentucky, patented land on Logan Creek on which his descendants are said to have lived a century or longer. He married on October 16, 1828, Nancy Harris, born ca. 1806 in Tennessee. Their marriage is recorded in Washington County, Missouri, marriages 1815-1850. This marriage produced 12 children, of whom many descendants are still living in Reynolds County today.

We know that Hannah Morris Thornton Copeland and Hettie Morris, who married Nathaniel Baker, were sisters of Caleb, George and Joshua Morris, but we have been unable to establish their parentage. A letter dated September 5, 1847, written by Landon and Hannah Copeland and George and Nancy Morris to Nathaniel and Hettie Baker mentions other members of the family and early places of residence in the county — crops, the economy of the area, etc. It also mentions an Abraham Morris who must be a family member. Isaac Baker, son of Hettie and Nathaniel, speaks of "Uncle Abraham Morris" in a letter to his father written at Fort Smith, Arkansas, and dated May 28, 1847. From these letters we surmise that Abraham Morris was another of the brothers or perhaps a brother of their father.

Land records prove the Thornton family homesteaded land here on Logan Creek near or adjoining the homestead of Landon Copeland. Their patent, dated October 30, 1857, to William Thornton from the U.S. Government, James Buchanan, President, describes the 120 acres as being "the west half of the southwest quarter of section twenty six and the northeast quarter of the southeast quarter of section twenty seven in township thirty north, range one east." George Franklin "Frank," son of William "Billy" Thornton, and his family lived on this farm until they moved to Dickens Valley. Inasmuch as we have never been able to learn the Christian name of the first husband of Hannah Morris, we wonder if the William Thornton named in the patent was that husband and the one who originally filed for this homestead.

Three children were born to the marriage of Landon and Hannah Morris Thornton Copeland. They were: Samuel, born on July 1, 1838; Elizabeth A. "Betsy", born on June 15, 1841, who married James "Jim" Weems in Missouri; and Amy Ann "Anna", born January 15, 1844, who married William or Isiah Daniels in Missouri. Williams Daniels was the name given in a family letter, but Isiah Daniels is the name shown on the death certificate found in Texas death records of Jim Daniels, their oldest son. Mississippi was given as the birth state of Jim Daniels' father. We tried unsuccessfully to tie him in with one of the three different families of Daniels known to have been in Reynolds and Wayne Counties these many years.

The Weems and Daniels families are said to have come to Texas before 1877 and were living near Alvarado in Johnson County when Samuel Copeland brought his family to Texas in 1877. In fact, a letter written by George Baker and Ferman Copeland, son of Samuel, dated July 17, 1881, and headed Alvarado, Johnson County, Texas, reads, in part: "We have seen Van's folks & Daniels & Weems lives in about 8 miles of Vans. We staid there last Saturday night. They air all well & Jim is as big a talker as ever & all getting a long very well." We believe the "Van" they write of is Van B. Thornton, step brother of Betsy Weems and Anna Daniels.

Landon and Hannah Copeland lived out their lives on the farm in the Mills Community on Logan Creek, raising his children, her children and their children, who married the children of their neighbors. Landon died on June 26, 1850, at Logan Creek, Missouri, and is buried in the family cemetery on his farm, near his father and at least three of his sons. Hannah was living when the federal census was taken that year, but we do not know how long she survived.

He died just a scant two months before the end of his elected four-year term in the first governing body of Reynolds County. When the election was held on August 20, 1850, Landon's brother, Dale Copeland, was one of the men elected for justice of the county court.

Landon Copeland left a legacy of good will to his fellow man, as well as a legacy of service to his community and the new Reynolds County. He also left five sons to perpetuate this service and the Copeland name. These five sons contributed much to early Reynolds County.

William and Lot, just boys when the family settled on Logan Creek to homestead land, grew to maturity there and became successful farmers and merchants. They chose adjoining farms on Logan Creek, built homes, and raised their families there. They married sisters, daughters of James and Sina Huff Ellington, who had come to Missouri in 1829. Sina, the only daughter of Joseph Huff, a wealthy successful man, had inherited substantially from her father. James Ellington went to California in the gold rush of 1849, but Sina stayed in Missouri with their five children, holding on to her inheritance, which, according to rumors, she did not share with her husband. On January 3, 1856, she entered 120 acres of land on which the town of Ellington now stands. President Franklin Pierce signed the government patent. With her own closely guarded money, she paid the necessary fee to obtain the land. James Ellington returned to Barnesville, but Sina refused to live with him. He returned to California and was murdered by robbers.

William Copeland married Mary "Polly" Ellington and they had six children: Elizabeth, born in 1849; Mary Jane, born in 1851, who married Gilbert Dickson; Sina Catherine, born in 1853, who married James Moore; Moses Lemroe, born in 1855, who married Margaret Anna Rose; William Anderson, born in 1858, who married Mary E. "Mamie" Moore; and Lucy, born in 1861. Polly Copeland died on December 4, 1864, and William married Margaret Elizabeth Tubbs. Their children were: Sarah Ann, born in 1866, who married Will Shunkwiler; James G., born in 1867, who married Lucy Blanche Buford. He taught in the Mills School in 1882 or 1883. When he died at 26 years of age, he was a graduate of St. Louis Medical College and had studied much under Dr. William Anderson "Doc Bill" Copeland, his older brother; Juliette E. "Julia", born in 1869, who married William H. Reed; Harry F., 1870-1877; John Alexander Logan, born in 1871, who married Cora Lula Burks; and Samuel S. Copeland, 1875-1904.

Lot Copeland, born in 1827, married Elizabeth "Betsy" Ellington ca. 1846 and they had four children before his untimely death about 1859 in Ellington. Their four children were: John born 1847 married (1) Amy Alma Hart and had Lura Ellen born 1871, who married William Barnes; Amy Alma born 1872 married Edmund G. Haywood. (2) Maranda Moore and they had nine children: Lavada Iowa 1877-1941 married James W. Brewer; Lott J. (twin) 1878-1948 m Ida May Johnson; William (twin) 1878-1879; Polly E. 1881-1896; Walter (twin) 1881-1887; Ora Olive "Ollie" 1885-late 1940's; Mollie Garfield 1887-1906; Josetta 1889-1890; and Benjamin 1891-1968 married Imogene "Imo" Daniels.

Lot J. and Benjamin Copeland were co-owners in Ellington Hardware and Manufacturing Company for some years. During a part of this time, Ben served on the board of education of the public schools. In 1925-1926, he was presiding judge of Reynolds County. Lot J. Copeland served on the board of trustees when Ellington was incorporated as a village in 1911. Lot J. also worked with his father in the blacksmith business.

Landon Copeland, 1849-1916, was the second child of Lot and Betsy Copeland. He married Polly A. Moore and they had nine children: Thomas A., 1875-1897; Lydia, who married Wesley Baxter Dickson; Fred Otis, 1876-1958, who married Emily Smith; William "Bill", born in 1878, who married Clara Pogue; Harry, 1880-1958, who married Ethel Luanna Mann; Sina E. 1883-1951, who married James Virgil Rayfield; James A., 1886-1888; Lyman Beacher, 1889-1901; and Essie, 1892-1961, who married Frank Hargrove.

Artimissa Copeland, 1852-1927, was the third child of Lot and Betsy. She married Anderson Massie in 1879 and bore him seven children in their 14 years of marriage. Their children were: Charles Lemro, 1880-1968, who married Delphia Allen; Elizabeth "Lizzie", 1881-1953, who married Franklin M. Stout; Louisa Anna, 1883-1960, who married Luther J. Fears; Isaac Edward, 1884-1958, who married Mary Jane Dement; Emma Olive, 1886-1969, who married George Washington Casey; Mollie Harriet, 1888-1937, who married Jerrson E. Brawley; and Laura Jane, 1891-1983, who married Luther W. Braddy.

Louisa Copeland, 1854-1905, the fourth and last child of Lott and Betsy, married William Chilton Webb in 1877. They had three children: Jim, born in 1877; Mary Ann, 1881-1905; and Dessie, 1886-1972, who married Edward Roy Mefford.

Landon's third son was James Copeland, born August 12, 1831. He was obviously a farmer, but information on him is quite scarce. Files of Delsa Lesh show: ". . . the land Abstract of the farm of Ralph & Helen Neely, joining Ray Copeland, shows James L. Copeland as the first owner. The land was transferred to Marion Copeland on May 30, 1888." This farm is in Doe Run Valley and appears to have been homesteaded by James L. Copeland.

The fourth son, Lewis Copeland, born February 17, 1837, married Lucinda Johnson in 1853. He was killed by bushwhackers during the Civil War. They had one child, James M. "Jim" Copeland, 1855-1929. He first married Mary Linn Carter and they had a child, John, born in Reynolds County, who died in infancy. Jim's second wife was Sina Ellington, daughter of John Ellington and Helen Thompson. Jim and Sina Copeland had four children: Lewis Monroe "Luke" born February 10, 1887 married Grace Roy in 1912. Their children are: William Anderson "Bill" born December 25, 1913 Webb Creek married Hazel Smith in 1935; Hartford born 1916 married Agnes Vann in 1935; James Haden born 1917 unmarried; Leroy born 1928 married Hazel Alexander; and Lawrence "Max" born 1933 married Verneal Murray. William A., one of twins born April 24, 1888, to Jim and Sina, was accidentally shot and killed by his brother Luke on December 26, 1901. His twin, Catie, died at five months. Both are buried in the family cemetery on Webb Creek. John P. born November 21, 1894 was the fourth child of Jim and Sina Copeland. He married Roxie Hoskins in 1919 and they had five children: Edna born 1920 married Ray Miller; Lewis T. 1923-1947 married Dot_____; Eugene born 1926 married Darlene _____; George born 1928; and Bob born 1932. John P. Copeland served his county in World War I in the Medical Department. In civilian life, he was a rural school teacher and a merchant. He died in 1959 and is buried in Yount Memorial Cemetery, as are others of his family. This family lives in the Garwood Community in far south Reynolds County.

Samuel Copeland, born July 1, 1838, in Ripley County, was the fifth son of Landon. He married first in ca. 1859, Mahala Burdmon, born ca. 1840 in Arkansas. They farmed in Ripley and Wayne Counties. Their children were: M. Ferman "F.C." 1860-1940, married Lucy Baker, 1864-1937, daughter of John Baker and Elizabeth Jane Barnes; Amy Ann 1862-1949, married Jim Smith; Deby Jane, 1864-1864; James M. "Jim" 1865-1953, married Laura Belle Wear; Margaret, 1867-1937, married Joe Eaton; John, 1869-1937, married Cynthia Baker, sister of Lucy; and Emily 1873-1965, married Charles Henry Atkinson. Sam and Mahala Copeland were in Webb Township, Barnesville, in the 1870 census of Reynolds County, but were in Wayne County in 1873 when Emily was born. Mahala died February 8, 1875, probably in Wayne County. She was likely buried there.

Samuel Copeland married Virginia Bowers on November 26, 1876, in Reynolds County and the ceremony was performed by Thomas Barnes, J.P. Virginia, born April 3, 1845 in North Carolina, was a daughter of Calvin Sydney Bowers, born early 1800, and Ruthay Whitcley, born November 23, 1815. They married in 1830. Ruthay was a daughter of William Whitley, who came from England to Edgecombe County, North Carolina, in the late 1700's, and Mary How (Howe), whose father was a half-breed Cherokee Indian. The Bowers were pioneers to Reynolds County from North Carolina in about 1847.

Sam and Virginia and Sam's seven children started for Texas soon after the marriage in 1876, but they spent most of the next year in Marion County, Arkansas. They arrived in Bell County, Texas, at Christmas, 1877. After some visiting of family in Johnson County, Texas, they returned to the Cedar Knob Community and settled just across the Lampasas River from the farm home of John Baker. In this community they raised their family of 12 children, Sam's seven by his first marriage and the five born to him and Virginia. These five children, all of Sam's grandchildren, and many of his great-grandchildren were born in the same community where Sam and Virginia started in 1877. They continued to farm throughout their lives and their children followed in their footsteps. Sam Copeland died on December

19, 1916 and Virginia died July 2, 1899. Both are buried in Cedar Knob Cemetery, as are many of their descendants. Their children were: Magradia "Grade", 1878-1953, unmarried; Landon Clarence, 1880-1945, married Delie Arnold; Minnie, 1884-1970, unmarried; William Samuel "Bill", 1888-1975, married Libbie Cora Tarver; and Joe Lemroe, 1892-1918, unmarried.

John Baker, born in 1838 in Ripley County, married Elizabeth Jane Barnes, born in 1843 in Ripley County, the daughter of Thomas Barnes, Sr., and Polly Stinson, in 1859 in Reynolds County. They brought their family to Texas ca. 1870 and settled in the Cedar Knob Community in southwestern Bell County, where they lived out their lives. John was a son of Nathaniel Baker, born in 1798 in Maryland, whose parents were Manning Baker, born in 1776 in Maryland, and Rebecca Clare, born in 1778 in Maryland. They married on September 13, 1796, in Baltimore, Maryland, and had four children when they died in ca. 1812, soon after the birth of their son, John. Their children were separated among the family. Fourteen-year-old Nathaniel ran away from his family and went with some emigrants to the Bellevue Valley in Missouri. There is said to have been an Elisha Baker with a son, Elija, living at Gotaway, near Ironton in Washington County in the early days of the settling of Missouri. James Bell has found in research of early families of Missouri that John, Andrew and Elisha Baker were part of a settlement of eight or ten families in the small community of Alley Mills (or Mines) in 1796. Perhaps these were relatives of Nathaniel Baker.

Whether or not Nathaniel Baker found family in Missouri, he did not return to Maryland and had no contact with his family there until shortly before May 25, 1846, 34 years later! Nathaniel Baker had married in ca. 1823 to Hettie Morris, born 1804 in Kentucky, and they had eight of the nine children born to their marriage. Their ninth child was born that September and was named by his sister Elizabeth in far-away Maryland. They had married in Wayne County and were there in the 1830 census, in Ripley County in the 1840 census; and in Shannon County in the 1850 census. Both are said to have died ca. 1865, and their last years were likely spent in the Hen Peck Community, Carter Township, Carter County, near their daughter Susannah, who was married to George Washington Clark. They were buried on the Clark farm. Nathaniel and Hettie's children were: Susannah, 1824-1886; Isaac, 1827-after 1861; George, 1828-1883; son, 1833-1849; Drucilla, born in 1835; John E. Baker, 1838-1915; Merrier (Mary), born in 1841; Minerva Jane, born in 1844, married James Maberry; they were in the 1880 census of Carter County with seven children; Rebecca Frances, born September 1, 1846, and died March 18, 1934, in Bell County, Texas. She married William Galbraith, born in 1840 in Iowa, in 1869 in Reynolds County. They had three children when Galbraith died probably about 1880. He is probably buried in the cemetery on the old Sam Galbraith farm in Hen Peck Community near Van Buren in Carter County. Rebecca brought their three children to her brother John's home in Bell County and they lived out their lives there.

John E. Baker died on July 7, 1915 and Elizabeth Jane Barnes Baker died November 5, 1920. Both are buried in Cedar Knob Cemetery. Their children were: George Washington Baker 1859-1923 married first Nancy Louisa Lane who died in 1892 leaving him with a 13-month-old son. Within the year of her death, George returned to Reynolds County and married his childhood sweetheart, Mrs. Mary Elizabeth Allen Massie, widow of Alfred Nathan Massie. He brought his bride and her five Massie children to Bell county and they started a family of their own. They had seven children, plus George's first and Mary's five, making a total of thirteen who all grew up together and were a close-knit family. George's brothers and sisters were: Meary Hattie 1862-1863; Lucy given above; William Clare 1867-1870; John Edward 1869-1914; married Mary Emmeline Gilbreath 1870-1954; Cynthia given above; Martha Ellen 1875-1938 married James William Thornton; David Clinton 1878-1884; Luke 1882-1932 married Mettie Inez Hatter; and Sarah Elizabeth 1885-1970 unwed.

Thomas Barnes, Sr., born March 9, 1804 in Wilkes County, North Carolina, descended from John Barnes, Sr., born in 1735 in Ireland, who married Elizabeth Hamilton and emigrated to America in 1760, settling in New Perth, New York. There their son, Edward, was born ca. 1770. He emigrated to North Carolina and raised a large family there, one of whom was Thomas Barnes, Sr., who married prior to 1826 and had three children by his first wife, who died ca. 1830. He married Polly Stinson, born April 29, 1812 on March 27, 1831 in North Carolina and they had two children by 1835, when they came to Iron County. They settled at Pilot Knob, where they farmed two years, moving on down to Logan Creek in 1837. Their settlement there was called "Barnesville" for Thomas Barnes. He owned a water mill on Logan Creek and did milling. He also operated a distillery for a number of years. He bought land and engaged in farming throughout his lifetime. They attended a Methodist Episcopal church and he was a stauch supporter and charter member of the Masonic Lodge. There were 12 Barnes children and most of them raised large families. Barnes descendants are legion in Reynolds County.

Thomas Barnes children were: James born 1826 married Lucinda Pyles; Rebecca born 1828; William Thomas 1829-1865 married Elizabeth Brooks; Sarah 1832-1916 married William "Billy" Thornton 1823-1902; Thomas Stinson 1835-1915 married (1) Caroline Leggett (Legate) (2) Esther Mary Eddings and (3) Ellana Chitwood, had a total of 16 children; Josiah B. 1837-1903 married Cecily _____; John S. 1839-1862 served Union Army in the Civil War, died in service; Mary Ann 1841-after 1894 married Smith White Cotton, had eight children; Elizabeth Jane 1843-1920 married John E. Baker, had ten children; Edward 1845-1884 married Cynthia Elizabeth Crownover, had seven children; Nancy Caroline "Nant" 1848-1933 married Nelson Barton, had eight children; and Martha Emaline 1851-1925 married Gladden Tubbs 1843-1933, has six children.

Thomas Barnes, Sr., died on December 10, 1857, and Polly Stinson Barnes died November 22, 1863. Both are buried in the vicinity of Ellington, Missouri, though we have never learned the exact cemetery.

The Copeland name has been well perpetuated in Texas. Samuel's seven sons sired 17 grandsons, 23 great-grandsons, 20 great-great-grandsons and one great-great-great-grandson as of January 1980. This tabulation is only of those of the Copeland name — only sons of sons!

William Copeland, who was named with Lot, Landon, Cary, Dale and Andrew as having been in early Washington County, Missouri, with these Copeland, moved on into Overton County, Tennessee. He married and raised a large family there. We believe he was a younger brother of Lot Copeland.

William Copeland, born on July 12, 1783, in North Carolina, married Margery Carmac, born on June 13, 1785, in Virginia, in 1805. Their children were: Sarah Hill, born on September 5, 1807; Hazel, born on February 2, 1809; Cornelias, born on February 22, 1811; Jessie, born on January 12, 1813; Letty Sprawle, born on March 27, 1815; Tadoc Thornton, born on March 11, 1817; Isaac, born on June 15, 1820; Jacob, born on January 28, 1822; Retta, born on March 19, 1824; Elizana, born on December 26, 1826; John Fletcher, born on February 2, 1829; Syrena, born on March 11, 1831; and Richard Browning, born on January 6, 1833. William Copeland died before the 1860 census was taken in Reynolds County. His wife died after the census was taken in 1870.

William Copeland brought his family back to Reynolds County in the late 1840's. He is listed as Family #32 on the 1850 census of Reynolds County: William Copeland, 66, North Carolina; Margery, 64, Virginia; Eliza A., 23, Tennessee; John, 21, Tennessee; Serena, 18, Tennessee; and Richard, 17, Tennessee. Nearby, Family #38 is Isaac Copeland, 29, Tennessee; Elizabeth, 25, Tennessee; Charles, three, Tennessee; and Jessee, one month. We believe this William Copeland is the one listed with our early Copeland.

Isaac Copeland, seventh child of William, was listed in 1850, 1860, 1870 and 1880 censuses of Reynolds County, and incorrectly listed as the oldest child of Landon Copeland in Genealogy of the Families of Copeland-Morris Baker-Barnes and Related Families, written and published in 1980 by Eula Venita Copeland Guess and Althea Copeland Taylor.

Isaac Copeland, born on June 20, 1820, Tennessee, married ca. 1846 in Tennessee, Elizabeth _____ and they had Charles Harrison, born in 1847 in Tennessee, and Jessee, born in 1849 in Missouri. So Isaac, son of William Copeland, born in 1783 in North Carolina, came to Reynolds County, Missouri, near our Copeland's, before 1849. On the 1860 census of Reynolds County, Black River Township, Isaac is listed with Mary, 27, Tennessee and the following children: Charles, 14; Jessee, 12; Lemuel, 7; Francis, 5; and John, five months — all boys and all except Charles born in Missouri. The 1870 census of Reynolds County lists: Isaac; Mary; Jessee, 21; Lemuel, 17; Francis, 14; John, 10; Isaac, five; and Luther, one — still all boys. This census shows Isaac Copeland has land valued at $600. The 1880 census was the first one showing the birth state of each parent of every person listed. Logan Township, Reynolds County, in 1880 lists: Isaac Copeland, 60, Tennessee, father born in North Carolina, mother born in Virginia; Mary, 49, Tennessee, father born in North Carolina, mother born in Virginia; John, 18, Tennessee, Tennessee, Tennessee; Isaac W., 13, Missouri, Tennessee, Tennessee; Sydney L., 11, Missouri, Tennessee, Tennessee. This is proof positive that Isaac is the son of William and Margery Copeland.

Isaac Copeland is thought to have remained in Reynolds County until 1895 or 1896. Courthouse records at Centerville lists #109 sale of land from I. Copeland and wife to T.S. Barnes dated July 3, 1877 — proving Isaac's wife was alive at that time. We have in our files a quit-claim deed dated May 14, 1883 from James. T. Dobbins to Isaac Copeland concerning 120 acres of land in Reynolds County. Isaac was a farmer through the years, but somewhere along the way he became a minister of the gospel. Both the Iron County marriage book 1857-1873 and Carter County marriage book 1861-1881 have records of marriages performed by Rev. Isaac Copeland.

Rev. Isaac Copeland, June 20, 1820-November 20 1904, shares a huge bronze monument with his son Charles H., September 12, 1848-April 8, 1931, and Josephine, wife of Charles H., December 1, 1854-March 2, 1922 in the cemetery in Collinsville, Grayson County, Texas. Others of his family are buried in the large lot. Isaac Copeland is said to have lived around with relatives in Reynolds County until about 1895 or 1896 and then went to Texas to join his sons.

Charles Harrison Copeland, born on September 12, 1848 in Tennessee, married Josephine Trammel, born on December 1, 1854, on December 25, 1873 in Missouri. Their marriage is listed in Vol. 1, Reynolds County Marriages 1870-1891. Their oldest son, Albert, was born in December of 1875 in Missouri. They came to Grayson County, Texas, between 1875 and 1878. Their second son, William Marshall "Bill", was born in March of 1880 in Texas. Elizabeth, their daughter, was born in January of 1884 in Texas. They farmed around Collinsville in Grayson County.

Jessee Copeland, second son of Isaac, was born in 1849 in Missouri. His wife was Sarah Jane _____, born in 1854 in Missouri. They came to Texas in 1876 and their son, Jasper D., was born in 1876. The 1900 census of Montague County, Texas, lists Jasper D., as 24, born in May of 1876 in Texas.

Others of Isaac Copeland's family came to Grayson County, Texas. Some of them are buried on the same lot as Isaac in Collinsville Cemetery. There are still many descendents of Isaac Copeland living in that area, and some in Fort Worth, Tarrant County, Texas.

Submitted by Mrs. Althea Copeland Taylor, 1705-A Forest Trail, Temple, Texas 76502, great-great-granddaughter of Landon Copeland.

COLLIN C. CAMPBELL

The justices of the county court who had been chosen by the governor of Missouri in 1845 to organize and bring into being Reynolds County were given the authority to select a qualified person to serve them as their clerk. This person would also serve as circuit clerk. Collin C. Campbell was chosen. When the first county election was held in 1846, Collin C. Campbell was elected to the position.

Very little was learned of this man even though the compiler of this book attempted to find a descendant or a person who had done research on the Campbell family. Information we give here must be credited to Wanda Leigh Eidson of Weatherford, Texas, who sent us a page from the Haden/Hyden Family Book.

The first trace we find of Collin C. Campbell was in 1837 when he is shown as postmaster in Caledonia, Washington County, Missouri. His marriage is found in Madison County, Missouri, the following year — January 3, 1838 to Lucy Ann Eidson, daughter of Henry and Mary Buford Eidson, who came to Washington County, Missouri in 1814 in company of Mary's parents, William and Annie Pate Buford.

Collin C. Campbell was born May 10, 1811, in Greensburg, Westmoreland County, Pennsylvania. He came to Missouri in the 1830's, but whether his parents came at that time has not been determined. A Moses Campbell found in Madison and Washington Counties could be his father, but we have little proof.

When the post office was re-established at Lesterville, Missouri, in 1842, Collin C. Campbell was postmaster.

In 1849-50, he resigned his position as county and circuit clerk of Reynolds County and moved to Jefferson City, Missouri. He remained there only a short time, as he is found in Johnson County, Missouri, living near the town of Knob Noster a short time later.

Information in the Haden/Hyden Family Book indicates he attended St. Louis Medical College. We have no proof that he practiced medicine while in Reynolds County, but that his profession in Johnson County. He spent his remaining days in the Knob Noster Community and died there December 30, 1876. His wife, Lucy Ann Eidson, was born in Bellevue Valley on February 20, 1818 and died February 6, 1893.

Collin and Lucy Ann Campbell's oldest child was Mary E., born on January 24, 1839, in Fredericktown, Madison County, Missouri. She married Dr. Charles Franklin Mercer on September 8, 1856, and they had four children before her untimely death on February 17, 1862.

William Henry Campbell, born on May 19, 1841, at Fredericktown, was their second child. He attended Jefferson Medical College and took final exams for graduation in 1864. These were exams in the institutes of medicine;

anatomy, obstetrics, chemistry, surgery, materia medica, practice of medicine. His great knowledge of medicine would not have saved him from every man's fate — he died on April 15, 1867. So many persons for reasons beyond our understanding are not allowed time to fulfill promising careers.

Collin's third child, Lucy Ann Campbell, was born on September 7, 1846 at Lesterville, Missouri, and died May 6, 1847. The fourth child, Collin C. Campbell, Jr., born September 7, 1846, at Lesterville, was accidentally killed on September 3, 1863, in Pettis County, Missouri, by a pistol ball shot, according to information found in the family Bible.

Alexander Eugene Campbell, born September 18, 1849, at Lesterville, was their fifth child. He died September 25, 1868. George Washington Campbell, born September 17, 1853, in Johnson County, was the sixth child. He died August 15, 1885.

Seventh, Emma Lucy Campbell, was born on February 14, 1856, and died in 1942. She was married on September 24, 1878, to Jacob Swingle and they had seven children.

John Virgil Campbell was the eighth child of Collin and Lucy Ann. He was born April 6, 1858, and died in 1928. He married Nancy A. Robertson on September 22, 1879 and they had four children. Professionally, John was an undertaker at Knob Noster.

Collin C. Campbell spent only about seven years in Reynolds County, but his name will always be a part of this county's beginning years. James Crownover, Landon Copeland and William Love undoubtedly made a wise choice when they chose Collin C. Campbell as their first clerk.

WILLIAM CULLEN LOVE

William Cullen Love was one of the three justices of the county court appointed by the governor of Missouri in 1845. This court was formed by an act of the Missouri General Assembly on February 25, 1845, and was given the authority to aid in the advancement of the new county.

When Love died in 1891, his grandson, Joshua Carty, who had lived with his grandfather from birth until his graduation from Washington University School of Law, certainly knew his grandfather's achievements well. It was his grandfather's money that had enabled Joshua to obtain his law degree. The fondness and admiration for his grandfather is certainly shown in the obituary that follows, written by Joshua Carty.

"A veteran of the War of 1812 died at the residence of A.J. Carty near Ironton on Wednesday, June 10, 1891. William Cullen Love, aged 96 years, 5 months and 15 days. Mr. Love was born on December 25, 1794 in Wilkes County, North Carolina. His father was a native of Scotland. His mother was an American, born of Scot-Irish parentage. He was left fatherless at an early age and was taken to be raised by Benj. Martin, a rich planter and an excellent man. His childhood and youth was one common to that day, yet by dint of perseverance and through the generosity of Mr. Martin, he succeeded in obtaining a fair education. He ran away from home in 1813 and joined the U.S. Army, this country being at war with Great Britain at that time. He enlisted in a regiment of horse dragoons of which Thomas H. Benton, Missouri's great senator, was a lieutenant colonel. This regiment was disbanded in a short time and the young soldier found himself away from home without money or friends; and without yet having been in a fight.

"Nothing daunted, however, he traveled on foot across the state of East Tennessee to where General Coffee was recruiting soldiers for Jackson's Army in the south. He enlisted at once and was appointed recruiting officer by Gen. Coffee in which capacity he was engaged for six or eight months, visiting all the prominent towns in Tennessee. In the spring of 1814, he was permanently assigned duty as orderly-sergeant of Wm. O. Butler's Company of the 44th U.S. Regular Infantry, and the command was ordered to join Jackson in Creek County.

"He arrived too late to participate in the fight at Horseshoe Bend, but in time to accompany Jackson to Pensacola, Florida. Here the recruits were initiated into real war, and led the assault on the main town. In this fight, the young orderly-sergeant took a manly part. He was one of the first to reach the Spanish flag to haul it down and raise the Stars and Stripes instead. From Pensacola, Jackson went to New Orleans where on December 22, 1814, the first battle was fought. Skirmishes, picket fighting, and sorties kept the opposing enemies watchful of each other until the morning of the 8th of January, 1815, when Packingham's Army, the 'Conquerors of Napoleon' was hurled against the Kentucky and Tennessee backwoodsmen to meet a fearful fate and a bloody repulse. In this battle this beardless youth who was just a few days past twenty, did his part well. He was first to observe the approach of the enemy, having gone to the river bank to draw the ration of the day. He ran back to the company, ordered the men up, armed and to occupy their positions. No sooner had this been done than the enemy was within rifle range. If fell his lot to have charge of his company during the battle. His captain was acting major, the first lieutenant was sick and the second lieutenant was disabled by a wound received at Pensacola. The 44th Regiment held the key of the breastworks, the center, and against this Packingham in person led the King's and Queen's Regiment. The result is well-known. It may not be out of place to say that Mr. Love always contended that the popular impression that the Americans were entrenched behind a breastwork of cotton bales in the battle of January 8th, was erroneous. Not a cotton bale was used then. They were used for temporary breastwork before the first of January.

"After this battle came peace and discharge. The young soldier returned to North Carolina where, in July, 1816, he was married to Miss Sarah M. Bryan. In 1818, they moved to Cumberland County, Kentucky, where he followed farming for two years. In 1820, they moved to Missouri, settling on Black River in what is now Reynolds County near Edgehill in June of that year. Here he lived, worked, raised his family and was, at last buried. He was the father of eight children and raised seven to manhood and womanhood. Of these, only one, Elvira, his youngest daughter survives him. She is the wife of A.J. Carty. His oldest daughter was the wife of R.S. Browne of Washington County. His second daughter was the wife of W.J. Goggin of Reynolds County. His oldest son, Capt. James H. Love, was a prominent citizen of Searcy County, Arkansas. His second son, Dr. John H. Love, lived on Black River in Iron County. His third son, A.J. Love, died in 1866; and his youngest son, R.E.B. Love, died unmarried in 1862. His wife died in 1860; and since that time he has resided with his youngest daughter. He was great-great-great-grandfather . . . six generations alive at the same time.

"In his prime he was a man of splendid physique, six feet two inches tall, weighing 180 pounds, was straight as an Indian, capable of enduring untold dangers and privation, and endowed with a constitution that seemed would never give away. He never shunned exposure, in fact, seemed to court it. He never stopped for snow or rain. He is among the last of the race of pioneers who feared no dangers, shunned no privation . . . a race of giants raised up by the Almighty to conquer the wilderness. In politics, he was a lifelong and consistent Jackson Democrat. He cast his first vote for James Monroe for President in 1816, and has voted for nineteen Democratic candidates for President, in all, since then. Mr. Love was patriotic, honest, brave and generous. He loved his family, his friends, his country and the truth. He held, at different times, several official positions, though never an office seeker. He was noted for his frugality. He worked to the utmost of his strength as long as he

95

could. He was interred on Friday, June 12, 1891, in the family cemetery on the old homestead near Edgehill. He is gone. For nearly a century, he successfully met and conquered danger and disease, to gradually waste away at last before the inevitable decay of nature. May his ashes rest in peace."

William Cullen Love, like almost everyone in this early period, was a farmer, but he also held a number of appointed and elective offices in Washington, Shannon and Reynolds Counties during a fifty year period. He was appointed justice of the peace in Black River Township, Washington County, by Governor John Miller in 1828 and 1832. This area was made a part of Shannon County in 1841, and William C. Love was a justice of the county court for that county, being appointed that year. Reynolds County was formed in 1845 and William was destined to serve in its first year as justice of the county court. The last known office he held was a justice of the county court in 1872 for a six-year term. He was then 78 years old, and to ride a horse from his farm at Edgehill to the county seat at Centerville, a distance of about 30 miles round trip, would tax a much younger man today beyond his limit.

There is some indication that William Cullen Love may have gone to California during the gold rush in 1849. A number of men from this area are known to have gone. Here, again, he would have been rather old for such an undertaking, but as we have established, he had extraordinary physical endurance and could have made the trip. If he did go, he was back home by 1860, as he was shown on the census record of Reynolds County that year.

A story told by Clifford Adams and recorded by Edward Randolph Adams is the only proof we have that William C. Love went to California in those years of "gold mania" which gripped and tingled the very "inner soul" of almost every man in America and caused many to head in that direction in great haste. Most returned home poorer than they were before they left. However, William was one of the few exceptions. We quote:

"Billy Love, grandfather of Bob Love and great-grandfather of Arthur Love, lived at Edgehill, Missouri, on what was later known as Fred Oesch Farm. It is now owned by one of the Cawley brothers, I think. In the gold rush of 1849, he left his family and went with a group overland to California. Johnny Latham was in the group and a man named Smith, who was killed by the Indians on the way. Billy stayed long enough to make a large sum of money. He returned safely overland again, bringing his money with him.

"When Billy heard that Price was making a raid through southern Missouri in 1864, he decided to put his money, most of which he still had, in a St. Louis bank. Some of the money, perhaps most of it, was in gold. Billy had his daughter, Anna, leave hurriedly for St. Louis with the money. She had to go by horse to Potosi and catch a train there via Mineral Point for St. Louis. Anna was a resourceful young woman and made the round trip successfully, leaving the money safely in a St. Louis bank.

"Later Billy used some or all of the money to buy a farm of more than 400 acres on Stouts Creek near Ironton. He moved his family to this farm and lived there the rest of his life of almost 100 years. The farm went later to Billy's grandson, Love Carty, and is now owned by Frank Adams."

This story, told by Clifford Adams, is accurate in almost every detail. Although William C. Love was shown on the 1850 census in Black River Township, he could have been enumerated by his family to the census taker, even though he was 2000 miles away. He also bought the Moses Carty place for his son, Dr. John H. Love, in the 1860's, lending credence to this gold rush story.

In Wilkes County, North Carolina, we find the marriage of William Love and Sally Bryan on February 24, 1816. Their first child, James Harrison Love, was born in Wilkes County on July 13, 1817. Soon after this, William and Sarah left North Carolina and moved to Cumberland County, Kentucky, where William is found on the 1820 census of that county. There in Cumberland County, their second child, Diana Mary Ann Love, was born on November 19, 1819. Their third child, Margaret Caroline Love, was born on October 14, 1821, at Edgehill, Missouri. These births would seem to agree with the obituary, stating that William left North Carolina in 1818, stayed in Kentucky two years, and moved on to Missouri in 1820.

Five more children were born at Edgehill: John Hartwell Love on May 12, 1824; William Milan Love on January 29, 1826; Andrew Jackson Love on December 22, 1828; Elvira Love on March 30, 1830; and Robert Edward Bryan Love on April 10, 1832.

James Harrison Love, the oldest child, was born in Wilkes County, North Carolina on July 13, 1817. He married Mary "Polly" Jamison on January 26, 1837. They soon moved to Searcy County, Arkansas.

He served as a private in Company B, 1st Arkansas Cavalry in the Mexican War under the command of Col. Archibold Yell. He enlisted in Washington, Hempstead County, Arkansas, in July of 1846 and was honorably discharged at Camargo, Mexico, about July 1, 1847. During the Civil War, "Harry" raised at least two companies for the Confederacy and served for a time as captain in each. On August 5, 1861, he enlisted in Company K, 14th Arkansas Infantry in Yellville under Col. F.P. Powers, resigning his command on July 18, 1862. Then, on February 9, 1863, he raised another company which formed Company C of John F. Hill's Regiment of 7th Arkansas Cavalry enlisting at Searcy County for a three-year period. He was described in his discharge papers as being six feet two inches tall, blue eyes, dark hair, and light complexion. His father's, William Cullen Love's, discharge, dated April 6, 1815, gave a very similar description: six feet, blue eyes, sandy hair, and light complexion.

James Harrison Love was married twice more. His second marriage was to Miriah Sinclair, and his third was to Mary Louise Cash Arnold on October 25, 1868. He died at St. Joe, Searcy County, Arkansas, on November 24, 1887.

Diana Mary Ann Love, the second child, was born in Cumberland County, Kentucky, on November 19, 1819. In 1842, she married R. Soloman Browne, a Presbyterian minister who had been married twice before and was twenty years her senior. They lived in Washington County, Missouri, where you will find them on the 1850 census. In 1873, they moved to Salem, Dent County, Missouri. Mary Ann died there in 1877 and Soloman died in 1888. This marriage produced nine children, but, perhaps, only six live to maturity as the will of William Cullen Love only names six.

Child number three, Margaret Caroline Love, was born October 14, 1821, at Edgehill, Missouri, being one of the first children of white parentage to be born in that community. She married William J. "Buck" Goggin in about 1843. William, the son of Green Berry and Elizabeth Carty Goggin, was born in Cumberland County, Kentucky, in May of 1824. This marriage produced eight children. Margaret Love Goggin died on June 3, 1878, and William Goggin succumbed to the inevitable in January of 1903.

Dr. John Hartwell Love, born on May 12, 1824, was the fourth child. He married Julia Cain on March 29, 1848. She was a daughter of Robert and Catherine Maxwell (?) Cain of Washington County. They are shown on the 1850 census of Washington County, but were in Arkansas in 1851. They eventually returned to the area near where they were born.

Eight children were born to John H. and Julia Cain Love, but some did not survive to adulthood. John H. Love died on April 20, 1872, and Julia died March 3, 1903. Dr. Love and most of his family fought, but lost to, the dreaded and fatal disease of tuberculosis, which claimed a number of Love descendants at an early age.

William Milan Love, the fifth child, was born at Edgehill on January 29, 1826, and died November 22, 1833, not being granted the time necessary to develop and contribute to life's cycle. Many millions of children have been denied this chance and thousands of parents have tried to find some logic, some reason, for such an untimely tragedy, but all explanations seem empty, vain, and without merit or purpose.

Child number six, Andrew Jackson Love, was born December 22, 1828, at Edgehill. He married Mary _____. Andrew died in 1866 without any known children.

Elvira Love, born on March 30, 1830, at Edgehill, was the seventh child. She was the only one of William Cullen Love's children who out-lived him. She married Andrew J. Carty, the son of Joshua and Charlotte Mallow Carty. Eight children were born to this union, but only three would reach maturity.

The youngest child, Robert Edward Bryan Love, was born at Edgehill on April 10, 1832. He, undoubtedly, was named for his maternal grandfather, but we have not been able to prove this. He was the first postmaster when the post office was established at Edgehill in 1854. This post office was closed during the Civil War, and, when it re-opened in 1871, William Cullen Love was postmaster. Robert Love had died in 1862.

William Cullen Love's brother, Robert King Love, 1790-1843, moved to Missouri and Edgehill in 1830, after spending a number of years in Lincoln County, Tennessee. It was there he married Margaret Catherine Davis in 1821. Margaret was born in 1801. Robert moved his family to the farm owned by William and remained there until his death in 1843. Margaret had died five years earlier. Robert King Love was probably somewhat handicapped by poor health, or had perhaps inherited his father's knack for misfortune. He accumulated very little worldly riches, according to the report by William Cullen Love, administrator of Robert's estate.

The amount of $183.3475 was inherited by the following six children: William Robert Love, 1823-1985, married Sarah P. Larimore in 1844; John Andrew Love, 1825-1889, married Christian Richeson in 1843; Dollarson (Dallason) Sweat Love, 1828-1913, married Sarah Jane Cole; Eliza Love, 1830-1906, married first David Vassey and second _____ Buck; Sarah A. Love, 1832-1905, married V.B. Carty; and Mary Adalade Love, 1835-1863, married William Huitt.

Space will not permit us to provide you with all the information we have found pertaining to the later generations of Robert King Love, but some work has been done in a book entitled Love-Loomis Family History, by the late Burt Weed Loomis, Ph.D., 1963.

Let us now return to records from the birthplace of William Cullen Love in Wilkes County, North Carolina, and to the year 1805, keeping in mind that the obituary stated he was left fatherless at an early age and was raised by Benjamin Martin. On a small fragmented document, filed in the Bastardy Bonds of Wilkes County, is found the following grand jury presentation: "October Term 1805, the Grand Jury of Wilkes County presents the children of John Love, shoemaker, said children being in a state of sufferance." Two land transactions about this time shows further the financial hardship this family was confronted with. On May 1, 1805, the Wilkes County sheriff sold land lost by John Love, action taken by David Watkins. And, in September, more land was lost by John Love in a sheriff's sale. This action was taken by James Sheppard. Some of this land had been inherited by John Love's wife, Margaret, from her father, Robert King, who had died in 1799.

In the Wilkes County marriages, we found the marriage bond of John Love and "Peggy" King, dated May 23, 1789. The 1790 federal census shows they had one daughter. In the 1800 census they had one daughter and four sons. John was over 45 and Margaret "Peggy" was between 26 and 45 years old.

An indenture found in Wilkes County and dated October 30, 1810, reveals where the county court bonds William Love to Benjamine Martin. We quote in part: "Doth put; place and bind unto the said Benj. Martin, an orphan boy named William Love of the age of fifteen years next Christmas with the said Benj. Martin to live after the manner of apprentice and servant until the said apprentice shall attain the age of twenty-one years." A second indenture, also dated October 30, 1810, binds William's brother, James, who was 11 years old, to Thomas Parks.

They were fortunate to be bound to these two prominent and wealthy families. We have no record of what happened to James, but our William, undoubtedly, gained valuable experience with the Martins that contributed later to his moderate success in life from a very humble beginning.

In the federal census for 1810, Wilkes County, North Carolina, "Peggy" King is shown with two males, 10-16, one male 16-26, two females under 10, one female 16-26, and one female (Peggy) over 45 years old. We have already identified three boys, Robert, William and James. Agnes Love, who married Isaac Wilcockson on November 9, 1817, is almost certainly a daughter, as William was bondsman. Another likely daughter would be Nancy Love, who married David Wilcockson on November. 1, 1828. David and Isaac were securities for A.W. Finley's bond when he was appointed administrator of Margaret Love's brief estate settlement in 1838.

William Love's grandfather, Robert King, died in 1799 and left a will which was probated in the July term and witnessed by Spencer Adam. He left everything to his wife, Mary Ann, to do with as she wished. Mary Ann and John Love were appointed administrators. In Wilkes County Will Book #1, on a badly torn page, is an inventory of the estate of Robert King, deceased February Term 1800. "2 cows and calf, 1 horse, 1 pot, 1 dutch (page torn) . . . 1 dish (page torn) . . . 3 bacons, 1 set of knives and forks, 2 pair cards, 1 bed and furniture, some books (page torn) . . . dollars in hand of John Love."

In the North Carolina census for Wilkes County, Robert King is listed as being over 60 years old in 1787. The Old Roaring River Primitive Baptist Church in Wilkes County, North Carolina, was constituted in 1779. In the minutes of that church was found the following information on Robert and Mary Ann King: "On Saturday the 8th of July, 1786, the church setting in order, undertook to reprove Bro. King for selling corn at 20 pr barrel — for which he agreed he would not do again. He also agreed to pay the man 5 pds of his money bak." "Satterday 20 Sept., 1786, the church delegated Bro. Robert King (with others) to attend the association at Bro. Petty's meeting house" "Cald meeting Satterday 1st August 1789, Bro. Larrance (and others) to go talk with sister King" "November 9th 1793, report made to the church that sister King had transgressed by drinking too much and church delegated Bro. Hammon (and others) to go labour with her" "2nd Satterday Dec 1793, church had some told about sister King and agreed to bare with her till next meeting" "Jan meeting 1794, report made to church that Sister King was not able to come to meeting."

In 1761, a Robert King bought 320 acres in Rowan County, North Carolina. In 1765, this land was sold by Robert and Mary Ann King. A Richard and Margaret (Barley) King are believed to be the parents of this Robert. The name Margaret fits, as that was the name of our "Peggy" King Love. Spencer

Adams, who witnessed the will of Robert King, was from Rowan County, research had revealed, lending support to the study that our Robert King had lived in Rowan County before coming to Wilkes and, therefore, is the son of Richard.

Sarah M. Bryan Love, the wife of William Cullen Love, was born in Virginia on June 14, 1794. Sarah's father was a doctor, educated in Pennsylvania. We do not know his given name. Family tradition says he was related to Rebecca Bryan Boone, wife of Daniel Boone. Rebecca, who was born in 1738, was the daughter of Joseph Bryan. Joseph's parents were Morgan and Martha Strode Bryan, who were married in Chester County, Pennsylvania, in 1719. Morgan Bryan moved his family to Roanoke County, Virginia, in 1730. Then, on to the Yadkin River, Wilkes County, North Carolina, in 1748. It is not known whether all his children followed him to North Carolina. Perhaps some of them remained in Virginia where they later met the Harrisons when they moved to Pennsylvania County. Roanoke and Pennsylvania were adjacent counties in this early period. Morgan and Martha Strode Bryan had ten children: Joseph, Eleanor, James, Mary, Samuel, Morgan Jr., John, William, Thomas and Sarah.

William, a younger brother of Morgan, came to America from Ireland with Morgan in 1718. William Bryan, who was born in Bandridge County Down, Northern Ireland, in 1685, married Margaret _____ before coming to America. They settled in Pennsylvania, then followed Morgan to Roanoke County, Virginia, where William remained until death claimed him in 1789, at the age of 104. This marriage produced four known children: John Andrew, James, William Jr., and Mary. David, whom we find in Roanoke County in the 1740's, may also be a son.

Somewhere out of these two Bryan families, undoubtedly, came our Doctor Bryan. The name Robert Edward Bryan has been used in every generation since the death of the doctor, giving cause to speculate this could be the given name we have been searching for. Dr. Bryan is believed to have moved from Virginia to the Yadkin River, North Carolina, in about 1800. He had a drinking problem which eventually ruined his life and did irreparable damage to his wife, Lucy Harrison Bryan. His drinking problem also brought financial ruin. Lucy died of a "broken heart" and the doctor soon drowned in the Yadkin River, leaving two small daughters, Sarah and a sister.

The two girls were taken to be raised by their mother's sisters. Sarah was taken by Diana Harrison Martin, and her sister was taken by Sarah Harrison Thurman. Diana Harrison Martin was the wife of Benjamine Martin, whom our William Cullen Love was apprenticed to in 1810. Sarah Harrison Thurman was the wife of Capt. Thomas Thurman. The Thurmans soon moved to Georgia and Sarah Bryan never saw her sister again.

In the 1880 federal census of Iron County, Missouri, William Cullen Love says his father was born in Scotland and his mother in Pennsylvania. His obituary says his father was born in Scotland and his mother in Pennsylvania.

In the book, Facts from Missouri History, by Goodspeed, (1889), William Robert Love, who was a prominent resident of Dent County, Missouri, states: "My father, Robert King Love, was born in Wilkes County, North Carolina, in 1790. My grandfather was John Love, who was born in Scotland."

William Cullen Love made a will and named all his grandchildren except those of his son, James, and his daughter, Elvira, as they were still living when the will was made. However, James Harrison Love died in 1887 and William continued to avoid the inevitable for four more years.

The grandchildren mentioned in the will as children of Mary Love Browne were: Harrison H. Browne, Robert Soloman Browne, Willard F. Browne, Charles Browne, Francis C. Browne, and Andrew J. Browne.

The grandchildren mentioned as descending from Caroline Love Goggin were: Elizabeth, the wife of James Bell; Sterling P. Goggin; Lee Goggin; Green Berry Goggin; Robert E. B. Goggin; and Mary Goggin.

The grandchildren shown in the will who descended from John H. Love were: Cornelis J. Love; Martha A. Love; Margaret Love; Robert C. Love; and Lucy Love.

Elvira Love Carty had three children who lived to maturity. They were Robert Love Carty, Joshua Carty, and Joanna Carty.

James Harrison Love had: Susan Love, Hannibal Love, Sidney A. Love, Sarah Catherine Love, Edward A. Love, and James Cash Love.

Robert Love Carty, son of Andrew and Elvira Love Carty, was born on September 30, 1868, and spent his entire life in the same household as his grandfather until William's death in 1891. He had been given a good education and was not a man prone to boastful exaggeration. In a letter he wrote to Otha Love in Leachville, Arkansas, dated May 16, 1935, he writes: "I cannot tell you how far away she was from Benjamine Harrison, the signer of the Declaration of Independence; but she (his grandmother, Sarah M. Bryan Love) was a second cousin of William Henry Harrison, the President."

William C. Love was the great, great grandfather of the author of this book.

REFERENCES

Rose Ann Burns Mitchell, Poulsbo, Washington
Otha Love Wilhelm, Monkton, Maryland
William Symonds, Ironton, Missouri
Edna Bond Ripley, Arcadia, Missouri
Mrs. W.O. Absher, North Wilkesboro, North Carolina
Mary Ann Thurston Thornton, Sedalia, Colorado
Burt Weems Loomis, Ph.D., Potosi, Missouri

JAMES MAXWELL ALIAS "DON DIEGO MAXWELL"

James Maxwell was born in the British Isles, most probably Ireland. He studied in Spain for the priesthood. His Spanish connections would prove a great asset to him after coming to America.

In 1796, the Rev. James Maxwell was appointed pastor of the Catholic Church at Ste. Genevieve, Missouri. He was well educated, was held in high esteem by the Spanish government, often being selected to a position of authority. After the Louisiana Purchase, the priest continued to have power and influence in the Territory of Louisiana and the Missouri Territory. He was appointed by the President of the United States to the Council of Nine after Missouri became a Territory in 1812 and was chosen chairman by this group.

James Maxwell had become curate of Ste. Genevieve and vicar general of Illinois by 1799, when he applied for a huge Spanish land grant on Black River in present day Reynolds County. (A curate is a clergyman who assists a vicar or rector. A vicar general in the Anglican Church is a layman serving as a deputy to an archbishop or bishop.) This grant was for 112,896 arpents or approximately 96,000 acres. (An arpent represents about .85 acres.) We will quote from the record:

"To Don Carlos Dehauk Delassus, Lieutenant Colonel in the Royal Armies and Lieutenant Governor of Upper Louisiana:

"Don Diego Maxwell, curate of Ste. Genevieve and Vicar General of Illinois, with all the respect due to you, represents that the Most Excellent Duke De Aleudia, Minister of State and Universal Despacho of the Indies, having manifested his desire that catholics from Ireland should come to settle themselves in this colony of Louisiana, knowing them to be faithful subjects and affectionate to the Spanish Government on account of their religion, as appears by the annexed letter of Don Thomas O'Ryan, Chaplain of honor of his Majesty and Confessor of the Queen, our lady, written to the petitioner in the English language, by order of his Excellency, the above named Minister, the government engaging to have a church built for them in their settlement and leaving to the judgement of the petitioner to solicit the government the quantity of land of the royal domain which he will think necessary for himself and said settlers. There being some vacant lands belonging to the domain, upon which no settlement has been made to this day, situated between Black River and the Current which are branches of the White River at the distance of from thirty to thirty five leagues from this town; therefore the petitioner humbly supplicates that you will condescend to take the necessary measures in order to enable him to obtain from the government, in full property, the concession of four leagues square making the quantity of 112,896 Arpents of land in superfices, in the said place, and for the aforementioned purpose; the petitioner having no object but the advantage to his Majesty's service and Salvation of the Souls which shall be confined to his care. He at the same time informs you that several of the above mentioned Irish Catholics induced by him, have already arrived from Ireland, and that many others are coming, and now on their way, with a part of his own family not without great expenses and cost to your petitioner, for which he hopes to be remunerated by the government. And if not, by God and the gratitudes of those poor people, for having rescued them from the British tyranny and persecution to which they were exposed on account of their religion. This Favor, solicited by the petitioner, he hopes to obtain from the generosity of the government which you represent in this part of the colony, as be conformable to the intentions of his Majesty, communicated by his Minister. Meanwhile, he will pray God to preserve your important life many years.

"Ste. Genevieve, October 15, 1799, Diego Maxwell

Charles D. DeLassus, the Lieutenant Governor, granted this request November 3, 1799, and the land was surveyed, dated and certified February 9, 1806.

The land board rejected this claim as early as 1806 because the claimant had not met the consideration of which this grant was founded, which was an obligation to bring Irish Roman Catholic emigrants and form a settlement. James Maxwell claimed the reason for not having complied was the existing war and the subsequent prohibition of emigration from Ireland.

The land board, which consisted of John C. Lucas, Clement B. Penrose, and Frederick Bates, again rejected the claim in 1810, but, somehow, like so many Spanish grants, the litigation lingered on until 1835, when a new land board was of the unanimous opinion that this claim "ought not to be confirmed, the conditions not having been complied with."

On September 5, 1799, Maxwell again asked the Spanish government for 3,000 arpents of land for his two brothers with their respective families and other persons of his kindred, who were coming to join him to avoid persecution in their native England. This land was near New Bourbon, where James Maxwell lived. The lieutenant governor of Upper Louisiana, DeLassus, granted this request, also.

In 1808 the Louisiana Academy was established and James Maxwell was one of the trustees. The trustees submitted a letter to the Senate and House of Representatives of the United States. This letter stated:

"The inhabitants of the District of Ste. Genevieve and the Territory of Louisiana are anxious to procure the means and opportunity of diffusing knowledge and information among the rising generation, have by Voluntary Subscription raised a fund toward establishing an Academy for the instruction of youth." This letter goes on to say: "Said institutions are induced to look to the government of the United States for such aid and support . . . "

The local citizens by subscription made up $1,904 cash and $814 for material and labor. A number of these contributor were men of distinction who had played an important role in the territory and who would later make their mark in Missouri history.

James Maxwell undoubtedly never lived on the Maxwell Reserve on Black River. Possibly, he had never set foot on the entire 96,000 acres. But the long, drawn-out litigation that lasted nearly thirty years prevented Reynolds County from getting a lot of pioneers that it would have otherwise.

James Maxwell, who was born in 1742, died on May 28, 1814. He was thrown from his horse after leaving church service and died the following day from the injuries incurred. He was given the highest honor at his death by being buried in the church at Ste. Genevieve. Only three people have been so honored.

The huge reserve passed on to his two nephews, John P. and Hugh H. Maxwell, who tried — as their uncle had done — to hold on to the grant.

John Rice Jones took the seat vacated by the death of Father Maxwell in 1814 in the Council of Nine and William Neely was made presiding officer.

Father Gibault, who had been vicar-general before Father Maxwell, was reprimanded by Bishop Carroll of Baltimore for selling land belonging to the church for his individual gain. After Father Maxwell became vicar-general of Upper Louisiana, he also rebuked Father Gibault for being so lenient in collecting legal fees for marriages and marriage banns and for marrying a Mr. Randall and Miss Sarah Waller, a minor, without her parents' consent. Father Maxwell further advised him that heretofore he had granted him his protection and favorable report as to his conduct to the bishop, who had requested him to keep a watchful eye upon him, but if he continued in his present conduct, he would have to pursue a different course.

It is apparent the Father Gibault was not then in favor with the ecclesiastical authorities. This apparently came about by land sales in the Kaskaskia and Cahokia area which the priest had sold to John Rice Jones and Nicholas Jarrot. Father Maxwell, although he had obtained huge land grants, avoided problems with the church.

The original description of the land would be impossible to comprehend as the survey record reads: "I do certify that the above plot represents 112,898 Arpens French Measure situated on the forks of Black River about 80 miles west of Cape Girardeau, beginning on a hackbury on the NE bank of the South Fork of Black River running N. 60 E. 280 poles to a branch 960 ot Middle Fork 450 to Branch 500 to N. Fork 430 to branch 440 to White Oak corner from thence S. 30 E. 150 to Branch 3190 to Branch 20 to Black Oak corner S. 60 W 1320 to the river 2040 to stake N 30 W 3360 to the beginning."

One corner of the reserve started near Centerville and ran Northeast to the headwaters of the Taum Sauk Creek, then Southeast to the vicinity of Cloride in Iron County, then Southwest to an area southeast of Redford, then to its starting point near Centerville — an area four leagues or twelve miles square by modern terminology.

After Rev. James Maxwell's death, the two heirs were successful in getting the United States Congress in 1816 to pass the following act: "Be it enacted by the Senate and the House of Representatives of the United States of America in Congress assembled, that all the rights, title and interest of the United States, of in and do any real estate whereof a certain James Maxwell died seized on the 28th day of May one thousand eight hundred and fourteen, be, and the same is hereby released unto John P. Maxwell of the Missouri Territory and Hugh H. Maxwell of the Territory of Illinois, nephews of the James Maxwell, and the same is hereby vested in the said John P. Maxwell, Hugh H. Maxwell and their heirs forever as fully as if they were citizens of the United States, on the said fourteenth day of May one thousand eight hundred and fourteen, saving and reserving to all persons, other than the United States, any right, title or interest of, in and to the premises aforesaid, whereof the said James Maxwell died seized as fully and amply as if this law had not been passed. Approved April 17, 1816."

John P. Maxwell died leaving Hugh H. Maxwell his only heir. Hugh apparently had three children: Sophie Angelique, Lucian B., and Ferdinand Maxwell. Sophie Angelique Maxwell married Joseph Michael Chenn.

The Catholic church where Rev. Maxwell was buried has a plaque that reads, "Rev. James Maxwell died 28 May 1814, age 72."

REFERENCES

Missouri Archives
History of Missouri, by Houck
Ste. Genevieve Catholic Church records
The District of Ste. Genevieve, by Lucille Basler

JOHN BUFORD

John Buford, the son of William and Annie Pate Buford, was born May 28, 1793, in Bedford County, Virginia.

John and his descendants were destined to become some of the most respected and influential families ever to live in Reynolds County.

John was chosen to be surveyor by the governor of Missouri when Reynolds County was formed in 1845. He had served Shannon County as their surveyor, being appointed in 1842.

John Buford would continue to serve as surveyor of Reynolds County until he was elected state representative of Missouri for three consecutive terms, 1850, 1852, 1854. He was again appointed surveyor in 1857 to serve the unexpired term of Joseph Ketcherside.

According to the headstone at John Buford's grave, located on the farm where he lived and now known as the Dobbins Cemetery, he came to Reynolds County in 1825. This is the date inscribed on his headstone. He was certainly not the first white man to come to the county, but a very early settler.

John Buford married Elizabeth "Betty" Davis Ervin on January 2, 1827. Elizabeth had married Alexander Irvin in Albermarle County, Virginia, and they had lived there until his early death. Elizabeth had then joined other members of her family in their trip to Missouri.

John's parents, William and Annie Pate Buford, were married October 20, 1791, in Bedford County, Virginia. Some time in the early part of 1800 they moved to Breckenridge, Kentucky, and then on to the Belleview Valley in Washington County, Missouri, in about 1814.

It has been written that William Buford had great wealth, owning hundreds of slaves. Some wealth was apparent, as many land transactions would indicated he was a man of some means. The 1830 census shows him with 27 slaves and his son, John, with nine slaves.

William and Annie Pate Buford had seven known children: John, born May 28, 1793; Mary "Polly", born November 1, 1794, married Henry Eidson; Abraham; Nancy, married Bartlett W. Yeargain on August 31, 1831; William Jr.; Pate, born August 26, 1808; and James M. Nancy Buford Yeargain died August 15, 1832 and Bartlett died August 18, 1859.

William Buford's many land purchases included a section of land (640 acres) near the three forks of the Black River. This was a part of the Maxwell Reserve and one of its best parts, with deep alluvial bottom soil. It represented the finest form of land this country had to offer. William bought this land in 1818 and gave it to John. William Buford died January 17, 1842. His wife, Annie Pate, must have died after the 1840 census was taken, as a woman advanced in years was shown in William Buford's household.

John Buford and his wife, Elizabeth, were the parents of 13 children, which included three sets of twins. Five of these children died in infancy.

Another died before he reached 20 years.

Their first child, Nancy, was born October 18, 1827. She married William Carty in 1848. He was a son of Moses and Elizabeth Carty.

Mary was their second child. She was born June 24, 1829. Her first marriage was to Andrew Robinson in 1847. Andrew was a son of John L. and Sarah Bryan Robinson. After Andrew Robinson's death, Mary married Daniel Horney. Mary Buford Horney died in 1915.

Henry and Elizabeth were the first set of twins born to John and Elizabeth Irvin Buford. They were born in 1831. Henry died in infancy, but Elizabeth survived and married B.F. Campbell in about 1850. Elizabeth and her husband both died in 1856.

Martha Jane was the fifth child. She was born December 24, 1832, and married Hugh P. Faulkenberry in 1848. They are shown on the 1850 census of Reynolds County. Martha Jane Buford Faulkenberry died September 17, 1902.

A second set of twins, John and William Buford, were born in 1833 and died at birth.

James Buford, born March 1, 1835, was the eighth child of John and Elizabeth Irvin Buford. He died in 1853 unmarried.

Children nine and ten, Abraham and Lucy, were born May 1, 1840. Abraham Buford married America Moore in 1865 and they became progenitors of a number of Reynolds County's most successful and talented citizens. America was a daughter of William and Mary Westmoreland Moore, who came to Reynolds County from North Carolina in 1857. Lucy Buford married John P. George on October 18, 1860. He was a son of Andrew Lewis George and Mary Jane Eidson.

Another set of twins were born to John and Elizabeth Irvin Buford in 1843. They were Margaret and Sarah, children eleven and twelve. Both died in infancy.

Eliza Buford, born July 10, 1846, was the last child born to them. She married Henry Robinson and they had no children. After Henry's death, Eliza married Thomas D. Imboden in 1870. She died in 1896.

The Lesterville area was once known as "Buford", named for John Buford, but this name gradually disappeared and Lesterville became the accepted name in the 1830's.

John and Elizabeth Buford were Baptists in their belief and, without doubt, were early members of The Black River Baptist Church. However, they are not shown on the membership in 1850.

Searching the land records of Iron and Reynolds Counties, one is amazed at the numerous transactions involving John Buford and his brother, Pate Buford.

John Buford died March 28, 1874, and his wife, Elizabeth, who was born August 10, 1802, died November 10, 1863. Both were buried in the Dobbins

Cemetery on the old home place, a cemetery no longer habitable because of age and neglect.

The Buford family had had a long and successful life in America. They have excelled in many fields since before the Revolutionary War and they continue to display those same characteristics yet today.

Compiled and written by: Kathryn McKenzie Vickery
P.O. Box 94
Ellington, MO 63638
and
James E. Bell
P.O. Box 287
Black, MO 63625

REFERENCES
History and Genealogy of the Buford Family in America with Records of a Number of Allied Families, by Captain Marcus Bainbridge Buford, San Francisco, California, 1903. Revised and Enlarged by George Washington Buford and Mildred Buford Minter in 1924.

PATE BUFORD

Pate Buford, fondly known as the "Father of Reynolds County", was born August 26, 1808, in Bedford County, Virginia. He migrated with his parents, William and Annie Pate Buford to Bellview Valley, in Washington County, Missouri, in about 1814. They settled on land near the Buford Mountains, which were named for his father, William Buford.

Here Pate grew to manhood and married Arlotte Carty, who was born May 20, 1811, in Cumberland County, Kentucky. She was a daughter of James and Sarah Copeland Carty, who were pioneers to Cumberland County, Kentucky, in 1803 and pioneers to Washington County, Missouri, in about 1820. James was the eldest son of John Carty, born prior to 1755. The first documentation of the location of John Carty was the birth of his son, James, on August 11, 1774 in Surry County, North Carolina. Sarah "Sally" Copeland Carty was a sister of Lot Copeland, born ca. 1772 in Surry County, North Carolina. The Cartys and Copelands were likely neighbors in Surry County, North Carolina, when James and Sally married about 1797.

James and Sally Carty had the following children: Joseph, born November 20, 1789, who married Julia Jamison; Elizabeth, born March 20, 1801, who married Green Berry Goggin; Amy Ann, born September 25, 1803, who married William Cape; Joshua, born July 28, 1806, who married Charlotte Mallow; Nancy, born August 11, 1808, who married Milton Goggin; Arlotte; Califurnia, born September 18, 1814, who married Thomas Buford, a first cousin of Pate Buford; Adromache, born March 18, 1818, who married John Jamison; and John I.C., born November 5, 1821, who apparently did not marry.

Pate Buford moved often and was always dealing in land, buying and selling. It would be almost impossible to pin-point his location at any given time.

He was selected state representative of Shannon County in 1844, and, being a transplant product of Black River, he started almost immediately to push for the formation of Reynolds County, thus the pet name "Father of Reynolds County". After Reynolds County was formed in 1845, Pate was destined to serve as the county's first representative in 1846. He again represented Reynolds County in the General Assembly in 1860. The Civil War was soon raging and it is not clear who served in 1862.

The children of Pate and Arlotte Carty Buford were: Sarah A., who was born December 11, 1831 and died November 5, 1850; James, who was born September 21, 1834, married Lettie Susan Stoner on December 18, 1855 — this marriage ended in divorce and he married Marie Louise Bacon on January 28, 1867. James Buford was prominent in Iron County as a politician, farmer, and saw-mill entrepreneur. Third child, Nancy, died in infancy; William, who was born April 7, 1838, married Iowa Gulliver on December 20, 1860. She was a daughter of William H. Gulliver. William was elected presiding judge of the county court of Iron County, Missouri, for three terms. Fifth child, John, died in infancy; Green was accidentally killed by Milton Gallaher while serving with a unit of the Confederacy camped near Bloomfield, Missouri, during the Civil War. Milton was also from Reynolds County, being a son of George and Serena Miner Gallaher. Seventh child, Milton, died in infancy; Simeon E., who was born September 1, 1849, married Eliza A. Packard. Simeon held numerous political offices in Iron County and spent some time in Reynolds County.

Arlotte Carty Buford died of measles on August 14, 1858. Pate then married Delilah Chitwood, a daughter of Hugh and Jane Nicholas Chitwood. Hugh was born October 27, 1812, in Scott County, Tennessee, and died August 22, 1885. Jane Nicholas Chitwood was born January 15, 1815, and died October 26, 1891.

Children of Pate and Delilah Chitwood Buford were: Jane, who was born March 9, 1861, married Peter Ruhl on October 22, 1879; Paschal, who was born March 22, 1864, married Sarah R. Middleton, daughter of William R. and Sarah J. Middleton, on March 3, 1885; Thomas, who was born March 16, 1867, married a Miss Sinclair; George W., who was born September 9, 1869, married Faora Seal on May 20, 1896; a twin to George W. died at birth; Charles, who was born February 1, 1872, married Laura Clark, and, after Laura's death, Ollie Campbell.

Pate Buford held political office in Iron County after its formation in 1857, being county assessor.

Thomas Buford, a first cousin of John and Pate Buford, was the son of John and Rhoda Shrewbury Buford. He married Califurnia Carty on June 28, 1831, in Washington County, Missouri.

Their children were: John, born in August of 1833; Nancy, who was born March 4, 1836; James Carty Monroe, who was born December 16, 1839; Rhoda Jane, who was born October 16, 1842; Sarah, who was born April 14, 1844; William, who was born February 14, 1847, was killed April 16, 1865, on Webb Creek, Reynolds County, Missouri, by the Federal soldiers on the closing day of the Civil War.

The log house which has been credited with being the oldest building in Reynolds County was built about 1847. Rhoda Buford Carty, who lived until May 14, 1931, always told her descendants that her family moved into this new home when she was very young, five years old.

Pate Buford died on June 5, 1875, and was buried in the Eidson Cemetery in Iron County, Missouri.

REFERENCES

History and Genealogy of the Buford Family in America with Records of a Number of Allied Families, by Captain Marcus Bainbridge Buford, San Francisco, California, 1903. Revised and Enlarged by George Washington Buford and Mildred Buford Minter in 1924.

John Carty and 4000 Descendants, by Jamison, Cauley, Bell and Jaycox, 1979.

MARVIN MUNGER

Marvin Munger was appointed by the governor of Missouri in 1845 to serve as sheriff until an election could be held. He ran and was elected sheriff and collector in 1846. Marvin had served Shannon, the parent county of Reynolds, as sheriff in 1842.

During the 1800's, Marvin Munger's descendants married into the Shy, Parks, and Goggin families, who all contributed greatly to the political, social and religious growth of the region.

The Mungers who settled in Reynolds County trace their ancestry to Nicholas, who probably came from County Surrey in England as a small boy about 1639. The name Munger, in its various spellings, is found also among the Germans and the Dutch. Many of Nicholas' descendants have used other spellings of the name.

Little is known of Nicholas. His father's given name is unknown, but his mother's given name was probably Frances, wife of Henry Goldham or Goldam, her second husband, who was an early settler of New Haven and Guilford, New Haven County, Connecticut. Nicholas became a Freeman in 1652, so he was born no later than 1630-1.

Nicholas was married at Guilford on January 2, 1659/60 to Sarah Hall, who, according to some writers, was a daughter of William and Sarah Hall, both born at Rolvendon, County Kent, England. Nicholas died on October 16, 1668, at the East Parish of Guilford and Sarah then married Dennis Crampton. Sarah died January 31, 1689.

There were two sons from this couple, John, born on April 26, 1660, and Samuel, born in 1662-5, both in the East Parish of Guilford. John's descendants will not be discussed, as this family is well traced to 1914 in The Munger Book, by J.B. Munger.

Samuel was married on October 16, 1688, in Guilford to Sarah Hand, who was born March 2, 1664, at East Guilford. She was the daughter of Joseph Hand and Jane Wright. Their children, all born at the East Parish of Guilford, were: Samuel, born February 7, 1689/90; Joseph, born January 19, 1693/4; Sarah, born March 16, 1695/6; Deliverance, born March 12, 1697/8; Nathaniel, born February 26, 1699/1700; James, born May 1, 1701; Ann, born February 1, 1703/4; and Jane, born February 27, 1705/6. Both the Hand and Wright families were early Connecticut settlers from England. Samuel died in the East Parish of Guilford on March 5, 1717/8. Sarah married, second, Charles Woodworth. Sarah died August 1, 1751.

The younger Samuel was married on April 6, 1710, in Guilford, to Dorothy Evarts. She was born in 1683 and was a daughter of James Evart and Lydia Guttridge (Goodrich). Children, the first five born at the East Parish of Guilford, the sixth at Hampton, Windham County, Connecticut, and the remaining two at unknown locations, are: Submit, born January 5, 1711; Samuel and Nathaniel, born October 5, 1712; Elnathan, born July 14, 1714; Dorothy, date unknown; Joseph, born in July of 1719; Rebecca and Sarah, dates unknown. The Guttridges and Evarts were both English families. There is no record of the death or burial of Samuel and Dorothy. Samuel was a miller and farmer. His family appears to have moved to Hampton after 1714 and by 1725 to Brimfield, Hampden County, Massachusetts.

Nathaniel married first on July 1, 1736 to Elizabeth Bullen, who was born on June 21, 1718. She was a daughter of John Bullen. Children, all born in Brimfield, were: Jehiel, who was born June 3, 1737; Jessee, born April 5, 1739; Jonathon, born September 5, 1741; John, born April 29, 1744; Elizabeth, born July 7, 1746; Ephraim, born July 22, 1749; Solomon, born July 11, 1751; Eunice, born July 17, 1754; and Ichabod, born August 11, 1756. Elizabeth died on November 21, 1787, at the West Parish of South Brimfield (New Wales) and Nathaniel married Fear Shaw, of Ware, Hampshire County, Massachusetts. in June of 1788. Nathaniel was employed in the county's service in 1747 and in 1754-1756 for defense of the western frontiers.

Jehiel first married Mary Rogers, who died with her child at its birth. He then married Elsie Rogers in 1758. Their children were: Esther, who was born May 17, 1759, in Brimfield; Nathaniel, born April 25, 1762; Lydia, born April 24, 1764; Moses, born October 21, 1769; Polly, born January 17, 1773; Jehiel, born February 6, 1775; Sarah, born June 14, 1776; and Rebecca, born 1780. The last seven children were born in the West Parish of Brimfield. Jehiel married Mrs. Abigal Shepard third, on July 8, 1811, after Elsie Rogers died at Whiting, Addison County, Vermont, on April 20, 1798. Abigal Shepard Munger died, also at Whiting, in 1812. Jehiel and Abigal are buried in the old graveyard in the rear of the Baptist Church they attended in Whiting. Jehiel died in Whiting on August 3, 1817.

Captain Jehiel's name appears on the lists of soldiers belonging to several different regiments during the Revolutionary War.

Nathaniel probably left Brimfield before his father left in 1787. Nathaniel married Beulah Cox in 1786, and there is no record of them in Whiting except for the birth of their first four children: Olive and Clarissa, born February 17, 1787; Clark, born June 13, 1789; Jehiel, born April 26, 1790; Marvin, born in 1797-8; Nathaniel and Sarah, both born in the 1790s at Charleston, Montgomery County, New York; and Ira, born in the 1790s in Lima, New York. Nathaniel died at Lima in 1798, and Beulah died at Royalton, New York, on January 11, 1841.

Nathaniel was also a soldier of the Revolution, serving from July to December of 1780, with service at West Point, Orange County, New York.

Marvin came to Missouri about 1818 and married Salina Lewis on October 28, 1819 in Belleview Valley, Iron County, Missouri. She was born November 29, 1796, in Norwich, Windsor County, Vermont, and was the daughter of Ashael Lewis and Eunice Welch. Their children, all born at Munger's Mill, Reynolds County, were: Martha, born January 11, 1822; Orrin, born January 2, 1824; Lewis Preston, born July 21, 1826; Francis Marion, born April 19, 1834; Moses Wilbur, born October 6, 1836; and Mary Clementine, born August 31, 1839. The Lewis family, according to Pioneer Families in America, had moved to Ohio in 1816 and went from there to Kentucky. In 1819 they came to Missouri in keel boats, landing at Ste. Genevieve and settling in Washington County. Salina's brother, Rufus, later moved with his family to Montgomery County, where his children married and lived. This Lewis family came from England, the father immigrant was John Lewis, who died in December of 1676 in New London, New London County, Connecticut. Other early English Connecticut settler families in Salina's ancestry were Borden, Hough, Calkins, Scoville and Huntley.

Marvin settled with his family at the head of the Black River where he built the first grist mill in that part of Missouri. The place was early called Munger's Mill, but was later known as Munger until the post office there closed in 1934. Marvin was the first postmaster at Munger's Mill, appointed on March 24, 1840(?). Alfred Julian Munger, a grandson of Marvin, was postmaster at the time the postoffice closed.

In 1845, the Munger's Mill community became a part of Reynolds County. Marvin served this area in a number of capacities: Baptist minister, teacher, justice of the peace, sheriff and collector in Ripley County; and in Reynolds County as the first sheriff, in 1845, and collector. He built the first frame house in Reynolds County before the Civil War. The house was still occupied by his grandson, Ira Clarence, as late as 1928.

Marvin no doubt played an important part in the organization of the Black River Baptist Church, which was founded in 1833 and located on the Middle Fork of the Black River in the present-day community of Black, Reynolds County. He may have served as the church's first minister and also served as a messenger to the associational meeting held at sister churches in the 1840s. Later he belonged to the Baptist Church at Cedar Grove in Iron County, that church being closer to his home at Munger's Mill.

Marvin died at his home on the East Fork of the Black River of congestive chills on March 13, 1863.

Ira Munger is listed in the 1840 census for Black River, Washington County, between 30 and 40 years old and is believed to have been the brother of Marvin. On August 2, 1845, Ira was appointed by the governor as a temporary justice of the peace of Reynolds County. He was the first postmaster at Centerville, Reynolds County, appointed February 2, 1846. Another brother, Clark, according to The Munger Book, who lived in Hartland, New York, was visiting Marvin in 1850, died early in the morning following his arrival and was buried at Munger's Mill.

Martha married William Andrews and moved to Montgomery County, Missouri. She does not appear in the 1850 census for Missouri, but the book, A Reminiscent History of the Ozark Region, mentions that, in 1894, she was still living, but widowed.

Orrin married Malinda Shy on March 2, 1848. She was born on May 4, 1826, a daughter of Eli Shy and Mary Elizabeth Smith. Their children were: Sarah Jane, born June 19, 1850, in Reynolds County; Nathaniel, born March 1, 1852; Mary S., born October 24, 1854; Martha, born February 17, 1857; Elizabeth M. Born May 10, 1859; Elvina, born January 3, 1862; and Madilena, born May 11, 1864. All were born in Missouri. According to family tradition, Orrin died in the Confederate service at Memphis, Shelby County, Tennessee, in 1862 (1863?), where his brother Lewis Preston also died in the service in 1863. The official Confederate Army records list approximately 20 Mungers who served in the Civil War with a Dudley Munger (No family connection has been found with the Reynolds County Mungers.) being the only one assigned to a Missouri army unit. Neither of these Munger brothers are listed in the records. Orrin was appointed a justice of the peace in Reynolds County in 1864, which places a question on the family tradition about his being killed earlier in the service. Malinda died on March 10, 1904, in Lufkin, Angelina County, Texas. In 1860 the family lived in Black River Township.

Sarah Jane married James Warren Wilson on July 5, 1866, at Centerville. He was born December 1, 1843, in Tishomingo County, Mississippi, a son of Jacob Wilson and Jemine Burgess. Their children were: Jacob Orrin, born September 17, 1867; William Nathaniel, born February 20, 1870; Mary Bell, born November 1, 1872; Hangford, born about 1874, died April 2, 1889, buried in Dobbins Cemetery, Reynolds County; Alfred Howell, born August 8, 1875; Thomas Monroe, born September 19, 1878; Norman Wentworth, born September 28, 1881; (Mont?) Edwin, born June 9, 1884; unnamed twins, born February 9, 1887, died the same day; Virgil Irving, born September 21, 1890; and Otto Munger, born November 26, 1892. James Warren died November 26, 1912, in Birchtree, Shannon County, Missouri. The family lived in Lesterville Township 1880-1900, where he was a farmer.

Nathaniel married Mary Boby on December 28, 1871. Mary was born in 1844-5 in South Carolina. Their children, all born in Missouri, were: Martha Jane, born October 2, 1872; Ida O., born May 21, 1875; James A., born June 13, 1877; Annie F., born December 5, 1879; Mont (?) H., May 6, 1883; unnamed daughter, born May 24, 1885, in Lesterville, Reynolds County, and died the same day; Lana Myrtle, born July 27, 1886; unidentified child, February 10, 1893; and Marvin F., March 3, 1896. Mary died on March 12, 1896. Tombstones without dates for Mary and a son are in the Pleasant Hill Cemetery in Reynolds County. The family lived in Carter Township, Carter County, Missouri, in 1900. He was identified as a farmer.

Mary S. married George Wash Hunter on November 7, 1869. He was born in 1847-8 in Mississippi. They had six children.

Martha died in August of 1863 (1857?) and is buried in Dobbins Cemetery.

Elizabeth M. married Henley Nelson Campbell on December 20, 1877, in Reynolds County. He was born in September of 1856 in Tennessee. Their children were: D.J., born in 1880; Mont E., born in June of 1882; Freddie A., born in January of 1885; Robert L., born in October of 1887; George B., born in May of 1890; Birdie M., born in May of 1893; James M., born in January of 1894; and William N., born in April of 1896. All were born in Missouri. D.J. is not found in later censuses, so it is presumed that the child died before 1900. The family lived in Liberty Township, Iron County.

Elvina married John Vinson on December 24, 1884 in Reynolds County. If he is the John Vinson listed in the 1880 census for Reynolds County, John was born in 1850-51 in Missouri. They had four children. Elvina was shown as a school teacher in the Reynolds County census of 1880.

Madilena married Sterling P. Irvin on November 3, 1885, in Lesterville. Sterling was born in 1862-3 in Missouri, the son of Samuel H. and Mary M. Irvin. They had four children.

Lewis Preston married Myra Jane Parks on August 1, 1847, in Lesterville. She was born December 23, 1832 in Lesterville, the daughter of Marshall Parks and Mary Williams. Their children were: Mary Salome, born October 1, 1848; Rosanna O., born August 22, 1851; Marshall M., born December 26, 1854; Salina C., born March 11, 1856; Ulissus S., born May 9, 1858; Preston Clark, born September 18, 1860; and Alfred A., born September 7, 1863. All were born in Missouri. Lewis Preston was a farmer and a carpenter. He died in 1863 as mentioned before. Myra Jane married second William Alcorn, who was born in 1830-1 in Illinois. They had one daughter, Delora. The 1860 census for Iron Township, Iron County, listed with William Alcorn: Sarah H., age 17, born in Illinois; Joseph A., age 10; Elizabeth J., age 7; John W., age 5; Martha L. age 3; and Mary C., age 4 months. The Black River Township census for 1870 included Alcorn children: Joseph, 1850-1 (Joseph H., December 10, 1850?); Jane and John, 1851-2; Martha, 1856-7; Mary, 1858-9; William, 1860-1; Henry, 1861-2; and Nancy, 1865-6; and Marshall, Salina, Clark and Alfred Munger with Myra Jane and William. The Alcorn family lived in Lesterville.

Mary Salome married William Alexander Ramsey in 1868 in Reynolds County. William was born in December of 1845 in North Carolina, the son of Sanders Taylor Ramsey and Leah Light. In the 1880 census, their children were: Lurena Belle, age 12; and Preston Taylor, age 10. Both were born in Missouri. William Alexander served in the Confederate Army from the summer of 1864 until the end of the war. The family lived in Iron County until about 1879, then spent four years in St. Francois County. In 1883, they moved to Shannon County, where in 1900 they lived in Bartlett Township. William Alexander was a farmer and carpenter and also served, starting in 1892, as an associate justice of the Shannon County Court.

Marshall M. married Eugenia L. Zolman on September 5, 1878 in Farmington, in St. Francois County. She was born January 20, 1857, near Farmington and was the daughter of Joel and Louiza Zolman. Their children were: Charles M., born August 11, 1879 in Farmington; Harrie L., born December 8, 1881 in Farmington, died February 22, 1884; Laura Alice, born June 8, 1884 in Farmington; Roy Luman, born September 12, 1886, in Eureka Springs, Carroll County, Arkansas; Ethel L., born March 8, 1890, in Eureka Springs; Harvey E., born August 19, 1892 in Eureka Springs; and Alfred A., born August 22, 1896, in Arkansas. Marshall M. was ordained to the ministry on March 15, 1896, by the First Missionary Baptist Church of Eureka Springs. In 1900 the family was living in Cedar Township, Carroll County.

Preston Clark married Helen M. White on July 17, 1891, in Florence, Lauderdale County, Alabama. Helen was born May 20, 1868, in Florence, the daughter of William T. and Susan White. Their children were: Cecil Clark, born June 17, 1897; and Helen Eugenia, born September 13, 1899. Preston Clark was a carpenter and about 1914 lived in Evansville, Vanderburg County, Indiana.

Moses Wilbur married Adeline "Nancy" Light on April 2, 1863 at Munger's Mill. She was born in February of 1838 or 1839 in North Carolina, the daughter of Isreal and Mary Light. Their children, all born at Munger's Mill, were: Cordelia, born January 18, 1864; Amy, born February 15, 1866; Alfred Julian, born October 2, 1867; Minnie L., born November 30, 1871; Ira Clarence, born October 27, 1873; Mary Ollie, born February 2, 1875; Clara C., born February 12, 1877; and Watson M., born February 29, 1880. Moses Wilbur was a farmer and he was born, lived and died (August 6, 1922) on the old homestead at Munger's Mill. Nancy died February 6, 1902. They are buried in the Fitzgerald Cemetery, Reynolds County. There is a tombstone for Samanthia Munger dated October 5, 1867 with the age at three years, seven months, two days, the daughter of M.W. and A. Munger. The resulting birth date of March 3, 1864, conflicts with Cordelia's birth date and it had not been determined which is correct. Four children had died by the time the 1910 census was taken. Moses Wilbur was postmaster at Munger's Mill in 1910. The Light family came from either Belgium or Germany.

Cordelia married August Charles Tiefenauer in 1882-3. According to his tombstone in the Fitzgerald Cemetery, he was born on October 6, 1861, in Switzerland. His parents were John Baptist and Mary Ann Tiefenauer. Their children were: Lucy Estelle, born October 27, 1885; Charles Edgar, born February 27, 1887; Rose, born about 1888, died before the 1900 census; Flora M., born December 10, 1889; William H., born October 10, 1890; Walter F., born March 13, 1894; George Andrew, born January 25, 1896; Grace L. born, May 19, 1898, died April 1, 1901; Thomas Elza, born August 11, 1900; and Bessie V., December 1, 1904. All were born at Munger. August died June 9, 1908 (June 9, 1902 on tombstone). The 1900 census shows the family living in both Arcadia Township and Kaolin Township, Iron County, where he farmed.

Amy died October 11, 1867, and is buried in the Fitzgerald Cemetery.

Alfred Julian was married first on February 12, 1893 to Nellie "Ella"

Thompson, the daughter of Joseph Thompson. Their children were: William Ara, born November 25, 1893; Daisy and Bessie, probably all born at Munger. The two daughters, born two years apart, died young and are buried in the Fitzgerald Cemetery, apparently without markers. Alfred Julian was married second on October 25, 1899 to Sarah O'Bryan Rich. She was born July 6, 1875, in Hog Eye, Missouri, the daughter of John Kelley O'Bryan and Lutrecia Bond. Their children were: Lola Belle, born October 2, 1900; Othal Homer, born August 28, 1903; Goldie Viola, born January 12, 1905; Grace Adelle, born April 25, 1907; Alfred Truman, born July 13, 1909; Essie Leota, born September 16, 1912; Clyde Eldon, born January 19, 1915; and Orrin Lloyd, born January 10, 1922. All were born at Munger. Sarah Anna had previously married Joseph Alexander Rich on January 2, 1895. He was born in 1883-4 in Missouri, and was probably the son of R.A. and Mary Rich. Their children were: Milborn Oswald, born November 26, 1895, died March 26, 1896; and Ezra Dow, born August 26, 1897. Both were probably born in Missouri. Joseph Alexander Rich died February 13, 1898. Alfred Julian died February 16, 1944, at Belleview, Iron County, and Sarah died July 30, 1951, in St. Louis. The couple is buried in the Fitzgerald Cemetery. Alfred Julian was the last postmaster at Munger where he lived until 1939 when he moved to Farmington for a short time before moving to Belleview.

Minnie married Alexander McClure O'Bryan on October 21, 1895 at Munger. He was born in November of 1867 in Virginia and was a brother of Sarah Anna O'Bryan, above. Their children were: Virdie S., born in January of 1897; Kelly W., born January 9, 1900; Lona, born March 28, 1901; Charity, born May 31, 1903; Marshall, born November 26, 1905; Lora, born September 13, 1907; and Paul and Silas, born August 12, 1909. All were born at Munger. The couple had lost two children by the 1900 census. Alexander McClure died May 17, 1936, near Desloge, St. Francois County, and Minnie died September 28, 1960, at Farmington. They are buried in the Methodist Cemetery at Caledonia, Washington County.

Ira Clarence was married first to Rhona Fitzgerald on September 25, 1898, at Munger. Rhona was born November 6, 1881, at Munger, the daughter of John Fitzgerald and Elisema Schrum. Their children were: Lemuel Tesro, born March 21, 1905; unnamed daughter, still born 1906-7; Oscar Marshall, born April 26, 1908; Andrew Jackson, born September 20, 1909; Lottie Belle, born August 6, 1911, and Lewis Donald, born January 28, 1913. All were born at Munger. Ira Clarence's second marriage was to Elizabeth "Lizzie" McNail Sizemore on November 9, 1935 at Munger. She was born in March of 1875 at Munger and was the daughter of Joe and Mary McNail. Ira Clarence died May 27, 1942, in Ironton, Iron County, and Rhona died June 27, 1915, at Black. They are buried in the Fitzgerald Cemetery. Elizabeth died about 1950 at St. Louis and is buried in the Caledonia Methodist Cemetery. The family lived in Lesterville Township.

Mary Ollie married Fritz Mund in 1893-4. He was born in November of

1871 in Missouri. Their children were: Josie, born in November of 1894; Lillie, born in January of 1896; Effie, born in November of 1898; Maud, born 1906, died 1917; Alice, born in 1908, also died in 1917; and Ruth, born in 1914. All were probably born in Missouri. Mary Ollie died in 1948 at Pilot Knob in Iron County. Fritz died in 1946 on his farm. The first two children were not shown in the 1900 census, so they probably died before that time. The family lived in Lesterville Township, where Fritz was a farmer.

Clara C. married Edward E. Nugent, who was born about 1860, possibly in Wisconsin. Their children were: Ralph, born July 30, 1897, at Munger; Marie, born April 16, 1902, at St. Louis; unidentified twins, born 1903-4, died in infancy; Myrtle, born November 4, 1905, at Sawyer in Iron County, died in infancy; unnamed son, born in 1906, still born; Francis, born July 30, 1908; and Estelleene, born March 21, 1909. Children without birth places shown were born at Iron Mountain, St. Francois County. Edward E. died about 1909 at Iron Mountain of pneumonia, the result of being chilled when the Iron Lake dam broke. He is buried in St. Louis. The 1910 census lists only children: Ralph, Maria, Myrtle, and Frank with their mother, living in St. Francois County.

Watson M. "Waty" married Charles L. Fitzgerald on September 26, 1900. Charles was born in 1879 in Missouri and was the brother of Rhona, who married "Waty's" brother, Ira Clarence. Their children were: Bula I., born August 7, 1901; Buren F., born May 12, 1903; Paul W. born October 22, 1905; Bessie May, born October 25, 1907; Hazel, born October 20, 1908; Hartford, born January 23, 1911; Golden and Goldie, born March 6, 1913; Doyle Lewis, born May 11, 1914; Woodrow Marshall, born November 17, 1915, at Monterey in Reynolds County; and Russell T., born December 10, 1918. All except Woodrow Marshall born at Munger. Charles L. died in 1943 and "Waty" died in 1967 at Ellington. The couple is buried in the Ellington Cemetery.

Mary Clementine married Isreal Light about 1860. Isreal was born in December of 1838 in North Carolina, a brother of Adeline, who married Moses Wilbur. Their children were: Francis Marion, born in March of 1860; Albert C., born in September of 1861; and Emma, born in 1869-70. All were born in Missouri. The 1880 census adds William H., age 11 (August 1873 in later census), and L. Jesseemarie, age 3, both born in Missouri. A son, Preston Lewis, died in 1867, according to a tombstone in the Fitzgerald Cemetery. Mary Clementine died in 1929. The family lived in Lesterville Township, where he farmed.

Francis Marion married Mary Salome Parks on August 23, 1858 at Lesterville. She was born December 23, 1832, at Lesterville and was a sister of Myra, wife of Lewis Preston. Their children were: William Andrew, born March 30, 1861, at Lesterville; Marshall Marvin, born February 5, 1863; Orrin Lafayette, born March 23, 1865; Letha M., born January 11, 1867; Mary Demaris, born February 5, 1869; and George W., born March 9, 1871.

The latter children were all born at Munger's Mill. Mary Salome died March 20, 1914, at Piedmont, in Wayne County, Missouri, and is buried in the Dexter Cemetery, Stoddard County, Missouri. Francis Marion died November 18 (September 29?) 1890 at Lesterville and is buried in the Dobbins Cemetery. The 1860 census indicates he was a blacksmith. There is a tombstone in the Dobbins Cemetery for Malinda Munger, who died in 1867. This is probably the daughter, Letha M.

Goodspeed's Reminiscent History of the Ozark Region indicates that Francis Marion served in the Confederate Army under General Price, but only for a short time because of sickness. However, just as for his two brothers, no official record of his service has been found.

The Munger Book indicates that this family moved to Texas about 1878 but remained there only one year before returning to Lesterville.

William Andrew married Alice N. "Allie" Moore on January 11, 1888, in Reynolds County. She was born on March 17, 1868, in Missouri, and was the daughter of Dr. John W. Moore and Zerelda Jamison. William Andrew died October 18, 1888, at Centerville, and is buried in the Dobbins Cemetery. An infant son of William and Nancy died in 1885 and is buried in the same cemetery. This poses the questions of whether or not Alice was known as Nancy, or if William Andrew had and earlier marriage or if the son's death date is incorrect. "Allie's" second marriage was to Aaron Murdock "Dick" Shriver on December 24, 1890 in Reynolds County. He was the son of Aaron Proctor Shriver and Nancy Jean Hunter Lapiere. (Aaron appears on the 1880 census as Aaron Lapere.) They had one daughter, Nita N., born in November 1881-2 in Missouri. They were divorced before 1910 when "Allie" and her daughter were listed with "Allie's" father in the census. "Allie" married William W. Allen on February 15, 1913. "Allie" died on April 26, 1929, and, with W.W. Allen, is buried in the Ellington Cemetery.

Marshall Marvin married Sarah Ella Shy at Centerville on September 5, 1887. She was the daughter of Alfred Howe Shy and Sarah Jane Goggin. Their children were: Thomas Orrin, born July 19, 1888, in Escondido, San Diego County, California; Myra Ina, born January 28, 1890, at Centerville; unnamed daughter, born December 1, 1891 at Centerville; unnamed son, born July 10, 1892, in Centerville; William Andrew, born December 26, 1893, at Centerville; Harry Shy, born July 19, 1896, at Bonne Terre, St. Francois County; Mary Calphurnia, born July 11, 1899 at Farmington; Marvin Marshall, born December 1, 1901, in Enid, Garfield County, Oklahoma Territory; Sarah Ella, born February 28, 1903, at Harper, Harper County, Kansas; Georgia Pauline, born July 4, 1906, at Enid; and Frances Amy, born July 23, 1909, at Blackwell, Kay County, Oklahoma. As of 1986, five of these are still living and at the time Marshall Marvin and Sarah Ella have 163 descendants. Marshall Marvin died March 28, 1938, and Sarah Ella died March 3, 1948, both in Stillwater, Payne County, Oklahoma. They are buried in the Grace Hill Cemetery at Perry, Noble County, Oklahoma.

Marshall Marvin studied law as a young man, as did his two brothers, but chose the ministry for his life profession and was ordained a Baptist minister in Missouri. He was also a school teacher. Shortly after their marriage, the couple moved to Escondido, California, accompanying Sarah Ella's brother, Thomas Jefferson Shy, and his family. "Tommy" Shy was seeking a warmer and drier climate as treatment for his tuberculosis. The family must have returned to Reynolds County in 1889, as their second child was born there in January of 1890. The next ten years were spent serving pastorates in Centerville, Lesterville, Bonne Terre and Farmington. The family's moves can be traced by the birth places of the children. On September 19, 1895, M.M. Munger was elected pastor of the Pleasant Exchange Baptist Church (later Ellington Baptist Church) at Ellington.

Orrin Layfayette married Minnie Marvin Lee on December 13, 1890, in Van Buren, Carter County, Missouri. Minnie was born in August of 1870 in Missouri, the daughter of Arch Lee of Madison County, Missouri. This Lee family came from Virginia and is related to the famous Lee families of Virginia. Their children were: Lucille; Archie; Damaris June Lee, born August 12, 1896, in Van Buren; Orrin Lee, born January 5, 1899, in Van Buren; George Ronald, born in April of 1903 (?), in Greenville, Wayne County, Missouri; and Mary Lee, born February 19, 1907, in Greenville. Minnie Marvin was educated at the State Normal School and was a member of the Methodist Episcopal Church. Orrin Layfayette attended schools at Farmington and at Carlton Institute and after assisting his father on the farm until 1888, went to Carter County. There he took the position of deputy clerk in the county clerk's office, later the office of deputy sheriff and county collector and in 1889 he was elected sheriff of Carter County and served two terms. After 1891 he studied law and was admitted to the bar in 1893. He began his practice in Van Buren. In 1893 he became the owner of The Van Buren Current Local newspaper at that city. The family moved to Wayne County about 1900 where he practiced his profession in Greenville until 1910. At that time they moved to Piedmont, Missouri, where he lived until his death. Orrin Layfayette died on August 13, 1928, at Piedmont in Wayne County.

Mary Demaris married George W. Cross on July 5, 1891, at Centerville. George was born March 30, 1872, at Sturgeon, Boone County, Missouri, the son of Samuel F. and Susan F. Cross. They had two daughters: Glenn F., born in August of 1892 in Missouri; and Carrie Salome, born in May of 1896 in Missouri. They lived at Piedmont, at Cape Girardeau, Cape Girardeau County, where he owned a printing business and newspaper, and Salina, Saline County, Kansas. They later moved to Ponca City, Kay County, Oklahoma, where George owned and operated a printing business. George was a great lover of bird dogs and quail hunting. George died on August 24, 1949, and Mary Demaris died on July 3, 1963, both at Ponca City, where they are buried in the IOOF Cemetery.

George W. married Lottie C. Campbell on March 30, 1895, at Van Buren. She was born in March of 1876 in Missouri, the daughter of Celeste Dabney Campbell. Their children were: Eugene Marvin, born July 1, 1896, at Van Buren; Paul Martel, born in March of 1898, in Missouri; Orrin Lee; Frances Campbell, born in March of 1900 in Missouri; Mary F., born in 1902-3; and Robert O., born in 1907-8 in Missouri. George W. was an attorney and newspaper man. He was associated with his brother, Orrin Layfayette, both in the newspaper business and law practice. George W. married Beulah Lucas Trotter on March 10, 1917. They had one daughter, Marjorie. Beulah had two sons and a daughter from her first marriage. George W. died at Bloomfield, Stoddard County, Missouri. He was prosecuting attorney of Carter County from 1895 to 1899 and of Stoddard County from 1917 to 1921. He was a member of the state legislature from Stoddard County at one time. He served as chairman of the Board of Regents at the Southeast Missouri State Teachers College in the 1930s, was a vice-president of the Missouri State Bar Association and president of the Stoddard County Bar Association.

At the age of 18, George W. went to Carter County and taught at the Beaver Dam School and later attended the Farmington Baptist College. Upon leaving college, he resumed teaching school then moved to Van Buren to learn the printing trade. With his brother, he secured The Van Buren Current Local and operated it for a short time. He entered law school in St. Louis and in 1893 was admitted to the bar to practice before Judge Green in Reynolds County. He started his law practice with his brother, Orrin, in January of 1894 in Van Buren, where in November of 1894 he was elected prosecuting attorney of Carter County. George W. died in Bloomfield, Stoddard County.

Nathaniel Munger, "the singing teacher", one of the Lesterville Baptist Church as described in the book, John Carty and 4000 Descendants, which cited the oldest Lesterville Baptist Church records, has not been adequately identified to place in this Munger family.

The following Mungers contributed considerable information on this family: Mrs. Fred R. (Fern) Munger Merrifield, Mrs. Robert R. (Frances) Munger Cloud, Marvin Marshall Munger, Rev. Lloyd and Lois Munger, Mrs. O.E. (Lottie) Munger Francis and Mrs. Robert (Lora) Munger Fitzgerald.

SHY

It is not known when or from where the Shys came to America but the family probably came from England. The earliest Shy record in England, according to Latter Day Saints Church index records, is for a Mary Shy who married a William Nottingham in County Bedford in 1654. A token number of later Shys are listed for Berkshire, Durham, Hertford, Kent, Norfolk, Oxford, Wiltshire, and York Counties, and London. A Humphrey Shy was in Barbados in 1679, witnessing a will for Thomas Tount. The 1706 tax rolls of the Spesutin Hundred in Baltimore County, Maryland, included a Thomas Shy, possibly the first record of the name in this country. The name is found spelled Shye, Shi, Shie and Shies and possibly some early Skys were actually Shys. A Shie family of German extraction is in the United States.

The first identified ancestor of the Shys in Reynolds County is John Shy, Sr., of Caswell County, North Carolina. He was born about 1720 (was over 60 on 1786 tax rolls), married Racheal ?, probably about 1760, and he died in late 1790 or early 1791, in Caswell County. The couple had nine children who reached adulthood, including Robert. Racheal's will of October 1, 1804, executed in Caswell County, identified all the children with the exception of John Jr., who had died by that time.

Robert, born ca. 1772, in Orange County, North Carolina, married Sarah Stalcup on January 11, 1797, in Orange County. She was born ca. 1778, and was the daughter of Tobias Stalcop. This Stalcop family has been traced back from Sarah five generations to John Anderson Stalcop who came to America from Sweden about 1665 in the Swedish ship Key of Kalmar, as a cook. The immigrant's father, Andriess Anderson, lived in Sweden and his mother, Christina Goalbrandt, was from Holland. After his marriage, Robert first appeared in the 1800 census of Caswell County. His family included one boy under 10, one girl under 10, and one slave, in addition to the parents. He purchased 240 acres of land in northern Sumner County, Tennessee, on December 7, 1801.

According to A Reminiscent History of the Ozark Region, Robert, his wife and four of his children, Samuel, Seaborn, Eli, and Sarah, the wife of James Lee, with their families, started west from Kentucky in 1830 with the intention of locating in the vicinity of where Little Rock, Arkansas, now is and where Robert owned a section of land. However, upon reaching New Madrid, Missouri, Robert was taken ill with cholera and died. His widow and three of their four children died soon after. After their deaths nothing was ever done with the Arkansas land. Now alone, Eli located with his family in the area where Reynolds County is now located.

The 1830 Missouri census found Robert, Simeon, Eli and Levi C. Shy in New Madrid County. While the tradition above indicates all the sons but Eli died after 1830, Canby, Ebon (Seaborn?), Samuel, Sarah and Sebrum (Seaborn?) appeared in the 1840 census for New Madrid County. Sarah, age between 50 and 60 in that census, must have been Robert's surviving wife. Samuel and Thomas Shy were in Pike County, Missouri, in that census. This raises the question of which sons, or other family members, actually died in the New Madrid cholera epidemic of the 1830s.

The will of Robert, dated April 8, 1834, and filed in New Madrid County November 17, 1836, mentioned the following children: Racheal (deceased), Jessee (Franklin), Robert, Jr., Melinda, John, Samuel, Eli, Elmira, Sarah and Seaburn (probably not listed according to age). The wife, Sarah, was appointed executrix of the estate and her name appears a number of times in the court records related to the estate. Her name last appears on December 3, 1842, and her estate is first mentioned in New Madrid County court records of February 15, 1843, so it appears she died between those dates. Robert willed the Arkansas land to Robert, Jr., Seaburn and Sarah, the children still at home.

Sarah's estate was distributed to Samuel, John, Eli, Elvira Anthony, Sarah Lee, the heirs of Robert Jr., Thomas D. Harrison and wife (either Racheal or Melinda) and Sebrun. Jessee and either Rachael or Melinda were not included and there is no explanation in the records.

Racheal married a Boyles. Robert's will mentioned her as deceased with daughters Minerva and Lydia still living.

The section on the Shy family in the Carty book relates that the Eli Shy family traveled up the Black River in boats, "cordelling" (pulling with ropes) the boats when necessary. The family settled first in the Belleview Valley area where they lived for about one year and then moved to Lesterville where they settled on a farm. Eli's name is found often as a messenger to the annual meetings of the Baptist Church Franklin Association representing the Black River Baptist Church.

Eli was born in Sumner County, Tennessee, on January 3, 1802. He married Mary Elizabeth "Ally" Smith on January 17, 1824, in Sumner County. Ally was born June 20, 1807, in Mercer County, Kentucky. Their children were: Martha Jane, born November 4, 1824; Melinda, born May 4, 1826; Alfred Howe, born January 11, 1829, in Sumner County; Sarah Ann, born September 21, 1831, in Missouri; John Wesley, born March 2, 1835, in Missouri; Robert Mitchell, born in 1837 in Missouri; Elmina, born April 6, 1839, in Missouri; William F., born November 6, 1841 (September 10, 1842?) in Missouri; Mary Elizabeth, born October 2, 1845, at Lesterville; and Minerva, born September 31, 1849, in Missouri. Eli died on May 6, 1855, in Lesterville, and Mary Elizabeth died November 13, 1876, in Lesterville. Both are buried in the Dobbins Cemetery. Eli served as messenger for the Black River Baptist Church in 1849 and the early 1850s.

Martha Jane married William Miner. They had two sons: John E., born October 5, 1842, died March 19, 1845; and William H., born April 15, 1845, died June 30, 1845. Martha Jane died on May 4, 1845, in Reynolds County, and is buried in the Dobbins Cemetery, as are her two sons.

Melinda married Orrin Munger. As mentioned in the Munger section, this is the first Shy-Munger marriage.

Alfred Howe married Sarah Jane Goggin. She was born October 7, 1838, in Black, the daughter of Milton Goggin and Nancy Carty. Their children were: Nancy A.D., born October 30, 1856; Willie S., born February 27, 1858; Isabelle C., born October 20, 1862; Thomas Jefferson, born December 24, 1866; and Sarah Ella, born May 12, 1869, at Belleview. Probably all of these children were born at Belleview. Sarah Jane died March 17, 1910, and Alfred Howe died March 28, 1884. He is buried in the Dobbins Cemetery and she is buried in Centerville Cemetery. He was circuit clerk for a number of years in Reynolds County. Family tradition says that Alfred Howe operated a store in Ironton which was burned by the Federal troops during the Civil War. After this, the family moved to Eureka Springs, Arkansas. While there, they lost three children to diphtheria and, apparently discouraged, the family returned to Missouri. Like his father, he served in 1856 as messenger for the Black River Baptist Church. He was the postmaster at Belleview in 1867-8. The family later lived in Centerville.

Nancy A. died on February 18, 1865.

Willie S. died on May 15, 1863.

Isabelle C. "Belle" married Richard Irvin January on July 4, 1877, in Reynolds County. Richard was born October 26, 1850, in Oregon County, Missouri, and was a son of Joab F. January and Mary Movina Sanders Ward. Their children were: Minnie V., born in September of 1880 in Oregon County; Ella "C", born in March of 1882; Alfred Irvin, born March 15, 1884; Otto Jefferson, born August 14, 1888 (1886?); Carl C., born July 26, 1891; and Elmer R., born in July of 1895. All were born in Missouri. Belle died September 16, 1941, and Richard Irvin died February 2, 1923. Richard Irvin was a school teacher and later a lawyer, county clerk in 1882, prosecuting attorney in 1881 and county school commissioner. He engaged in the real estate business, his principal interest in the development of mining property. Isabelle C. was a student of Richard Irvin before they married. The 1900 census indicated the mother had lost five children. They are buried in the Centerville Cemetery. The family lived in Centerville. The January family is of French origin and the Ward family is of Irish.

Thomas Jefferson "Tommy" married Lenora Matheline "Nora" Parks on August 6, 1885, at Centerville. She was born February 6, 1868, at Centerville, the daughter of Andrew Jackson Parks and Lucinda Rayfield. Their children were: Halla Grocious (son), born May 27, 1886, at Centerville; Olive Bell, born March 20, 1888, in California; and Alfred Thomas, born May 4, 1889, in California. Thomas Jefferson died January 20, 1891, in Escondido, California, and Nora died August 7, 1937, at Centerville. They are buried in the Centerville Cemetery. Nora married William J. Hunter on June 7, 1893, in Centerville. He was born in 1864-5 in Missouri, the son of Samuel and Nancy A. Hunter. Their children were: Mabel Clare, born March 8, 1894, in Centerville; Alvin Ruel, born in December of 1895 in Missouri; and William Andrew, born November 22, 1897, in Missouri. William J. Hunter died in 1897. Nora married again after April 26, 1910, this time to Gentry Sloan.

Halla Grocious died in 1969 and is buried in the Centerville Cemetery.

Alfred Thomas married Bessie Chitwood on July 27, 1907, in Centerville. She was born on August 2, 1890, at Ellington, and was the daughter of Henry Thomas Chitwood and Fannie Mae Coleman. Their children were: Bernice (son), born 1907-8; Wilma, 1909-10; Irma; Jerry; Bess; Lenora;

Maxine; Billye; and Alfred T. (possibly not in order of birth). All were probably born in Missouri. Alfred Thomas died February 11, 1969, in Ironton, and Bessie died January 14, 1972, in Farmington. They are buried in the Centerville Cemetery. The 1910 census lists him as a farmer living in Carroll Township.

Sarah Ella married Marshal Marvin Munger and is discussed with the Munger family.

Sarah Ann married Green Berry Goggin on March 14, 1850, at Centerville. He was born May 10, 1827, in Cumberland County, Kentucky, the son of Milton Goggin and Nancy Carty. Their children were: Milton E., born December 30, 1850; William O., born June 17, 1852 (3?) in Reynolds County; Mary Jane, born January 28, 1856; Nancy C., born February 8, 1858; John Thomas, born September 3, 1860; Robert M., born March 18, 1863; Isabelle, born December 11, 1866; James A., born June 16, 1869; B.F., born November 16, 1872; and Alvin P., born September 14, 1874. All were born in Missouri. Green Berry's name is found in the Black River Baptist Church records for a period of 50 years. He was listed as a messenger to the associational meeting eleven times. Green Berry died February 11, 1900, and Sarah Ann died September 21, 1909. Both are buried in the Rayfield Cemetery. The family lived in Black River Township, where he farmed.

John Wesley died October 22, 1838, and is buried in the Dobbins Cemetery.

Robert Mitchell died December 13, 1867, and is buried in the Dobbins Cemetery.

Elmina married James Carter Monroe Buford. He was born December 16, 1839, in Missouri, the son of Thomas Buford and California (Califurnia) Carty. Their children were: Calphurnia, born June 1, 1861; Mary E., born February 27, 1863; William A., born April 20, 1864; John M.A., born October 22, 1868; Lucy J., born October 22, 1870; and Sarah Minerva, born March 1866 or 1871 (according to the Carty book). All were born in Missouri. James Carter Monroe died March 8, 1881, and Elmina died July 28, 1934. She is buried in the Centerville Cemetery. The family lived in Centerville in 1870.

William F. married Nancy Green Bell on March 18, 1866. She was born April 2, 1845, at Edgehill, the daughter of Thomas Newton Bell and Mahala Cain. Their children were: Thomas Alfred, born October 29, 1868; Mary Jane, born in July of 1870; James Monroe "Mip", born in September of 1872; Ann Zona, born in May or March of 1874; Lucius Eli, born in January of 1876; George Seaborn, born in October of 1877; Robert Walter, born April 3, 1879; Richard Irvin, born August 18, 1881; Hattie May, born in January of 1883; and Clarence Harmon, born in December of 1884. All were born in Missouri. William F. died January 12, 1911, at Lesterville, and Nancy Green died August 4, 1908. William F. spent his entire life on the farm where he was born and farmed. He also operated a business in Lesterville. He and his wife were long-term members of the Missionary Baptist Church. He served six months during the latter part of the Civil War as a member of the Confederate Army (Maj. M.L. Claridy's Brigade), having been forced into the service as a recruit, according to A Reminiscent History of the Ozark Region. The couple is buried in the Shy-Chadbourne Cemetery. The 1900 census indicates that two children had died by that time.

Thomas Alfred died March 15, 1869, and is buried in the Dobbins Cemetery.

Mary Jane married John F. Irvin on December 25, 1899 in Reynolds County. He was born in 1859-60 in Missouri, the son of Samuel H. and Mary M. Irvin. They had one son, Roy F. A John F. Irvin owned the Spot-Cash Mercantile Co. at Lesterville and was a traveling salesman for the Woolson Spice Co. of Toledo, Ohio. The book, Old Reynolds, indicates J.F. Irvin owned the J.F. Irvin Tie and Lumber Company of St. Louis. It is not clear if these are the same man. Mary Jane died in 1959. The family lived in Bismarck, Iron County.

James Monroe married Ella W. Cross on December 21, 1893, at Centerville. She was born 1877-8 in Missouri and was a sister of George W. Cross, who married Mary Demaris Munger. The 1910 census showed the family living in Cape Girardeau County, with a son, Frank (Franklin) W., age 15, and daughter Myrtle (Louise), age one(?). They also had children George and Clarence. The couple was divorced. James Monroe died in 1958 and is buried in the Lake Charles Cemetery, St. Louis.

Ann Zona married William Andrew Parks on December 21, 1893, at Centerville. He was born February 19, 1870, in Missouri, and was the son of James Henry Parks and Matilda Rayfield. Their children were: Archie Homer, born September 19, 1893; Johnnie Ruhman, born October 21, 1895; Alpha Irene, born in July of 1898; and Graham Willie, born May 16, 1903. All were probably born in Lesterville. William Andrew was killed in a sawmill accident on November 1, 1904, near Lesterville and Ann Zona died in 1917. They are buried in the Shy-Chadbourne Cemetery. The family lived in Lesterville Township where in 1900 he was farming. The mother had lost one child by the 1910 census.

Lucius Eli married Carrie Hunt on August 19, 1900, at Lesterville. She was born in May of 1880 in Missouri, and was a daughter of Ford T. and Nancy J. Hunt. Their children were: Hazel Bell; Joy; and Frederick R. Carrie died in 1949 and is buried in the Shy-Chadbourne Cemetery.

George Seaborn married Rose Dillon on December 22, 1901, at Lesterville. She was born 1879-80 in Missouri. Their children were: Clee (son) age 7; Paul, age 5; Williard, age 2 (according to the 1910 census); and Erma, born in February of 1910. All were born in Missouri. George Seaborn died in 1945 and is buried in the Shy-Chadbourne Cemetery. He was shown as a farmer in Lesterville Township in 1910.

Robert Walter married Ethel Thomas after 1910. Their children were Nancy Delma and Walter Owen. Robert Walter died in 1962 and is buried in the Shy-Chadbourne Cemetery. Ethel M. Shy, who was born September 9, 1890, and died October 31, 1962, is also buried in the Shy-Chadbourne Cemetery and it is assumed this is Robert Walter's wife.

Richard Irvin died in 1887 and is buried in the Shy-Chadbourne Cemetery.

Hattie May married Joseph Martin Baugh on May 16, 1909. He was born in 1884 in Missouri, and was the son of Rev. Josiah Baugh. Their children were: Wilma S., born in March of 1910; Vadis Dorcas; William Joseph; Clarence John and Dorothy Margaret. Hattie May died in 1960 and Joseph Martin died in 1961. They are buried in the Shy-Chadbourne Cemetery. The family lived in Lesterville Township in 1910, where he was farming.

Clarence Herman married Catherine Foley. Their children were Clarence Herman, Jr., and Jane. Clarance Herman died in 1934 and is buried in the Calvary Cemetery, Reynolds County (?).

Mary Elizabeth married William Riley Hill. He was born July 27, 1837 in Tennessee, the son of Oliver P. Hill and Polly Wilson. They had one son, William Addison, born July 13, 1866, in Missouri. Mary Elizabeth died July 5, 1870, in Lesterville, and William Riley died November 29, 1930, at Cantwell, Missouri. She is buried in the Dobbins Cemetery. They lived in Logan Township. "Bill" Hill married five more times, according to an article in the book, Old Reynolds.

Minerva died on July 29, 1853, and is buried in the Dobbins Cemetery.

Jesse Franklin married Mary Ellen "Polly" Miner in 1851. She was born January 25, 1827, in Reynolds County. She was the daughter of William Henry Miner and Lydia McGinnis. Their children were: Thomas Dawson, born April 8, 1852; and William Henry, born January 24, 1854, both in Centerville. Jesse Franklin died August 30, 1854, in Reynolds County, and is buried near Edgehill. The grave marker is lost. Polly's second husband was Hute Latham, according to the Carty book. The records of the Shy Cemetery show she was wife of J. (John) N. Latham, born November 23, 1823, in Virginia. The 1860, 1870, and 1880 Iron County censuses show the John and Mary E. Latham family living in Dent Township, with the two Shy boys and Houston, born in 1857-8, Christopher (the John C. mentioned below) and Sarah C. Latham, born in 1861-2. All were born in Missouri. John N. died November 14, 1899, and Polly died January 9, 1923, in Black. They are buried in the Shy Cemetery. Cemetery records show a son, John C. Latham, died July 29, 1869, at nine years, six months and 20 days. Polly had lost one child, according to the 1910 census.

Thomas Dawson married Margaret C. Carty on April 23, 1874, in Reynolds County. She was born on June 3, 1857, in Missouri. Her parents were William Carty and Nancy Buford. Their children were: William Henry, born in December of 1875; Charles, born May 30, 1878; Albert M., born in September of 1880; John, who died young; James, who died young; Zimrier, born November 8, 1888; Mary Jane "Jannie", born in April of 1892; and Sarah C. "Sally", born in May of 1895. All were born in Missouri. Thomas Dawson owned and lived on the farm in Black River Township, owned in 1979 by his grandson, Cornell Shy. Thomas Dawson died October 1, 1931, and Margaret C. died March 18, 1924. Both are buried in the Shy Cemetery.

William Henry is shown in the 1910 census unmarried and living with his parents. He died in 1946 and is buried in the Shy Cemetery. He did not marry.

Charles married Stella J. Goggin in 1907-8. She was born November 13, 1890, at Edgehill. She was the daughter of Green Berry and Sarah McMahon. Their children were: Clarence O., born November 8, 1908; Cornell, born December 15, 1919; and Ralph, born April 2, 1924. Charles died November 18, 1952, and Stella J. died in 1983 (?). Charles and Stella J. are buried in the Shy Cemetery. The family lived in Black River Township, where he farmed.

Albert M. married Eller G. (Ella Z.) Goggin on December 23, 1903, in Reynolds County. She was born March 2, 1885, in Missouri, the daughter of James G. Goggin and Sarah E. Bell. Their children were: Alvin L., age 5; Clyde M., age 3; and Zoa M., age 2, all born in Missouri, as shown in the 1910 census. Ella Z. died June 20, 1960, and is buried in the Shy Cemetery. Albert M. died September 6, 1924. The family lived in Black River Township in 1910, where he was a farmer.

Zimrier's first marriage was to Ethel Carrie Smith. She was born in November of 1892 in Missouri and was a daughter of Jackson and Mary A. Smith. Their children were: Ruby Marie, born July 24, 1912; and Leora Berniece, born May 5, 1915. Ethel Carrie died in 1919 and is buried in the Shy Cemetery. Zimrier next married Lena Agnes Barton. She was born April 12, 1904, the daughter of Squire Barton and Isabelle Dennison. Their children were: Alice Geraldine, born November 23, 1926, and Thomas Davidson, born October 12, 1928. Zimrier died July 26, 1981, and is buried in the Dennison Cemetery, north of Black.

Mary Jane married James Vessie Carty after April 18, 1910. He was born July 5, 1889, in Missouri, and was the son of Charles Thomas Carty and Eliza Joann Kline. Their children were: James Bernell, born December 30, 1913; Margaret Fae, born March 20, 1920; Mercedes, born August 28, 1928; and Mary Jo, born January 16, 1933.

Sarah C. married Albert Rayfield, who was possibly a son of John C. Rayfield.

William Henry married Nancy Annis January on July 16, 1875, in Reynolds County. She was born November 27, 1855, near Couch and Thayer, Oregon County, Missouri, and was a sister of Richard Irvin January, who married Isabelle C. Their children, all born at Black, were: Jesse Franklin, born April 29, 1876; John Christopher, born April 8, 1878; Alvin Greenberry, born February 11, 1880; Burt (?); Thomas Houston, born January 18, 1882; Sarah Ellen "Ella", born November 21, 1883, Cora Bell, born April 9,

1886; Joseph January, born June 30, 1888; Letha Maude, born April 9, 1891; William Albert, born July 11, 1893, and an unnamed infant who was born in 1896 and lived only three days. Nancy Annis died December 29, 1898, at home near Black, and is buried in the Shy Cemetery. William Henry next married May Millicent (later changed to May Mildred) Oliver on January 4, 1901, in Reynolds County. May was born on May 1, 1872, in Chicago, Cook County, Illinois. Their children were: Florence Azeal (later changed to Florence Helen), born November 24, 1901; Louie Randolph "Rannie", born October 27, 1903; Josephine Olive, born April 7, 1907; and Harold Irving, born July 31, 1908. All were born near Black. William H. died January 4, 1933, and May Mildred died February 5, 1968. Both died at home near Black. Both are buried in the Shy Cemetery. He was a farmer in Edgehill.

Jessie Franklin married Rose Ella Harrison on January 6, 1901, in Centerville. She was born July 5, 1878, near Centerville, the daughter of Jesse R. Harrison and Theodosia Mann. Their children were: Thelma, born September 22, 1901; Robert Harrison, born April 8, 1903; Lois, born December 6, 1908; and Lucille, born December 12, 1914. All were born in Centerville. In early manhood Jessie Franklin taught school for ten years, later entering the mercantile business. He first operated a store in Corridon, then moved to Ellington where he ran a store in 1907-8. Selling out there, he moved to Centerville where he operated a store. Later, he bought a farm on Upper Logan Creek and farmed there until he moved to Ellington in 1919. He purchased considerable real estate in the area and operated a store in Ellington for many years. Jessie Franklin died on May 26, 1954, in Ellington and Rose Ella died March 2, 1971, in St. Louis. The couple is buried in the Ellington Cemetery. Rose Ella, according to the book, Old Reynolds, gave Gladden Dale School its name.

According to family records, John Christopher first married Ella Robinett. She was born February 3, 1886, the daughter of Woodson Robinett and Nancy J. Goggin. They were only married a short time. John Christopher then married Doshia V. Faulkenberry Parmer in 1907-8. She was born in September of 1881 in Missouri, the daughter of James Faukenberry and Martha Welch. Their sons were: Laverne, born September 25, 1908, died November 15, 1909; Clifford, born November 28, 1910; and Leon, born April 5, 1917. All were born in Black. John Christopher died in October of 1936 at Black, and Doshia V. died in 1965. They are buried in the Shy Cemetery. The 1910 census indicates Doshia had lost one child but had a daughter, Roberta Parmer, who was born 1882-3, in Missouri. The family lived in Black River Township in 1910, where John Christopher was farming.

Alvine Greenberry's marriage was to Lucy Jane "Janey" Hawkins on December 29, 1905, in Reynolds County. She was born September 15, 1881, in Missouri and was the daughter of George W. Hawkins and Sarah A. Carty. The couple lost one child on October 4, 1906, and another child in infancy. Alvin Greenberry died August 30, 1962, and Janey died July 20, 1964. She is buried in the Black Cemetery. Alvin Greenberry was farming in Black River Township in 1910. Family records show Alvin Greenberry married, second to Hetty (?) Crump, so his death date must be incorrect.

Thomas Houston married Mattie Reed on June 6, 1909, in Lesterville. She was born April 24, 1884, at Edgehill, the daughter of H.T. Jefft Reed and Zorilda George. Thomas Houston attended State Normal School at Cape Girardeau, began teaching at age 17, and taught until he was 21, when he entered medical school at the University of Louisville. He was a medical doctor, practicing in Centerville. She served as a cashier in the Reynolds Savings Bank at Centerville. He died May 28, 1915, in Reynolds County, and she died May 22, 1971, at Belleview. They are buried in the Shy Cemetery.

Sarah Ellen "Ella" married Norman Robert White on April 1, 1903. He was born April 14, 1884, at Caledonia in Washington County and was the son of Edwin H. White and Georgia Ann Mason. Their children were: Ancel January, born January 17, 1906; and Lyle Norman, born September 14, 1907. Both were born at Caledonia. Norman Robert died October 1, 1956, at Rolla in Phelps County, and Sarah Ellen died September 15, 1962, at Ironton. They are buried in the Bellevue Presbyterian Cemetery, Caledonia. Norman Robert founded and operated a funeral home, first in Caledonia and later in Ironton. The 1900 census for Iron Township, Iron County, lists Norman R. with wife Nora W., born in January of 1875 in Missouri. The couple had been married one year and had no children.

Cora Bell married William H. Stevens on January 1, 1902, in Iron County. He was born July 29, 1881, the son of Mart Stevens and Nancy E. Jamison. Their children were: Gladys, born September 16, 1902; Elmer, born February 17, 1905; Lowell "Nick", born August 5 ?; Paul J. born April 18, 1909; and Ruby, born October 16, 1915. Cora Belle died October 30, 1976; and William H. died December 11, 1936. They are buried in the Shy Cemetery.

Joseph January, Sr., married Pauline Kenower on August 3, 1920, at Breckenridge, Caldwell County, Missouri. She was born January 8, 1897, at Breckenridge, the daughter of John Thomas Kenower and Ola Russel. Their children were: Joseph January, Jr., born April 26, 1921, at Breckenridge; Paul Russel, born May 13, 1923, at Breckenridge; and Barbara Lucille, born November 11, 1936, at Chillicothe, Livingston County, Missouri. John January, Sr. graduated from Southeast Missouri State College and received his law degree from the University of Missouri. He served in World Wars I and II. After practicing law in Breckenridge from 1920 to 1927, he and the family moved to Chillicothe, where he spent the rest of his life. He served as city attorney of Chillicothe and prosecuting attorney of Livingston County, and conducted his law practice until his death. John January, Sr., died February 22, 1963, and Pauline died May 5, 1980, both at Chillicothe. They are buried in the Resthaven Memorial Gardens, Chillicothe.

Letha Maude L. married Isaac Emory Baker. He was born February 13, 1882, in Missouri, the son of Joseph Calvin Baker and Sarah Margaret Plummer Hodkins. Their children were: Harold, born January 20, 1911; and Wilma, born in 1914, died in 1922. Isaac Emory died September 19, 1972, and Maude L. died June 16, 1938. They are buried in the Shy Cemetery.

William Albert "Bert" married Amanda "Mannye". He was living in Cambell, Missouri, in 1954 and died April 30, 1980.

Florence Helen did not marry and lived in Chicago, Cook County, Illinois.

Louie Randolph "Rannie" married Stella Copeland on May 18, 1935. They had one daughter, Janet May, born February 25, 1944, in Black. Louie Randolph died January 26, 1986, in Black, and is buried in the Shy Cemetery.

Josephine Olive married William W. Wood. In 1954 she was living in the Canal Zone, Panama.

Harold Irving married Esther Berniece Robinette on July 27, 1935. She was born April 5, 1918, the daughter of Oga Robinette and Eva Esther Adkins. Their children were: Burma Jo, born July 13, 1937; and William Harold, born November 16, 1940, both at Black. The family lived at Black.

The following Shys have not been identified with the Reynolds County family:

Samuel G., born in May of 1830, with (Eliza) Amanda, born in January of 1851, and Lucy E., age 2 months, all born in Missouri, appear in the 1870 census for Reynolds County. In the 1880 census, Laura Belle, age 5, and Samuel S., born in October of 1878, had been added to the family. Samuel G. died in 1906 and Eliza died in 1928. The couple is buried in the Shy-Chadbourne Cemetery. The 1900 Union Township, Iron County, census adds James T., born in August of 1881, and Omer H., born in April of 1887. Children all born in Missouri.

Samuel G.'s daughter, Lucy E., married John B. Hodges on November 19, 1888, in Reynolds County. He was born in November of 1867 in Missouri. Lucy E. died in 1962 and is buried in the Rayfield Cemetery. The family lived in Lesterville Township in 1900, where he was farming. John B. married Lena S. Senciboy on November 26, 1902, at Lesterville. She was born in March of 1882, in Missouri, the daughter of James C. and Mary Senciboy. According to the 1910 census, this was John B.'s fourth marriage. Lena S. had four children by 1910: John W., age 6; Willard J., age 3 (born June 6, 1907); Mildred H., age not recorded; and one child who must have died. All probably born in Missouri. Lena S. died 1954 and John B. died in 1962, both buried in the Rayfield Cemetery.

William, born January 14, 1828, died October 30, 1914, and is buried in Dobbins Cemetery.

The 1910 census lists Manda (?) A., age 89, born in Missouri, a widow, living on her own farm in Kaolin Township, Iron County.

Emma A.W. buried in Buffington Cemetery, Reynolds County. At her death in 1857, according to her tombstone, her age was one year, 10 months, 11 days, and she was the daughter of G. and A. Shy. The most logical parents are Alfred Howe and Sarah Jane Shy.

G.D., grandson, by grave of William and Nancy Shy in the Shy-Chadbourne Cemetery.

Miss Mary J., died at Lesterville, April 10, 1868, age 31 years, six months, eight days, appeared as item in the Ironton Register on May 7, 1868.

Mary Ann Thornton, Joseph January Shy, Jr., and Leon Shy provided a great deal of information on the Shys. Mrs. Wilma Currinton's information in the book, Old Reynolds, was most helpful.

PARKS

The immigrant ancestor of the Parks who settled in Reynolds County, Thomas, was born in the 1670s or 80s, probably in either England or Ireland, but possibly in Virginia. Family tradition has his father as either John or Thomas, who probably was in Virginia around 1670.

Thomas, a school teacher in 1692, lived in Albermarle County, Virginia, and later in Essex County, Virginia, where he died before March of 1761. Thomas had seven children: John, born May 6, 1708 (?); Samuel, born about 1710; Charles, born about 1714 in Essex County; Mary; Martha: Elizabeth, born 1720-5; and Thomas Jr., 1720-5. Their mother's name in unknown.

Charles' wife was named Susannah and the couple had at least three children: Charles Jr., born about 1744 in Albemarle County; John, born about 1750; and Reuben, born about 1760. It appears the family left Virginia about 1769 and settled in Wilkes County, North Carolina.

Charles, Jr.'s first marriage was about 1771 to Sarah, born about 1746 in Halifax County, Virginia. Their children were: John, born August 28, 1774, in Washington or Wilkes County, Georgia; Charles, born May 21, 1776; Abraham, born July 5, 1778; Theophilus, born July 12, 1780; Mary, born November 25, 1783; and Marshall, born August 5, 1787 (1794?). The latter children were all born in Washington, Wilkes or Elbert Counties, Georgia. Charles, Jr.s' second marriage was to Mary Bobo, widow of S. Lewis Bobo, probably after 1804 and Sarah's death. He died November 2, 1806, at Elbert County.

Marshall married Mary H. Williams on March 17, 1822, probably in Georgia. She was born March 27, 1796, in the part of Virginia that is now part of Kentucky and was the daughter of Theophilus and Margaret Williams. Their children, the first three born in Georgia, one in Washington County and the last four in Lesterville, were: Andrew Jackson, born November 13, 1823, in Elbert County; Elizabeth Jane, born May 31, 1826, died February 14, 1832; Myra Jane, born June 11, 1828, in Elbert County; James Henry, born

July 28, 1830, in Washington County, Missouri; Mary Salome, born December 23, 1832; Marshall Lafayette, born March 19, 1835; Walter William Tucker, born March 14, 1837; and George Washington, born July 20, 1840. Her grandfather, Thomas Williams, was born about 1730-5 and died by March 5, 1836, in Muscogee County, Georgia. Theophilus Williams died by 1850 in Bryan County, Georgia. Marshall served as justice of the Reynolds County Court in 1847 and with the County Court in 1849.

Marshall inherited his father's Georgia property, but sold it and had moved to Missouri by May 20, 1825, when he and Theophilus Williams were involved in the estate of Ruel L. Williams in Washington County. By 1832, Marshall and Mary were settled in Reynolds County, near Lesterville. Marshall died December 5(1?), 1870, and Mary on April 15, 1865, both in Lesterville. They are buried in Dobbins Cemetery. He served as messenger for the Black River Baptist Church in the 1840s and was the first postmaster of Lesterville, appointed on January 17, 1851.

Andrew Jackson married Lucinda Rayfield on October 15, 1846. She was born September 20, 1826, in Kentucky, the daughter of John and Nancy (King?) Rayfield. Their children were: Elizabeth Jane, born September 15, 1847; James Henry, born July 17, 1849, in Reynolds County; William Andrew, born May 8, 1851, died December 9, 1872; Mary Matilda, born in December of 1852, died July 20, 1853; Lucy Miriam, born December 4, 1853; Nancy Catherine, born October 9, 1855, died May 9, 1872; Beatrice Gertrude, born April 21, 1858; Sarah Ann, born April 6, 1860; Lenora Natholine, born February 6, 1868; and Robert Lafayette, born December 20, 1872. All were born in Missouri. Lucinda died in Reynolds County on January 25, 1916, and Andrew Jackson died November 23, 1892, at Lesterville. Both are buried in the cemetery located between the Burroughs and R.L. Parks farms (1961) along Highway 21 on the Middle Fork of the Black River in Reynolds County. The 1860 census shows his occupation as blacksmith. One census shows Robert Lafayette as a grandson of Andrew Jackson.

Elizabeth Jane married James N. Bowles on August 27, 1874, in Reynolds County. He was born August 29, 1837, in Pulaski (now Phelps) County, Missouri, the son of William and Nancy Bowles. Their children were: Walter, born in February of 1876; George W., born in August of 1877; Laura B., born in June of 1879; Doshia; Sarah L., born August 16, 1883; Cora, born September 14, 1885; Hattie, born in March of 1888; and Andrew, born March 10, 1890. All were born in Missouri. James N. had previously married Ruth Crownover in 1859. She was born in 1841-2 in Missouri, the daughter of James Crownover. Their children were: William C., born November 16, 1863; John A., born in 1866-7; James Albert, born September 15, 1869; and Martha, who died when she was about two years old. All were born in Missouri. Ruth died in 1873. James N. managed a family mercantile business in Centerville after his father died in 1857 until about 1911. He also operated a hotel there and owned a farm on Sinking Creek in Reynolds County. He and

Andrew Parks owned the county weekly, The Echo, eventually selling it to A.P. Shriver. James N. died at his home on Sinking Creek on February 7, 1930, and is buried in the Centerville Cemetery. Elizabeth Jane was still living in 1930. The 1900 census indicates the mother had nine children, all living, so there is one unidentified child. The 1910 census indicates she had ten children, six living at that time.

James Henry married Sarah Louisa Henderson on March 12, 1871, in Reynolds County. She was born July 19, 1849, in Missouri, and was the daughter of Sarah Henderson. Their children were: Mary Jane, born January 22, 1872, in Lesterville; Martha Esther, born April 17, 1873, in Lesterville; Leona, born November 23, 1875, in Lesterville; and Ottis Harold, born July 13, 1886, in Centerville. James Henry died January 22, 1920, at Black, and Sarah died October 28, 1910. They are buried in the Centerville Cemetery. The 1900 census indicates the mother had lost three children. The family lived in Carroll Township, where he farmed.

Lucy Mirriam married Thomas F. Wadlow on August 5, 1875, at Lesterville. He was born 1853-4 in Missouri, the son of John Wadlow and Cynthia Thorp. Their children were: George Walter, born in 1875-6; Otho M., born in 1876-7; Charles C., born January 8, 1878; William A., born in 1879-80; Edgar and Holla (Rolla?), born November 22, 1888, all born in Missouri. The family lived in Jackson Township in 1878-1880. Thomas F. served as county assessor in Reynolds County.

Beatrice Gertrude married Joseph A. Baker on June 15, 1876, in Reynolds County. He was born July 4, 1854, in Kentucky. Their children were: William Alexander, born in March of 1877 in Missouri; and James. Beatrice Gertrude died July 20, 1879. Joseph then married Martha A. Hunter on November 20, 1879, in Reynolds County. She was born in April of 1861, the daughter of Thomas M. and Phelissanna Hunter. The book, Old Reynolds, had an extensive article on this family. Joseph A. died May 8, 1879. Martha A. died August 10, 1936, and both are buried in the Centerville Cemetery.

Sarah Ann married William Henry Powers on June 15, 1883, in Reynolds County. He was born August 22, 1860, in Piedmont, Missouri. Their children were: Ethel Blanche, born March 1, 1884, in Centerville; Andrew Lee, born March 12, 1887, in Van Buren; Letha May, born March 15, 1889, in Centerville; William Talmage, born April 22, 1891, in Centerville; Richard Terrel, born August 15, 1895, in Missouri, died October 8, 1900; and Herbert, born August 24, 1900, in Missouri, died in December of 1903. William Henry died February 28, 1930, and she died August 1, 1941. He served as county treasurer of Reynolds County. In 1900 the family was living in Ellington.

Lenora Natholine's first marriage was to Thomas Jefferson Shy on August 6, 1885, in Centerville. This family is discussed with the Shy family.

Robert Lafayette married Ida Elizabeth Jamison on December 23, 1894, in Iron County. She was born December 27, 1876, in Missouri, the daughter of James Jasper Jamison and Lucy Carty. Their children were: Eugene Otto, born October 30, 1895 of Centerville; James Andrew, born September 28, 1897; Lucy Zerelda, born January 21, 1900; and Truman, born July 24, 1910. Robert Lafayette "Bob" was county assessor in Reynolds County from 1909 to 1912. He served as sheriff from 1913 through 1916 and as county clerk from 1919 to 1922. From 1927 through 1946 he served as collector of revenue and was recorder of deeds and circuit clerk in 1947 and 1948. He died October 13, 1948, and she died September 23, 1958. They are buried in the Rayfield Cemetery at Lesterville. In 1900, the family lived in Carroll Township, where he was shown as a farmer.

Myra Jane married Lewis Preston Munger. This family is discussed with the Mungers.

James Henry married Matilda Rayfield on October 13, 1853, at Centerville. She was born January 20, 1834, in Missouri, the sister of Lucinda who married James Henry's brother, Andrew Jackson. Their children were: Mary Lucinda, born August 28, 1854, at Centerville, died October 2, 1859; Nancy Elizabeth, born June 6, 1856, at Lesterville (did not marry); Sarah Francis, born December 16, 1857; Margaret Corelia, born November 27, 1859; Martha Price, born November 7, 1861; Cordelia Salome, born May 26, 1865; George Washington, born August 17, 1867, at Lesterville (did not marry); William Andrew, born February 19, 1870, at Lesterville; Lucy Jane, born May 8, 1872, at Lesterville; and John Marshall, born January 11, 1875, died August 3, 1878. All were born in Missouri. James Henry died October 20, 1892, at Lesterville, and Matilda died in October 20, 1918. The 1870 census shows Mary, age 13, but no Elizabeth or Cordelia, so the daughters must have had double given names. The family was living in Lesterville in 1900, and he was listed as a farmer in the census.

Sarah Francis married Tillman Roland Terry in 1898-9. He was born in October of 1849 in Tennessee. They had one son, William J. Bryan, born in September of 1900 in Missouri. She died December 23, 1939. Tillman Roland had previously married in 1866-7. The 1880 census, Kaolin Township, Iron County, listed with Tillman Roland: Ann, 1848-9, born in Tennessee; Lee, born in 1868-9, in Missouri; and Frank, born 1870-1, in Missouri. The 1900 census showed grandchildren: Hale G., born in February of 1885; Tillman O., born in November of 1887; and Anna E. Terry, born in October of 1890, living with Tillman Roland and Sarah Francis. The family lived in Kaolin Township in 1880-1910, where he farmed.

Margaret Corelia married William O. "Wib" Goggin September 14, 1882, at Lesterville. He was born June 17, 1852, in Reynolds County, the son of Green Berry Goggin and Sarah Ann Shy. Their children were: Edna Ethel, born June 22, 1883, died June 13, 1887; Oscar H., born January 12, 1885, died January 28, 1885; Viola May, born May 12, 1887; Walles T., born March 5, 1889; and Zona Pearl, born June 21, 1891, died July 11, 1892.

136

Margaret Corelia died October 5, 1892. In 1880 the family lived in Lesterville Township, where he farmed.

Martha Price married William Reed on October 6, 1881, in Reynolds County. He was born in April of 1861 in Missouri. Their children were Bertha, born in January of 1883; Nellie, born in August of 1884; Oather (?), born in July of 1886; Grace, born in October of 1888; Clara, born in March of 1893; Willie, born in August of 1895; Minnie, born October of 1897, and Alpha, born in April of 1900. All were born in Missouri. In 1900 the family lived in Carter Township, Carter County.

Cordelia Salome married Benjamin McNail "Mack" Howell, on January 21, 1886, at Lesterville. He was born July 26, 1859, at Centerville, the son of Gideon Howell and Sarah J. Crownover. Their children were: Antonia, born November 4, 1886, in Centerville; and Chloe. Benjamin McNail had previously married Alice Breckenridge of Caledonia on October 20, 1880. One child was born, who died in infancy. Alice died March 31, 1883. Benjamin McNail taught school for years in Reynolds County and served one term as county commissioner. In 1889 the family moved to Skagit County, Washington, where Cordelia Salome died in August of 1890. Benjamin McNail taught school several terms and was a deputy auditor of Skagit County. He later returned to Missouri, back to Washington, and in 1892 moved to Oregon, where he entered Williamette University. During that time he entered the ministry, serving as pastor at Brooks, in Salem County, Tangent, in Linn County, and Nehakson, Oregon. In August of 1898 he enlisted in the army and served in the Phillipines during the Spanish-American War. After the war, he returned to Salem, Marion County, Oregon, The couple had nine children, three dying in infancy. He served two terms as police judge of Falls City, Polk County, Oregon, and was serving his second term as city auditor at the time of his death. Benjamin McNail died July 1, 1930, in Falls City.

William Andrew married Ann Zona Shy, daughter of William F. Shy and Nancy Green Bell. This family is discussed with the Shy family.

Lucy Jane married Guy R. McHenry, Sr., on December 18, 1889, in Reynolds County. He was born in 1867-8 in Missouri, the son of J.H. and Catherine McHenry or Iron County. Their children were: Grace, born 1890-1; Byron, born in 1891-2; Leo, born in 1896-7; Hallie; Guy R. Jr., born in 1898-9; Clarence, born in 1893-4; Paul R., born June 26, 1904, and John R., born 1907-8. All were born in Missouri. Lucy died May 8, 1910. Guy managed a sawmill in Lesterville Township. Hallie was not listed in the 1910 census with this family.

George Washington did not marry. He died December 25, 1939.

Mary Salome married Francis Marion Munger and is discussed with the Munger family.

Marshall Lafayette married Tolitha Ann Vann on December 26, 1868. She was born April 28, 1852, at Evening Shade, Sharp County, Arkansas, and was the daughter of Jessie Vann and Jane Davis. Their children were: Mary

Jane, born October 20, 1869; Lucy Elizabeth, born December 24, 1871; Marshall Lee, born September 26, 1873; George Washington, born September 30, 1875, at Centerville; and Sarah Ellen, born July 11, 1878. All were probably born in Reynolds County. Marshall Lafayette died October 27, 1879. Tolitha Ann then married Franklin Moore Sanders, on February 23, 1881, in Centerville. He was born May 22, 1839, in Kentucky. Their children were: Delphia Ann, born December 9, 1881; Milford Henderson, born February 29, 1884; Araminta Antoinette, born January 21, 1886, at Sinking Creek in Reynolds County; Mary Elizabeth, born February 12, 1888; Moses, born March 9, 1890; Jesse Franklin, born June 24, 1892; and John Raney, born November 8, 1894. All were born in Reynolds County. Franklin Moore died November 6, 1923, in St. Louis. The Vann family lived at Scarborough, Tennessee, and in Arkansas, before moving to Missouri about 1855.

Marshall Lafayette was a school teacher and a farmer. Tolitha Ann, his wife, was a former student of his. She died March 15, 1901 (April 28, 1902?) at Lesterville, and is buried in the Knuckles Cemetery in Reynolds County. Franklin Moore Sanders then married Polly Ann Piles Brawley on August 23, 1903, at Dagonia in Reynolds County. She was born in September of 1867 in Missouri, the daughter of Amia Piles. Polly Ann Piles had previously married J.R. Brawley on December 30, 1885, in Reynolds County. The 1900 census lists Polly Ann as a widow with six children.

Mary Jane first married William M. Akins on February 13, 1889, in Reynolds County. He was born October 30, 1866, in Missouri, and was probably the son of David Alexander Akins and Catherine Caroline Brawley, listed in the 1870 Reynolds County census. Their children were: Louis O., born November 27, 1889; Lilah A., born in October of 1891; Tolitha C., born in November of 1893; David L., born in April of 1896; Edith A., born in March of 1900; Obie O., born December 28, 1904; and Lindell L., born May 7, 1910. All were born in Missouri. Mary Jane next married Samuel Davis. She died April 22, 1965, in Reynolds County, and William M. died August 17, 1948. They are buried in the Corridon-Reynolds County Cemetery. The family lived in Jackson Township, where William M. was a farmer and lived later in Logan Township.

Lucy Elizabeth married William Gentry Helvey July 16-23, 1889, in Reynolds County. He was born April 1, 1868, in Missouri, the son of James and Mary Helvey. Their children were: Fannie D., born in December of 1890 in Missouri; Archie T., born in February of 1895 in Missouri; Otho O., born February 14, 1901; and two others who died before the 1910 census. Lucy Elizabeth died December 20, 1959, near Centerville, and William Gentry died June 25, 1954. They are buried in the Pleasant Hill Cemetery. The family lived in Logan Township, where he farmed.

Marshall Lee married Ollie Dillard about 1893. She was born May 7, 1879, the daughter of George W. Dillard and Adaline Conway. He was accidentally shot and killed in 1898 in Reynolds County by his wife's 14-year-old brother. They had one daughter, Icey (Dicey?), born in January of 1899. Ollie died in childbirth and Icey was raised by her maternal grandparents.

George Washington "Barney" married Rosa Bell Christopher on July 29, 1894, in Centerville. She was born June 19, 1877, in Reynolds County, the daughter of William Thomas Christopher, Jr., born September 8, 1854, in Illinois, and Mary Ann Counts. Their children were: Floy Madelena, born April 19, 1895, in Centerville; Perry Franklin, born October 19, 1896, at Centerville; Rosa Bell, born in July of 1901 in Desloge, St. Francois County, died one week old; Preston Lee, Sr., born August 27, 1905, Desloge; Christopher Columbus; born November 12, 1908, at Centerville; and Julie, born in February of 1914 at Centerville, died about one month old.

George Washington and Rosa Bell were divorced in 1919 and he moved with his sons to Wyoming in 1920. He died at Lovell, Big Horn County, Wyoming, on July 12, 1977. Rosa Bell's second marriage was to Joseph Medley and her third was to Robert Teasley. Rosa Bell died March 18, 1944, at St. Louis. George Washington spent most of his early life working as a timber inspector in Reynolds County. Later he worked on the railroad in Wyoming and on ranches in Wyoming and Montana. He is buried in the Lovell Cemetery.

Sarah Ellen married Lorenzo Dow "Dee" Knuckles (Jr.?) on October 14, 1894, at Logan's Creek, Reynolds County. He was born October 12, 1874, in Missouri, the son of Lorenzo Dow and Estis E. Knuckles. Their children were: Stella E., born in 1895-6; Roy L. born May 3, 1897; Cypheus L., born April 5, 1901; Johnnie; Esther E., born in 1902-3; Ethel and Telsa. All were born in Missouri. Dee died October 5, 1958, and Sarah Ellen died January 24, 1967, in Reynolds County. They are buried in the Pleasant Hill Cemetery, Reynolds County. The family lived in Logan Township, where he farmed.

Walter William Tucker did not marry and died October 23, 1863. In the Civil War he was in the Confederate Army, but deserted and joined the Federal Army.

George Washington married Mary Ella Larking December 10, 1874, in Reynolds County. She was probably the daughter who appears in the Reynolds County 1880 census with Sampson Larkin. Family tradition indicates they had one known daughter, although his will does not indicate any children. George Washington died April 14, 1876, in Reynolds County. It is probably that Mary Ella is the Mrs. Mary Parks who married James B. Barnes on October 11, 1883, in Reynolds County. The 1900 census shows James B. was born in August of 1859, and Mary Ella was born in February of 1857, both in Missouri. Their children were: Grover C., born in July of 1884; Allan G., born in July of 1888; Burns S. born in September of 1890; Bertha, born in August of 1892; Orrin, born in July of 1893; and Maud B., born in May of 1895. All were born in Missouri. That census shows she had borne six children with four living, which conflicts with six children listed. Mary Ella died before the 1910 census when James B. and children Thurman, 21, Byrns, 19, Della, 17, and Maude G. were living in Ellington with James B.'s mother, Celila Barnes.

The 1860 census shows that James B. was the son of Josiah and Cicily Barns (Barnes).

There was another Parks family living in Reynolds County in the 1800s, but no family connection has been made with this Parks family.

Janice and Lee Parks and Jaqueline Parks provided much of the material on the Parks family.

GOGGIN

Most of this material is taken from various parts of the John Carty book, but is sometimes rearranged and shortened to save space. The family name is found often as Goggins and sometimes Groggins, but is spelled here as Goggin.

"From the information that is available, we believe that our Goggin ancestors came from Queen County, Ireland, and arrived in Virginia in the 1740s. How many came and their relationship has not been determined." The Surnames of Ireland book shows that the surname Goggin derives from Cogan and Gogan in County Cork. Some Goggins in New England trace their ancestry to County Cork.

"When the Goggin family arrived in America, they settled along the Virginia coast. How long they lived there is not known, but within a few years they moved inland to Campbell, Bedford and Culpeper Counties in Virginia. George, Danial and perhaps another brother, David, moved to South Carolina. A Steven Goggin is recorded living on Flat Creek in Bedford County, in 1759. His relationship to the South Carolina Goggins has not been determined. Both lines used the name William often, but that was the only name common to the two families. The name of Steven's first wife is not known, but his second marriage was to Susanna Terry in 1772."

Stephen Sr. probably was the father of Steven Jr., Sarah, and John. It is not definite that the Goggin family in Reynolds County descended from Stephen, Sr.

The first known Goggin ancestor is William, who married Drusilla Jackman on December 8, 1785, in Lincoln County, Virginia, later part of Kentucky. Drusilla was born in Fauquier County, Virginia, in the late 1760s, the daughter of Richard Jackman and Mary Neavil (Neville).

The family moved to Cumberland County, Kentucky, about 1800-1. The book, History of Cumberland County, states: "William Goggin, 1760-1833, acquired large tracts of land in Lawson Bottom, north and south of Brownwood Landing. He built the Mansion Brick now in decay on C.W. Well's farm. A ferry was established known as John Robertson and John Cape Ferry in 1799, which name it held until 1808 when it became known as Goggin Ferry."

William's will names eleven children: Cynthia; Juble (Jubal); Polly; Malinda; Green Berry, born in 1798-9 in Lincoln County, Kentucky; Milton, born in 1801 in Cumberland County, Kentucky; Matilda; Jane; Harvey; Lucy; and Eliza Jane, born December 15, 1807. Drusilla died in Cumberland County in the 1820s and William died in 1833.

The Jackman family is first found in Virginia and is difficult to trace. Richard and Mary moved to Kentucky, where he died in Lincoln County in 1801. She died in Cumberland County in 1825. The Neville family is well documented to Mary from the immigrant, John Neville, born ca. 1612, England, and who came to America in 1634 in one of Lord Baltimore's ships, either the Dove or the Ark. John Neville died in June of 1664 in Calvert County, Maryland. Two American families that intermarried with the Nevilles in Virginia are Bohannan and Lott. Family researchers have not been able to connect this family line with the famous English Neville family.

Brothers Green Berry and Milton with their families, came to Washington County, Missouri, between July of 1828 and February 1830.

Green Berry married Elizabeth Carty before 1821 in Cumberland County. She was born March 20, 1801, in Surry County, North Carolina, the daughter of James Carty and Sarah "Sally" Copeland. Their children were: William J., born in May of 1824 in Cumberland County; Milton, born in 1827 in Cumberland County; Elizabeth, born in 1825-30; Jubal, born in 1836 at Edgehill in Reynolds County; Nancy, born in 1839 at Edgehill; and Drucilla, born in 1844 (February of 1846?) in Missouri. It is believed that Green Berry and Elizabeth were charter members of the Black River Baptist Church since Green Berry was listed as a messenger during the period 1838-1850. Green Berry died between 1846 and 1850 and Elizabeth died between 1850 and 1860, both at Edgehill. They are buried in the Goggin-Troutman Cemetery.

William J. "Buck" married Margaret Caroline Love in 1842-3. She was born October 14, 1821, at Edgehill, the daughter of William Cullen Love and Sarah M. "Sally" Bryan. Their children were: Elizabeth, born September 1, 1844, at Edgehill; Sarah J., born in 1847; Elvira, born in 1850; Green Berry, born August 4, 1853, at Edgehill; Mary, born December 20, 1857, at Edgehill; Robert Edward Bryan, born October 26, 1860, at Edgehill; Sterling Price, born April 2, 1861, at Edgehill; and Edward Lee, born in 1864 in Missouri. William J. was a farmer at Edgehill. He died in January of 1903 and Margaret died June 3, 1878, both at Edgehill. They are buried in the Goggin-Troutman Cemetery.

Elizabeth married James Henry Bell on March 8, 1864, in Iron County. He was born February 25, 1840, at Edgehill, the son of Thomas Newton Bell and Mahala Cain. Their children were: Hattie J., born February 25, 1865; William Gentry, born April 3, 1867, at Black; John Alexander, born May 25, 1870, at Black; Laura Ann, born March 8, 1873, at Black; Robert Franklin, born August 25, 1875, in Missouri; Andrew George, born January 12, 1879, at Black; and Mary Caroline, born September 2, 1882, at Black. Two children had died by the 1900 census. Elizabeth died April 1, 1913, at Chandler, Lincoln County, Oklahoma, and James Henry died September 27, 1917, at Ellington. Elizabeth is buried in the New Zion Cemetery at Chandler, Lincoln County, Oklahoma, and James Henry is buried in the Black Cemetery. The family lived in Black River Township, where he farmed.

Green Berry married Ella W. Richmond on April 10, 1881, in Reynolds County. She was born in September of 1864 in Missouri, the daughter of Dr. John R. and Rosella Richmond. Their children were: Rozella Caroline, born January 19, 1884, in Stoddard County, Missouri; Willard W. (A.?), born in April of 1890 in Missouri; Grover C., born in December of 1891 (1892?) in Missouri; Mable C., born April 18, 1898, at Edgehill; and Lela P., born in 1903 in Missouri. Ella W. died in 1908 and Green Berry died in 1910. They are buried in theGoggin-Troutman Cemetery. The mother had lost two children by the 1900 census. He farmed in Black River Township.

Mary married Joseph Black on January 5, 1886, at Middle Fork in Reynolds County. He was born in 1860 in Missouri, the son of George and Mary A. Black. Their children were: William Edgar, born October 26, 1886, and Joseph F., born September 22, 1890 (1889?). Both were born in Missouri. Mary and sons were living with her father in Reynolds County when the 1900 census was taken, Joseph having died before that time. Mary died September 14, 1946, Nikoma Park, Oklahoma County, Oklahoma, and is buried in the New Zion Cemetery, Chandler.

Robert Edward Bryan married Necie A. Robertson. She was born August 29, 1870, and was the daughter of Fay Robertson. Their children were: Caroline Zoe, born August 2, 1888; Winnie Davis, born November 6, 1890; Carlisle, born October 1, 1893; William Lafayette, April 14, 1895; Ottos, born March 22, 1899; Floy Vaiden, born September 13, 1901; unidentified son, born April 24, 1903; and Robert Edward Bryan Jr., born October 3, 1909. Robert Edward Bryan died March 2, 1925, and Necie A. died November 21, 1953. He was a medical doctor and practiced at St. Joe, Searcy County, Arkansas.

Sterling Price married Cassie B. Johnson in 1889-90. She was born in November of 1871 in Missouri. They adopted Stella Pettijohn, age 13 in 1910 census, born in Missouri, who married Richard Bell and had a large family. Sterling Price died October 29, 1930, and Cassie B. died in 1942. Cassie B. had lost one child before the 1900 census and a second between 1900 and 1910, according to the 1910 census. The family lived in Black River Township.

Edward Lee died March 28, 1887, while attending medical school. He is buried in the Goggin-Troutman Cemetery.

Milton "Mick" married Mary Jane Bell about 1852 in Reynolds County. She was born in January of 1834 in Reynolds County, the sister of James Henry Bell, who married Milton's niece, Elizabeth B. Their children were: William, born in April of 1853 in Missouri; Lucy A., born July 7, 1854;

Sarah, born in 1856; Lavada, born April 11, 1857; Thomas Green, born in 1859 in Black; Mahala E., born May 16, 1862, at Belleview; and Nancy. Milton was killed by Federal troops in 1865 while he was being transferred as a prisoner of war from Salem to Rolla. Mary Jane died August 7, 1906, near Redford, Reynolds County, and is buried in the Redford Cemetery.

William married Julia (?). She was born in April of 1877. Children shown in the 1900 census were Lottie, born in February of 1896, and Charles, born in February of 1899. Both were born in Missouri. In 1900 the family was in Iron Township, Iron County.

Lucy A. married James F. Rayfield on December 5, 1872, in Reynolds County. He was born in July of 1854 in Missouri, the son of William Rayfield and Lucy Boyd. Their children were: Sarah Joanna, born October 29, 1873; Leona, born March 3, 1876, at Centerville; Oather, born February 18, 1882; and Ida. Lucy A. died March 31, 1882, and is buried in the Rayfield Cemetery at Lesterville. James F. was a postmaster and merchant at Centerville. James F. next married Laura B. Laws on November 7, 1882, in Reynolds County. She was born in February of 1867 in Illinois, the daughter of James M. and Mary A. Laws. Their children were: Rolla W., born in November of 1883; Lenna H., born in May of 1885; Alice M., born in April of 1889; James C., born in August of 1893; Clyde J., born in 1894; Amy C., born in January of 1896; Dewey C., born in March of 1898; Golden R., born in 1900-1; and Floyd G., born n 1908-9. All were born in Missouri. James F. died in 1939 and is buried in the Ellington Cemetery. In 1910 the family lived in Logan Township, where he was farming. Laura B. had lost one child, according to the 1910 census.

Sarah married David H. Hartman August 25, 1896, in Iron County. He was born January 12, 1841, in Ohio, the son of John Dixon Hartman and Margaret Parker. They had one daughter, Minnie, born May 7, 1898, in Missouri. David's first wife was Ethlinda Black, born September 26, 1845, in Arkansas, the daughter of George and Mary Black. Their children were: John G., born July 14, 1863, in Iowa; Mary M., born February 6, 1866; Vianna M., born October 19, 1867; Sarah Isabel, born March 29, 1869; Donna (Donnie?), born November 1, 1871, died before 1883; William, born April 4, 1873, died before 1883; Rose E., born March 26, 1874; Philip D., born August 4, 1876; Leona, born October 9, 1878, died before 1888; and Ebenezer, April 24, 1880. The last nine children were probably born in Missouri. David died March 13, 1914. He was a farmer in Black River Township. The Hartman family, according to the Carty book, came from Pennsylvania. In 1900 the family was living in Iron Township, Iron County, where he was farming.

Lavada married James C. Harrison on March 15, 1877. He was born April 10, 1856, in Missouri, the son of William R. Harrison and Lucy B. Stewart. Their children were: Linnie, born April 1, 1878; William Milton, born October 14, 1879, in Redford; Thomas Walter, born March 20, 1882, in

Redford; Charles R., born June 11, 1885, in Redford; Carrie C., born January 3, 1889; and Everett F., born September 22, 1894, in Redford. Lavada died June 29, 1936, and James C. died September 23, 1933. Both are buried in the Redford Cemetery. The family lived in Logan Township, where he farmed.

Thomas Green married Sarah Catherine Carty on January 10, 1878, at Black. She was born September 2, 1863, in Black, the daughter of George Washington Carty and Elizabeth Rosanna Miner. Their children were: Willie C., born September 9, 1880; Minnie Bell, born November 23, 1881; Ida Elizabeth, born October 9, 1883, at Black; Evert T., born December 20, 1884; Nannie Ethel, born July 16, 1887, at Black; Robert Earnest, born April 27, 1889; Leora G., born August 18, 1890, at Corridon; Maggie M., born October 7, 1891, and Hallie Ray and Allie Gray, twins, born December 9, 1898, in Missouri. Thomas Green died February 26, 1902, at Lesterville, and is buried in the Rayfield Cemetery, Lesterville. Sarah Catherine died December 5, 1923, at Flat River, St. Francois County. The mother had lost three children by the 1910 census. Thomas Green was a farmer and the family lived in Black River Township.

Mahala E. married Frank Forman Gallaher on August 18, 1881, at Edgehill. He was born April 8, 1853, at Black, the son of George Gallaher, and Serena Miner. They had one daughter, Ella B., born September 9, 1882, in Missouri. Mahala died January 11, 1945, and Frank Forman died March 10, 1920. She is buried in the Riverview Cemetery, Portland, Multnomah County, Oregon. Frank Forman is buried in the Ellington Cemetery. The couple separated prior to May 10, 1896, when he married his third wife, Lillian Maude "Birdie" Temple, daughter of James O. Temple, at Barnsville (Ellington). Frank Forman had been married, first to Nancy C. Goggin, discussed later.

Nancy married John R. Harrison October 4, 1877, in Reynolds County. He was born 1857-8 in Missouri, the bròther of James C. Harrison, who married Nancy's sister, Lavada. Their children were: Lucy Jane, born in June of 1879 (tombstone shows October 16, 1874, with death date of September 16, 1884); and Thomas E., born May 27, 1881, died June 16, 1881. Both were born in Missouri. The children were buried in Rayfield Cemetery. In 1880 John R. was farming in Logan Township.

Jubal "Jube" married Martha F. Boyd. She was born in 1837 in Kentucky, the daughter of John Boyd and Elizabeth Lester. Their children were: John R., born in 1858 in Missouri; James G., born February 12, 1860, in Black; Artamissa Elizabeth, born October 3, 1863, in Missouri; Mary Jane, born October 26, 1866, in Missouri; and George W., born January 1, 1870, Missouri. Martha F. died July 3, 1913, in Black, after marrying second in 1906 to George W. Bell. This was also his second marriage. Martha and children lived in Black River Township in 1880. The family moved to Wright County, Missouri, some time after 1880. Jubal died before 1880.

John R. married Lydia A. Dennison on September 1, 1885, in Reynolds County. She was born in July of 1867 in Missouri, the daughter of Daniel Albert Dennison and Elizabeth Grien (Grimes?). Their children were: Lulu F., born in March of 1887; Walter, born July 12 1890; Clara Belle, born in February of 1893; and George Oscar, born April 24, 1900. All were born in Missouri. Clara Belle died February 17, 1907, and is buried in the Rayfield Cemetery. The 1910 census indicates the mother had lost four children. John R. was a farmer in Lesterville Township, living on the Middle Fork of the Black River.

James G. married Sarah E. Bell in 1880-1. She was born September 12, 1863, in Missouri, the daughter of George Washington Bell and Catherine Carty. Their children were: Effie M., born December 27, 1881; Lonnie T., born October 18, 1883; Eller G., born March 2, 1885; Harvey M., born June 6, 1888; Gentry T., born January 15, 1892; Tony Otto, born December 26, 1894; Alice Lucy, born January 24, 1896; Orso Clarence, born July 10, 1899; and Roy and Cloy, born February 1, 1902. All were born in Missouri. The twins were not listed in the 1910 census. James G. died February 8, 1935, and Sarah E. died July 14, 1937. He was a farmer in Black River Township. During the 1920s he hauled freight by wagon from the Missouri-Pacific railroad at Middlebrook, Iron County, to Black, making two or three trips a week.

Artamissa Elizabeth married William Herman Russell December 13, 1883, in Lesterville. He was born October 25, 1858, the son of James Russell and Mary Rose, who lived in Wayne County, Tennessee. Their children were: Walter James, born February 7, 1885, in Farmington; Alice Martha, born September 29, 1886; Anna Edith, born September 15, 1888; Rolla Herman, born April 21, 1890, in Reynolds County; Della Agness, born February 22, 1893, at Lesterville; John Edgar, born August 2, 1895, at Lesterville; Edna Ethel, born May 17, 1898, in Reynolds County; Fred Eli, born October 25, 1900, at Lesterville; Carrie Arlene, born April 26, 1903, at Lesterville; and Golda Mafetla, born January 25, 1906, in St Francois County. William Herman died November 7, 1913, and Artamissa Elizabeth died May 30, 1942. They are buried in the Pendleton Cemetery, Doe Roe, St. Francois County. After William's death, Artamissa Elizabeth lived near Elvins in St. Francois County. She was a member of the Longhboro Baptist Church.

Mary Jane married Reuben Valentine Sumpter on February 17, 1886, at Black. He was born January 3, 1848, in Missouri, the son of George and Anna Sumpter. Their children were: George Ethel Burt: born May 27, 1887; Martha Ann, born in April of 1889; Ernest Virgil, born May 3, 1891; James F., born August 9, 1893; John R., born in January of 1896; Virda A., born in May of 1900; Raymond; and Arlene. The family lived in Lesterville and later in what is now Iron County, near the headwaters of Neals Creek. Reuben served in Battery A, 1st Missouri Light Artillery, from November 25, 1864, to August 23, 1865, when he was only 16 years old. The couple separated about 1920. Reuben then married his fourth wife, Sarah. His first wife was Caroline Hawk and the second was Elizabeth Carty. Elizabeth was born May

23, 1850, in Missouri, the daughter of Greenberry V. Carty and Julia Ann Adams. Mary J. died March 18, 1947, in Oakland, Alamdeda County, California. Reuben Valentine died January 25, 1934, and is buried in the Masonic Cemetery at Oakland.

George W. married Lucinda J. "Lucy" Dennison on October 15, 1890, in Reynolds County. She was born November 18, 1871, in Missouri, the daughter of John Burch Dennison and Lucinda Trollinger Bell. Their children were: Sidney Herbert, born October 12, 1891; Laura M., born in September of 1893; Mary Myrtle, born in March of 1896; Anzona, born in March of 1898; Elsie; and Orville. All were born in Missouri. George W. died December 19, 1941, and is buried in the Bethlehem Cemetery in Reynolds County. The Dennison family came from Kentucky to Missouri about 1845-8, and the Trollinger family came from Tennessee. In 1900 the family lived in Black River Township, where he farmed.

Nancy was living with her mother in the 1850 census. She was converted in a Black River Baptist Church revival meeting held in November of 1853, and all trace of her has been lost since that time.

Drucilla's first marriage was to John Boyd, Jr., probably in 1858-9. He was born in 1840-1 in Missouri, the brother of Martha F. Boyd, who married Drucilla's brother, Jubal. They had a son, Green B., born in August of 1863 in Missouri. After a short marriage ending in divorce, she married Milton D. Gallaher. He was born November 8, 1837, in Missouri, the brother of Frank Forman Gallaher, who married Drucilla's cousin, Mahala E. Their children were: James Holman, born March 11, 1868, in Missouri; Charles H., born January 30, 1870, at Edgehill; John Thomas, born April 29, 1871, in Missouri; and Robert N., born in April of 1874, in Missouri. Milton's grandfather, David Gallaher, was one of the earliest settlers of Belleview Valley, arriving there in 1807. Milton died March 31, 1877, and is buried in the Love Cemetery at Edgehill. Drucilla died in 1902. Sons George, age 10, and William, age 8, are shown with this family in the 1870 Reynolds County census. Nancy, age nine, and Sarah, age five, are shown with their grandparents in the 1870 census. Another daughter, Syrenia F., is buried in the Love Cemetery in Reynolds County. The 1900 census lists Drucilla as a nurse, living in Black River Township, her son Robert N. with her. That census indicates she had seven children, four living.

Milton married Nancy Carty. She was born August 11, 1808, in Cumberland County, and was the sister of Elizabeth Carty, who married Green Berry, brother of Milton. Their children were: Green Berry, born May 10, 1827, in Cumberland County; William, born February 23, 1830, in Reynolds County; James W., born June 17, 1833, in Black; Sarah J., born October 7, 1838, in Black; and John Harvey, born December 9, 1845, in Black. Milton served as church clerk and as a trustee of the Black River Baptist Church. Milton died December 27, 1869, and Nancy died January 8, 1886, both at Black. She is buried at the Earl Baker farm (1976) near Black.

Green Berry married Sarah Ann Shy March 14, 1850. She was the daughter of Eli Shy and Mary Elizabeth Smith. This family is discussed with the Shy family.

Milton E. married Lizzie J. (Elizabeth J.?)in 1870-1. She was born June 11, 1846, in Kentucky. They had one daughter, Sallie Leu, born February 21, 1877, died November 3, 1892. Milton died February 1, 1911, and Lizzie J. died January 13, 1926. They are buried in the Rayfield Cemetery. In 1900, they lived in Lesterville Township, where he farmed and she was listed in the census as a hotel keeper.

William O.'s first marriage was to Sarah Jane Rayfield. She was born December 30, 1852, in Reynolds County, and was a sister of James F. Rayfield, who married Lucy A. Their children were: James F., born August 12, 1872, in Missouri; Thomas Green, born February 1, 1874; George W. born December 13, 1875; Mary Belle "Mollie", born August 4, 1878; and Charles M., born January 15, 1881. All were born in Missouri. Sarah Jane died August 5, 1881 in Reynolds County. William O. then married Margaret Corrila Parks on September 14, 1882, in Reynolds County. She was born November 27, 1859, in Missouri, the daughter of James Henry Parks and Matilda Rayfield. Their children, repeated from the Parks family listing: Edna Ethel, born June 22, 1883; Oscar H., born January 12, 1885; Viola May, born May 12, 1887; Walles T., born March 5, 1889; and Zona Pearl, born June 21, 1891. All were born in Missouri. William O. died December 25, 1895, in Reynolds County.

Mary Jane died March 22, 1906.

Nancy C. married Frank Forman Gallaher May 30 1872 in Reynolds County. He was born April 8, 1853, in Black. They had no children. Nancy C. died September 17, 1880, and is buried in the Love Cemetery, Edgehill. Frank Forman then married Nancy's cousin, Mahala E., discussed earlier.

John Thomas married Margaret N. Rayfield August 18, 1880. She was born July 13, 1861, the daughter of Andrew and Elizabeth Rayfield. Their children were: Andrew Green, born May 4, 1883; Sarah A.; Ralph O.; and Elza. The family moved in 1892 to Ingraham, Oklahoma Territory, on the Deep Fork River near Wellston.

Robert M. died August 18, 1866.

Isabelle's first marriage was to Andrew J. Rayfield on May 23, 1883, in Reynolds County. He was born in 1861-2 in Missouri, the brother of Sarah Jane, who married William O. They had one daughter, Anna, born October 13, 1884, in Missouri. Isabelle's second marriage was to Thomas Owen "Tommy" Bell on January 23, 1894. she was born in November of 1865, the son of George Washington Bell and Catherine Carty. They had one daughter, Zoa Dell, born October 23, 1895 (1896?), in Missouri. Thomas Owen died September 21, 1936, and Isabelle died August 17, 1952. They are buried in the Shy Cemetery in Black. Thomas Owen was a farmer in Black River Township.

James A. married Margaret J. "Mag" Carty on June 26, 1889, in Reynolds County. She was born November 22, 1872, in Missouri, the sister of Sarah Catherine, who married Thomas Green. Their children were: Milton Omer, born August 13, 1892; Ona Belle; Anna May, born January 24, 1894; Halla G. born July 23, 1897; and Ana P. born in April of 1900 in Missouri. Only Milton Omer survived to the 1910 census. James A. died December 1, 1926, and Mag died April 1, 1946. They are buried in the Black Cemetery. The family lived in Lesterville Township, where he farmed.

B.F. died October 16, 1873.

Alvin P. married Hattie May Adams December 11, 1902, in Centerville. She was born February 10, 1882, in Missouri, the daughter of Moses Adams and Malissa Campbell. Their children were: Della B., born September 30, 1903, in Missouri; Roy O., born October 18, 1906, in Missouri; and Pearl and Adam Ferrell, twins, born December 4, 1913. Hattie May died December 21, 1946, and Alvin P. died August 10, 1954. He is buried in the Rayfield Cemetery, Lesterville. The family lived in Lesterville Township, where he farmed.

William married Lettie Boyd. She was born April 19, 1833, in Kentucky, and was the sister of John Jr. and Martha F. Boyd, mentioned earlier. Their children were: Sarah Jane, born December 19, 1856; Milton T., born April 15, 1858; John B., born February 23, 1860; Green Berry, born January 16, 1862, in Reynolds County; and James William, born December 11, 1863, in Reynolds County. William, according to family tradition, was impressed into the Confederate service and died in Arkansas February 13, 1865. Lettie died February 23, 1919. The family lived in Arcadia Township, Iron County, in 1860 and the children were living in Dent Township, Iron County, in 1876. In 1910 Lettie was with her son, James William.

Milton T. married Margaret Lucretia Love March 4, 1885, at Middle Fork in Iron County. She was born February 12, 1858, at Edgehill, the daughter of Dr. John Hartwell Love and Judith Cain. Their children were: Verd Noel, born March 11, 1886; unidentified son, born May 28, 1888; Lucy Jane, born October 10, 1890; William Henry, born June 13, 1893; Minnie Almeda, born June 15, 1895; Ernest Green, born September 10, 1899; and Robert, born November 24, 1902. Milton T. died September 24, 1939, and Margaret Lucretia died December 29, 1944. The family later lived at Elvins, in the "lead belt" of Missouri.

John B. married Vianna Mae Hartman August 8, 1883, in Reynolds County. She was born October 19, 1867, in Missouri, the daughter of David H. Hartman and Ethlinda Black. Their children were: Irvin Richards, born in 1884; David William, born April 24, 1887; Gentry Oliver, born June 4, 1890; Rose Mae, born August 10, 1893; Harry A., born in October of 1895; and Gladys Lena, born August 19, 1906. All the children except Gladys Lena were born in Missouri. The family lived at Alva, Lee County, Florida. John B. died January 8, 1934, and she died June 12, 1934 at the home of her son,

Gentry, at Granite City, Madison County, Illinois. The couple is buried in the Edison Cemetery at Belleview.

Green Berry married Sarah Jane McMahan in 1889-90. She was born September 27, 1864, in Missouri, the daughter of John McMahan and Mary Richardson. Their children were: Stella Judy, born November 13, 1890, at Edgehill; Mae, born March 8, 1892, in Missouri; Anna F., born January 27, 1894, in Missouri; Alice Belle, born February 25, 1896, in Missouri; and John Raymond, born January 14, 1898, in Missouri. Green Berry died April 8, 1940, and is buried on the farm where he spent his entire life. Sarah Jane died August 16, 1964, nearly 100 years old. The family lived in 1910 in Kaolin Township, Iron County, where he farmed.

James William "Spicky" married Rebecca Lucinda Black in 1893-4. She was born January 8, 1872, in Missouri, the daughter of Coatsworth Pinckney Black and Nancy Thomas. Their children were: Otto, born October 8, 1893; Oliver, born January 30, 1896; Lettie G., born June 7, 1899; Nora M., born May 11, 1902; Salome A., born August 7, 1904; Nellie, born September 5, 1906; William Orville, born October 31, 1908; and Ruby Mae, born January 31, 1910 (?). All were born in Missouri. The family lived in Kaolin Township, Iron County, near his brother, Green Berry, in 1910 and later moved to a farm near Black, where James William died June 20, 1947. Rebecca Lucinda died July 4, 1929.

Sarah Jane married Tillman Terry. She died June 20, 1947. They had no children.

James W. married Sarah Catherine Bell before June of 1860. She was born December 6, 1842, in Missouri, the sister of James Henry Bell, who married James W.'s cousin, Elizabeth. Their children were: Franklin, born October 18, 1860; Nancy Jane, born March 13, 1863, in Missouri; Margaret Mandora, born May 23, 1865, in Missouri; Sarah S., born April 15, 1868, in Black; Mary Elizabeth, born February 17, 1870, in Missouri; and Alfred Shy, born March 23, 1874. The family lived between Black and Lesterville, where he farmed. James W. died in 1874 and Sarah Catherine died May 6, 1921. They are buried in the Black Cemetery.

Franklin died in infancy.

Nancy Jane married Woodson Robinett July 10, 1879, in Reynolds County. He was born in June of 1857 in Missouri, the son of Steven Robinett and Martha "Patsy" Miner. Their children were: James Franklin, born June 7, 1880; William Estelle, born December 31, 1884; Ella S., born February 3, 1886; Bertha Lee, born February 29, 1888; Omer J., born in August of 1890; Alfred, born in December of 1892; Oga, born April 24, 1895; Floy, born May 22, 1899; and Alice and Allie G., twins, born September 8, 1904. All were born in Missouri. Woodson died January 16, 1934, and Nancy Jane died October 25, 1937. They are buried in the Black Cemetery. He was a farmer in Black River Township.

Margaret Mandora "Dora" married William J. "Willie" Hawkins July 25, 1894, in Black. He was born April 15, 1871 (1870?), in Missouri, the son of George W. Hawkins and Sarah Carty. Their children were: Arthur Clyde, born April 22, 1895; James Lloyd, born August 29, 1898; and Mabel, born October 5, 1900. All were born in Missouri. William J. died June 21, 1911, and Margaret Mandora died January 1, 1939. They are buried in the Black Cemetery. Their daughter, Mabel, died before the 1910 census and is probably buried with her parents. He was a farmer in Black River Township.

Sarah S. married Dr. Fayette E. Stafford July 25, 1888, in Reynolds County. He was born June 19, 1860, in Pratt, Pratt County, Kansas. Their children were: Lee Roy, born in 1891; Monta, born May 14, 1894; Lora; Ernest, born March 8, 1897; Verna Blanche, born March 8, 1900. and Mable Elizabeth. The family lived in Dent County, Missouri, where Dr. Stafford practiced. Sarah S. died October 26, 1930, and Fayette E. died November 27, 1930.

Mary Elizabeth "Lizzie" married John George Carty February 5, 1891, in Reynolds County. He was born January 12, 1871, in Missouri, a brother of Sarah Catherine and Margaret C. Carty, mentioned earlier. Their children were: George Otis, born in February of 1892; Grace M., born December 13, 1896; Ava Belle, born in 1901; and Lowell, born in 1911. Mary Elizabeth died December 26, 1945; and John George died November 23, 1930. They are buried in the Black Cemetery.

Alfred Shy married Martha Eller Carty August 20, 1899, at Black in Reynolds County. She was born June 5, 1882, in Missouri, a sister of John George, Sarah Catherine and Margaret C. Carty. They had one son, Marvie Franklin, born May 29, 1900, in Missouri. Alfred Shy died September 8, 1914, a few days after being kicked by a mule. Martha Eller died November 17, 1939, from a kick by a cow. They are buried in the Black Cemetery. The family lived in Black River Township, where he farmed.

Sarah J. married Alfred Howe Shy. This family discussed with the Shy family.

John Harvey married Mary Louisa Sloan probably February 11, 1867, in Iron County. She was born January 1, 1846, in Missouri. Their children were William Harvey, born October 7, 1868, at Black; Charles Green, born March 7, 1871, at Black; Robert Edward Lee, born December 7, 1872; Sarah E., born April 1, 1874; Rhoda Bell, born March 15, 1877, at Black; James Milton, born March 31, 1878; Anne May, born February 16, 1880; Joshua C. and Nancy Calfern, twins, born January 26, 1882; Birdie, born in 1884; and Mary Ella, born January 18, 1889, died the same day. John Harvey was active in the Black River Baptist Church, where he was appointed trustee in 1870 and was church clerk for a number of years. Mary Louisa died in childbirth January 19, 1889. John Harvey then sold his land in 1890 and worked as a mail carrier, carrying the mail by horseback from Black to Ironton. He went to Oklahoma Territory and settled near Wellston, Lincoln County, in 1900, where he farmed and traded cattle until he died October 14, 1929. Mary Louisa is buried at the Wilmer Walker Farm Cemetery at Black. A tombstone there is marked Brenda B. Goggin-1884-infant, probably the Birdie listed above. The family lived in 1880 in Black River Township.

William Harvey married Nannie Christian February 15, 1895. She was born December 20, 1870, in Ohio. Their children were: Charles, born March 24, 1896, in Kentucky; May, born December 19, 1898; Roy A. born September 11, 1902; and Ruby Pearl, born August 16, 1907. William Harvey was a teacher in the Webb School, Reynolds County, but after the death of his mother in 1889, he gave up teaching and went to work in the lumber camps of southeast Missouri. From there he went to the coal mines of Kentucky, where he met Nannie in Cheona, Bell County, Kentucky. He was in a mine accident when left him with serious injuries and the family then went to Wellston, Oklahoma Territory, where he lived the remainder of his life. William Harvey died December 15, 1937, and Nannie died April 26, 1964.

Charles Green married Laura Chilcote March 21, 1901, in Reynolds County. She was born May 5, 1877, in Missouri, the daughter of Samuel R. Chilcote and Nancy J. Brown. Their children were: Montie Oscar, born July 21, 1902; Maude Marie, born March 27, 1904; Herbert William, born May 14, 1906; Ina opal, born April 28, 1908; and Bertha May, born October 18, 1910. The couple moved to near Wellston in 1902, where their children were born. Charles Green died February 26, 1911 and Laura died July 8, 1966. They are buried in the Rossville Cemetery, Rossville, Oklahoma.

Robert Edward Lee married Martha Elizabeth Wimmer in Lincoln County, Oklahoma Territory. She was born January 4, 1880, the daughter of Jacob Samuel Wimmer and Mary Aves Kincaid. Their children were: Blanche Aves, born December 27, 1902; Louisa Ellen, born September 6, 1906; Pearl Izola, born November 3, 1910; Lee Oliver, born February 24, 1914; and Minnie Alma, born March 5, 1917. Martha Elizabeth died October 8, 1929, and Robert Edward Lee died May 24, 1951.

Sarah E. "Sally" married John Alexander Bell February 28, 1900, at Chandler, Lincoln County, Oklahoma Territory. He was born May 25, 1870, at Black, the son of James H. Bell and Elizabeth Goggin. Their children were: Roy, born July 16, 1901, at Fallis, Oklahoma Territory; and Jessie, born October 9, 1903, at Dale, Oklahoma Territory. John Alexander grew up in St. Francois, Iron and Reynolds Counties. In the late 1890s he went to St. Louis, where he worked as a street car conductor. After serving in the Spanish-American War, he moved with his parents to Lincoln County, Oklahoma Territory, in 1899-1890. While working in Oklahoma City in 1908, he contracted tuberculosis and the family moved to Rockford, Colorado, making the trip by covered wagon. After moving to El Paso, El Paso County, Texas, for a short while, the family returned to Colorado and homesteaded in Baca County. After three years, they moved to a ranch near Marvel, LaPlato County, Colorado. Later the parents moved to Durango, La Plato County, where the couple spent the remainder of their lives. John Alexander died September 2, 1945, and Sarah E. died June 3, 1956, both in Durango.

Rhoda Bell married Wesley Young Hayles January 1, 1901. He was the son of William Hayles and Nancy Young. Their children were: Gladys Glee, born January 22, 1902; Hazel Hesel, born November 10, 1904; and Raymond Harold, born August 9, 1910. Rhoda Bell had moved to Oklahoma Territory in 1900, where she lived for about 60 years. She died January 14, 1966, in Los Angeles, California.

James Milton married Tressie May Wimmer, daughter of Jacob Samuel Wimmer and Mary Anes Kincaid. Their children were: Coy Alfred, born August 19, 1910, Andy Clifford, born July 11, 1912; Leonard Leon, born November 30, 1913; Violet Viola, born October 8, 1915; and an unidentified son. Tressie May died January 4, 1919, and James Milton died May 26, 1958.

Anne May married Matthew Steel Orr November 16, 1902, at Chandler in Lincoln County. Their children were: Grace, born June 22, 1905; Nelson Ellis, born August 22, 1911; and Pauline, born September 22, 1915. Anne May died December 29, 1931.

Joshua C. married Gertrude Waller April 12, 1912. She was born July 11, 188?. Their children were: John Riel, January 26, 1913; Harry Earl, born July 19, 1917; and Charley C., born May 4, 1919. Gertrude died November 25, 1964, and Joshua C. died May 7, 1970.

Nancy Calfern married Frank Jones. Their children were: Troy Franklin, born June 11, 1912; Ruble and Ruby, twins, born October 11, 1914; and Eva, born October 10, 1918. Nancy Calfern died December 2, 1955.

Birdie died (?) 21, 1889.

REFERENCES

A Reminiscent History of The Ozarks Region, Chicago, Goodspeed Bros.,1894

History of Belleview Valley, Caledonia Missouri, Belleview Valley Historical Society, 1983

Birth Records, Reynolds County, Missouri

Court Records, Reynolds County, Missouri

Court Records, Washington County, Missouri

Death Records, Reynolds County, Missouri

Old Reynolds, Ellinghouse, C.R. and others, Ellington, Missouri, Reynolds County Courier, 1978

A History of Black River Baptist Church, Estep, Flora Angel, 1969

Family Group Sheets File, Reynolds County Genealogical Society, 1985

Family Bible, Marshall Marvin and Sarah Ella Shy Munger

Family Records provided by too many people to adequately recognize.

History of The Pioneer Families of Missouri, St. Louis, Bryan and Rose, 1876

John Carty and 4000 Descendants, Jamison, John H., and others, Marceline, Missouri, Walsworth Publishing County, 1979

One Hundred Twenty One Cemeteries of Reynolds County, Missouri, Lesh, Delsa, and Stockton, Glenda, St. Louis

Ellington City Cemetery, Lesh, Delsa and Roger, 1976

Trails of Trials and Triumphs, Lesh, Delsa, 1985

Reynolds County, Missouri, Marriage Records, 1870-1891, Lesh, Delsa, Reynolds County Genealogical Society, Ellington, Missouri, 1985

The Munger Book, Munger, J.B., The Tuttle, Morehouse & Taylor County., Chicago, 1915

Obituaries File, Reynolds County Genealogical Society

Tax Roll, 1876, Iron County, Missouri

The Centerville Reformer, March 3, 1904–December 26, 1907, Centerville, Missouri

The Ellington Press, various issues, Ellington, Missouri

United States Census, 1790-1910

United States Mortality Schedules, Reynolds County, Missouri

Reynolds County, Missouri, Marriage Records, 1891-1900, Wilson, June, Reynolds County Genealogical Society, Ellington, Missouri, 1985

Reynolds County, Missouri, Marriage Records, 1901-1910, Wilson, June, Reynolds County Genealogical Society, Ellington, Missouri, 1985

Prepared by: John L. Lillibridge
19168 Bob-O-Link Drive
Hialeah, FL 33015

JAMES CROWNOVER

James Crownover, born July 17, 1810, in White of Franklin County, Tennessee, was probably the first Crownover in the State of Missouri. He was the son of Theodore (born between 1790-1800) and Mary Polly (Brawley) Crownover. They were married but a short time and had only one son named James. Little if anything is known of James's childhood. The circuit court records, dated January 17, 1825, in Murfreesboro, Tennessee, states that he was a bound apprentice to Levi Brawley to learn the trade of cabinetmaker. He was married to Sally Jordan, (born April 26, 1813, in Franklin County, Tennessee, died 1848-1850), the daughter of Levi and Fanny Townsend Jordan, on December 16, 1830, in Shelbyville, Shelby County, Illinois. Their first born was a son named Levi, born in 1832 in Illinois. James and his family moved to Missouri between 1832-1834 and settled in an area called Barnsville, which is now Ellington, Missouri.

Reynolds County was formed on February 25, 1845. Quoting from "Old Reynolds", published in Reynolds County, Missouri:

"Serving on the first county court by appointment of the governor were Landon Copeland, William C. Love, and James Crownover, all to serve until the first election the following year.

Also appointed by the governor were two other men who were to have key roles in the new county called Reynolds. He made Marvin Munger the first sheriff and John Buford the first surveyor. C.C. Campbell was appointed by the court as the first clerk of the county and circuit courts. These six pioneers — Copeland, Love, Crownover, Munger, Buford and Campbell — formed the first government of Reynolds County.

The first clerk of the county court was Collin C. Campbell, appointed to the office on May 5, 1845, to serve until the first election. This office was combined with that of clerk of the circuit court. Campbell held both positions. He was elected to the offices in August of 1846 and won a six-year term in the election in 1847, but he resigned in 1850. Next was James Crownover, who was elected in 1853, after being appointed to fill out Campbell's term. Crownover was elected in 1866 and held this office for many years.

The county and circuit clerk was one of the most demanding jobs during the early years of Reynolds County government. While the responsibilities of the county court changed from time to time, the work of this office was essential to maintain a stable situation in the county. In addition to clerking for the two courts, this office holder for a long time handled these chores for the probate court. Several years passed before Reynolds County had two distinct offices, one to clerk the county court, and another to clerk the circuit court. From the beginning the circuit clerk also was recorder of deeds."

The Reynolds County archives gives the exact date of James Crownover's election to county and circuit clerk, November 27, 1849. James held these offices until his death in the latter part of 1869 or early 1870. He was also post-master in Centerville, Missouri, for the years 1854-1859 and justice of the peace of Reynolds County. He was a member of the Black River Baptist Church.

The following is a list of real estate owned by James Crownover:

1. Block 9 - Lots 3, 4 and 5.
2. Block 10 - Lots 1, 2, 3, 4, 5, 6, 7 and 8.
3. Block 16 - Lots 1, 2, 7 and 8.
4. Block 18 - Lots 1, 2, 3, 4, 5, 6, 7 and 8.
5. Block 23 - Lot 4.
6. Block 24 - Lots 1, 2, 7 and 8.
7. Block 25 - Lots 1, 2, and fractional lots 7 and 8.

Total - 31 lots owned in Centerville, Missouri.

Reynolds County property owned by James Crownover:

1. November 16, 1857 - Theodore Crownover and wife Hannah to James Crownover, 240 acres.
2. December 1, 1858 - U.S. Patent by President James Buchanan to James Crownover, 40 acres.
3. September 1, 1859 - U.S. Patent by President James Buchanan to James Crownover, 160 acres.
4. January 18, 1870 - Edwards Barnes to James Crownover, 680 acres.
5. May 11, 1865 - Tax sale to James Crownover, 3.20 acres.
6. October 20, 1869 - Sheriff deed to James Crownover, 10 acres.
7. U.S. Patent by President James Buchanan to James Crownover, 80 acres.

Total owned in Reynolds County by James Crownover 1,213 acres.

The writer had copies of several "documents of great interest" from the old jail in Centerville, Reynolds County, Missouri, namely: U.S. land grants to James Crownover, signed by President Buchanan and to his sons, Levi and Theodore Crownover; documents written in longhand by James Crownover while he was in office as county clerk (He had a beautiful handwriting.); also, the probate will to the heirs of James Crownover, dated 1872, after his death.

James, Sally (Jordan) and Eliza Ann (Davis) Crownover are all buried in the Centerville Cemetery in Centerville, Missouri. A memorial in their honor was erected over their grave sites in June of 1984. The memorial was made possible through contributions of many of the Crownover descendants and related families.

Sally (Jordan) Crownover, born April 26, 1813, in Franklin County, Tennessee, died after the birth of her daughter Cynthia on or about September 17, 1848, in Centerville, Reynolds County, Missouri. Six children were born of this union. Sally was a daughter of Levi and Fanny (Townsend) Jordan. Levi was born August 21, 1793, in New Jersey and died between 1840-1850 in Missouri. He was justice of the peace in Shelby County, Illinois, in 1829 and was a member of Okaw Baptist Church in Shelby County, Illinois. Fanny

(Townsend) Jordan was born November 8, 1792, in Indiana. Four children were born to this union: R.W. Jordan (Ruben Wesley), born July 27, 1811, in Tennessee, died in Reynolds County, Missouri; Sally Jordan, born April 26, 1813, in Tennessee, died 1848-1850 in Centerville, Missouri; William Jordan, born April 12, 1817; and Polly Ann Jordan, born February 10, 1819.

Children of James and Sally Jordan Crownover were:

I. Levi Crownover, born in 1832 in Illinois, died in 1888 in Iron County, Missouri, married Rebecca Jan Erls (born in 1837, died in 1871), married March 22, 1855, six children:

1. Sarah Elizabeth (Crownover) Crafton, born in 1856, in Reynolds County, Missouri, died May 30, 1891, married William Henry Harrison Crafton on November 17, 1872 at Blairs Creek, Shannon County, Missouri, six children:

Lucinda Jane Crafton, born in September of 1873, died after four weeks of whooping cough.

Cynthia Evalen Crafton, born February 23, 1875, Shannon County, Missouri, died September 14, 1961, Centerville, Missouri, married Lewis J. Myres in September of 1896 in Centerville, Missouri, six children.

Mary Narcil (Molly) (Crafton) McGahan, born June 3, 1877, Shannon County, Missouri, died September 25, 1956, Eldorado, Kansas, married William V. McGahan on May 3, 1895.

Perry Levi Crafton, born January 22, 1880, Shannon County, Missouri, died April 1, 1955, in Illinois, married Alie Price in Reynolds County, Missouri.

George Monroe Crafton, born October 30, 1885, died ?, married Viola Starks.

Fannie Louis Crafton, born May 13, 1888, on Blairs Creek, Shannon County, Missouri, died ?, married William Kile. Moved to Breckenridge, Texas.

2. Hannah Lucinda (Crownover) Hart, second child of Levi and Rebecca Jane Crownover, born in 1858, in Reynolds County, Missouri, died 1894, in Van Buren, Carter County, Missouri, married Albert Hart (born October 15, 1852, died June 19, 1919) four children: James Luther Hart, born July 18, 1887, Jasper County, Missouri, died October 28, 1962 in St. Louis, Missouri, married Mabel Riefsteak.

Joseph Elmer Hart, born August 14, 1889, died in February of 1953, Reyno, Arkansas, married Nora Chitwood.

Martha Elizabeth Hart, born December 6, 1891, Blairs Creek, Shannon County, Missouri, died June 9, 1965, Winona Missouri, married first Bob Ferguson on September 10, 1907, three children:

Daisy Pearl Ferguson, born August 10, 1907, Blairs Creek, married first Walter Mooney on December 25, 1923, married second ? .

Elva Oma Ferguson, born November 7, 1909, Blairs Creek, married first Bill Warren in July of 1924, married second Mark Johnson on August 13,

1931, married third Artie Myers, December 14, 1946.

Orbie Chester Ferguson, born December 30, 1911, Rock Creek, Shannon County, Missouri, died November 2, 1912, Rock Creek, Shannon County, Missouri.

Second marriage of Martha Elizabeth Hart to Charles Albert Stark (born ?) married April 21, 1912, four children:

Edna Jean Stark, born March 27, 1919, Flip, Missouri, married Pyrtle Weaver in January of 1935.

Freda Pauline Stark, born July 3, 1921, Flip, Missouri, married Sam Smith on May 16, 1941.

Lucinda Ellen Stark, born July 5, 1923, at Freeport, Kansas, married Elmer R. Link on September 13, 1941.

Ethel Marie Stark, born August 10, 1925, Midco, Missouri, married Euel McDonald February 21, 1942.

John Clayton Hart, fourth child of Albert and Lucinda Hannah Hart, born September 22, 1893, Blairs Creek, died September 8, 1976, Poplar Bluff, Missouri, married Delia Buckner at Winona, Missouri.

3. Harm Crownover, third child of Levi and Rebecca Jane Crownover, born ? , died young.

4. Earl Crownover, fourth child of Levi and Rebecca Jane Crownover, born ? , died young.

5. James William Crownover, fifth child of Levi and Rebecca Jane Crownover, born in 1858, Reynolds County, Missouri, died in 1933, Redford, Reynolds County, Missouri, married Amanda Holland Ratliff (born October 30, 1870, Reynolds County, Missouri, died July 28, 1956, Annapolis, Reynolds County, Missouri), two children:

Effie Belle (Crownover) Bounds, Evans, born March 14, 1889, Redford, Reynolds County, Missouri, died April 9, 1979, Farmington, Missouri, married first Jessie Elisha Bounds in 1906, six children, second marriage to Thomas William Evans in 1911, five children.

Claty James Crownover, born April 26, 1891, Annapolis, Missouri, died January 20, 1947, St. Louis, Missouri, married Ursula Becky Moore (born May 22, 1895, Reynolds County, Missouri, died May 16, 1941 in St. Louis, Missouri), married June 15, 1913, Centerville, Missouri, four children:

Floyd Francis Crownover, born July 25, 1914, Reynolds County, Missouri, married first Esther Mae Powers on May 1, 1932 (born May 9, 1915, Cairo, Illinois), divorced in May of 1962, died March 9, 1985, four children:

Carl Edward Crownover, born August 15, 1933, St. Louis, Missouri, married Doris June Moore on December 27, 1952, East St. Louis, Missouri, two living children:

Dirk Crownover, born March 31, 1959, Pasadena California, married Kim Arlene Lee, August 20, 1981, El Toro, California, one child, Joshua Shane Crownover, born September 20, 1985, in Orange County, California.

Suzanne Renee (Crownover) Abbott, born October 21, 1961, Hollywood, California, married James Abbott, June 20, 1981, Orange County, California.

Robert Edward Crownover (second son of Floyd F. and Esther M. Crownover), born February 16, 1935, St. Louis, Missouri, married Rose Anel Lyons (born March 10, 1937, in Texas), three children:

Tammy Sue (Crownover) Gorza, born October 25, 1963, St. Louis, Missouri, married Luis Gorza, St. Louis Missouri, on January 20, 1984.

Robert Andrew Crownover, born January 5, 1965, St. Louis, Missouri.

Camie Rachelle Crownover, born November 11, 1980, St. Louis, Missouri.

Joyce Mae (Crownover) Sanders (third child of Floyd F. and Esther M. Crownover) born April 2, 1941, St. Louis, Missouri, married Richard William Sanders (born April 9, 1938, died 1985) three children:

Richard William Sanders, Jr., born April 2, 1963

Lesa Marie Sanders, born June 5, 1966

Collene Ann Sanders, born November 27, 1968.

All were born in St. Louis, Missouri.

Janet Marie (Crownover) Benthol (fourth child of Floyd F. and Esther Crownover, born April 25, 1942, at St. Louis, Missouri) three children: Raymond Charles Benthol, born September 22, 1964; Lisa Benthol, born June 2, 1968; Julie Ann Benthol, born July 25, 1970. All were born in Missouri.

Second marriage of Floyd F. Crownover to Pearl Grace (Roark) Lee, (born September 4, 1917, Bonnets Mill, Missouri) married on June 2, 1962, St. Louis, Missouri, one stepdaughter:

Jannette Roberta (Lee) Shoults, born March 12, 1939, St. Charles, Missouri, married Richard William Shoults on August 28, 1961, four children. Now residing in Fresno, California.

Joseph Daniel Shoults, born February 10, 1957, St. Louis, Missouri.

Sherry Lynn Shoults, born May 31, 1958, St. Louis, Missouri, married Mel Buchan June 16, 1979, in Clovis, California, two children.

Kimberly Jeanne Shoults, born September 11, 1962, St. Louis, Missouri, married Leslie Dean Logue on May 2, 1983, in Clovis, California, one child.

Cyndria Lee Shoults, born December 17, 1966, Kirkwood, Missouri.

Lowell Forrest Crownover, minister, brother of Floyd Crownover, born March 15, 1916, Reynolds County, Missouri, married Velma Lorene Petty (born May 25, 1921, Salem, Missouri), married on October 17, 1936, St. Charles, Missouri, four children:

Lowell James Crownover, Jr., born August 27, 1937, St. Louis, Missouri, married Phyliss Pauline Duty (born October 22, 1943, St. Louis, Missouri) married on April 6, 1961, St. Louis, Missouri, four children:

Debra Diane Crownover, born July 3, 1962, St. Louis, Missouri.

Sheryl Lynn Crownover, born November 15, 1963, St. Louis, Missouri.

Sandra Gail Crownover, born October 10, 1969, St. Louis, Missouri.

James Randell Crownover, born March 24, 1971, St. Louis, Missouri.

Gerald Lee Crownover, second child of Lowell and Velma Crownover, born April 2, 1939, St. Louis, Missouri, married first Esther Belenda McGill (born January 24, 1945) divorced, four children:

Wesley Allen Crownover, born November 20, 1963, St. Louis, Missouri.

Thomas Wayne Crownover, born August 6, 1966, St. Louis, Missouri.

Billy Gene Crownover, born April 18, 1969, St. Louis, Missouri.

Ricky Lee Crownover, born March 9, 1972.

Caroline Lorene (Crownover) Benton (third child of Lowell and Velma Crownover), born February 25, 1945, St. Louis, Missouri, married Rosco Darrell Benton (born February 18, 1944, Iron County, Missouri), married on May 27, 1964, two children:

Darrell Ray Benton, born December 8, 1964.

Donna Sue Benton, born February 14, 1965.

Both were born in St. Louis, Missouri.

Raymond Leon Crownover, minister, fourth child of Lowell and Velma Crownover, born November 22, 1954, Jefferson City, Missouri, married Kathrine Elmira Stewart (born January 6, 1954) on August 19, 1978, St. Louis, Missouri, one child:

Suzanna Louise Crownover, born October 23, 1981, St. Louis, Missouri.

Claty James Crownover, Jr., brother of Floyd F. Crownover, born April 16, 1917, Elvins, Missouri, died July 2, 1942 (drowned), House Springs, Missouri, married Corine N. Naile, (born January 8, 1920, St. Louis, Missouri, died July 22, 1973, Overland, Missouri) in 1941, one child:

Phillip Eugene Crownover, born January 28, 1942, St. Louis, Missouri, married Carole ? , two children.

Thelma Rae (Crownover) Wright, sister of Floyd Crownover, born September 4, 1920, West Fork, Missouri, died December 15, 1978, Vallejo, California, married Raymond Ferdinand Wright, (born June 3, 1917, St. Louis, Missouri, died October 27, 1978, Vallejo, California) on June 30, 1934, St. Louis, Missouri, eight children:

Thelma Rae Wright, born January 16, 1935, St. Louis, Missouri, married Houston Roy Greer on November 28, 1954.

Donald Raymond Wright, born June 21, 1936, St. Louis, Missouri, married Enge Maria Schlitzer on July 7, 1961, in California.

Arthur James Wright, born November 17, 1937, St. Louis, Missouri, married Mariam Carol Wheelan on February 8, 1958, in California.

Helen Marie Wright, born January 12, 1938, St. Louis, Missouri, died January 14, 1938.

Dorothy Jean Wright, born August 10, 1940, St. Louis, Missouri, married Charles Frank Bastgen on August 4, 1961, in California.

Steven Paul Wright, born November 27, 1941, St. Louis, Missouri, married Crystal Lee Nielson, on June 4, 1961, in California.

Lawrence Eugene Wright, born June 8, 1944, St. Louis, Missouri, married Patsy Ann De La Grange on August 10, 1963, in California.

Fredrick Richard Wright, born April 20, 1952, Albany, California, married Cheril Louise Cordingly November 4, 1970, in California.

6. Rebecca (Becky Lee) (Crownover) Fakes, sixth child of Levi and Rebecca Jane Erls, born in 1871, married Willie Fakes, children ? .

Levi Crownover lost his first wife, Rebecca Jane Erls during the birth of Rebecca Lee in 1871. His second wife was Susan Ann (Pinkley) Crossland (born April 23, 1840 in Missouri, died ?), one child:

Laura Frances (Crownover) Parker, born December 30, 1881, Sabula, Iron County, Missouri, married Alonzo (Lon) Parker on September 1, 1902, Ironton, Iron County, Missouri, died June 7, 1967, in Ironton, Missouri, eight children:

Joy Parker, born August 17, 1903, died September 5, 1903.

Vernon Alonzo Parker, born February 4, 1905, Reynolds, Missouri, married first Jewell Okey Schular, second June Yates, nine children.

Jessamine Isabelle Parker, born October 18, 1906, Reynolds, Missouri, married Clarence Oran Haynes on February 16, 1930, six children.

Paul Francis Parker, born August 27, 1909, Reynolds, Missouri, died September 4, 1974, married first Loretta Brown, second Alma Dettmer, three children.

Roy Clifford Parker, born August 27, 1909, Reynolds, Missouri, married Vada Inman on March 12, 1937, Arcadia, Missouri.

Hilda Claire Parker, born September 18, 1915, Reynolds, Missouri, married first Herman Leon White, second Bossen, third J. Boyer on December 31, 1964, three children.

Russell W. Parker, born November 17, 1917, Reynolds County, died in 1946.

Irvin Gay Parker, born March 30, 1920, Arcadia, Missouri, died June 29, 1940, married Eula Mae Vaugh, one child.

Freeda Mae Parker, born July 10, 1922, Arcadia, Missouri, married Mont Alfred Lashley on September 2, 1939 in Roselle, Iron County, Missouri, one son, one daughter.

II. Mary Ann Crownover, second child of James and Sally Crownover, born in 1834 in Centerville, Missouri, married John Fitzwaters (born in 1822), died February 12, 1867, four children:

Sarah Fitzwater, born in 1853, Reynolds County, Missouri.

Uriah Fitzwater, born in 1856, Reynolds County, Missouri.

Jasper Fitzwater, born in 1858, Reynolds County, Missouri.

Sintha Fitzwater, born in 1860, Reynolds County, Missouri.

III. Theodore (Dory) Crownover, third child of James and Sally Crownover, born September 8, 1835, in Centerville, Missouri, married Hannah Ann Erls (born April 13, 1840, in Indiana, died June 14, 1899), on May 30, 1855, St. Genevieve County, Missouri, died April 24, 1914, Kingdom Springs, Marion County, Arkansas, buried in Macoson Cemetery, Kingdom Springs, Marion

County, Arkansas. Nine children were born of this union:

1. James Harrom Crownover, born May 4, 1856, Centerville, Reynolds County, Missouri, died May 30, 1940, buried Greenlawn Cemetery, Springfield, Missouri. Married first Charity Chitwood on February 11, 1873, in Centerville, Missouri, two children:

Rebecca J. Crownover, born in 1873, married William Speer.

Lucy E. Crownover, born in 1874, married Columbus Honea.

Second marriage of James Harrom Crownover to Lucinda E. Scott (born May 15, 1856, died in 1903) on November 14, 1878, St. Francois County, Missouri, twelve children:

William J. Crownover, born in October of 1879, married Lulie Winett on January 8, 1903.

Clara Josephine Crownover, born in February of 1881, Reynolds County, Missouri, died in 1961, Marion County, Arkansas, married first Granville Poynter, second Thomas H. Clark, third Licklighter, six children.

Henry Burton Crownover, born in 1883, married Anna Weiher.

Hannah Theodocia Crownover, born in 1887, married Aubrey Harper.

Oscar Theodore Crownover, born in 1887, married Belle Moore.

Emma Lucinda Crownover, born in 1890, married James Johnson.

Mary Cordelia Crownover, born in 1892, married Spencer Cain.

James Washington Crownover, born in 1894, married Ulay Gann.

Ambrose L. Crownover, born in 1897, married Adie Garrison.

Hercy Levada Crownover, born in 1899, married ? .

Harold Eugene Crownover, born in 1901, married ? .

George Crownover, born in 1903, married ? .

2. William Riley Crownover, second child of James Harrom Crownover, born June 30, 1858, Reynolds County, Missouri, died January 17, 1913, Flippin, Arkansas, married December 24, 1905, to Hannah Frances (Julian) McDaniel in Harrison, Arkansas, three children:

Edith Lena Crownover, born June 8, 1907, married Charles Hopkins.

John Riley Crownover, born February 10, 1909, married Vestie Brook.

Pirgie Ester Crownover, born July 3, 1912, married Leonard Hopkins.

3. Levi Crownover, third child of Theodore and Hannah Crownover, born April 10, 1861, Reynolds County, Missouri, married Mary C. McGlossom (born in 1859), married on January 23, 1881, Howell County, Missouri, two (?) children:

Docia Crownover, born in 1891.

Victoria Crownover, born in 1895.

4. Sarah Jane Crownover, fourth child of Theodore and Hannah Crownover, born January 17, 1862, Reynolds County, Missouri, married first Walter Martin, three children, second John Ford, children (?). Children of Walter and Sarah Martin:

James Hiram Martin, born in 1882, married Laura Jones.

Louisa Martin, born in 1884, married William Monday.

Cynthia Martin, born in 1886, married first Ernest Coleman, second John West.

5. John Wesley Crownover, fifth child of Theodore and Hannah Crownover, born April 1, 1866, Centerville, Reynolds County, Missouri. No other information.

6. Cynthia Crownover, sixth child of Theodore and Hannah Crownover, born January 10, 1867, Reynolds County, Missouri, married Sam Julian on October 7, 1895, Howell County, Missouri, six children.

7. Fannie G. Crownover, seventh child, born in July of 1871, Reynolds County, Missouri, died September 26, 1928, married Nicholas B. Day on November 3, 1892, three (?) children.

8. Rebecca Lucinda Crownover, eighth child, born in 1874, married Samuel Alexander Gay, seven children.

9. ?

IV. Sarah Crownover, fourth child of James and Sally Crownover, born November 20, 1837, married Gideon Howell in 1852, died April 4, 1890 in Centerville, Missouri, seven children:

Benjamin Howell, born July 26, 1859, died June 31, 1929, Falls City, Oregon.

Clinton Dwitt Howell, born July 28, 1861, died March 24, 1936.

William Green Howell, born in 1864.

Martha Howell, born in 1866.

Laura Bell Howell, born in 1868.

Walter S. Howell, born in April 2, 1871, died January 6, 1888.

Henry Wilson Howell, born in 1879.

All were born in Reynolds County, Missouri.

V. Ruth Jane Crownover, fifth child of James and Sally Crownover, born in 1842, married James Bowles (born in August of 1837, died in February of 1930), died in 1873 in Centerville, Missouri, three (?) children:

William Crownover Bowles, born November 16, 1863, died September 20, 1895, married Margaret E. Brooks on May 1, 1884.

John Allen Bowles, born in 1867, died ? , married Mary E. Buford on November 4, 1886.

James Albert Bowles, born ? , married Lucy J. Callahan. One child, Martha Bowles, born ? , died at two years.

VI. John Crownover, sixth child of James and Sally Crownover, born in 1845, died in 1850-1860, at Centerville, Missouri.

VII.Cynthia Elizabeth Crownover, seventh child of James and Sally Crownover, born September 17, 1848, died December 23, 1903, Victoria, Jefferson County, Missouri, married first Edward Barnes (born July 17, 1845, Reynolds County, Missouri, died 1883-1887) on December 5, 1867, Centerville, Missouri. Six children were born to this union. Her second marriage to James Marion Cudniff January 7, 1887. One daughter was born of this union. The Barnes-Cudniff family moved to Hillsboro, Jefferson County,

Missouri, where they lived until all were married.

Six children of Edward Barnes and Cynthia Elizabeth (Crownover) Barnes:

Robert Barnes, born August 16, 1868, Centerville, Reynolds County, Missouri, died in Texas September 20, 1870, place of burial unknown.

Sarah Jane Barnes, born March 4, 1871, in Missouri, died January 7, 1947, married Jess Freeman, ca. 1893 in Missouri.

Ida Barnes, born April 6, 1873, died June 5, 1874.

Henry Thomas Barnes, born April 28, 1875, Centerville, Missouri, died July 23, 1920, in San Francisco, California, buried in Bakersfield, California, married Sarah Irene Pinson, two children.

Walter Charles Barnes, born October 21, 1877, Centerville, Missouri, died December 27, 1957, Kaft County, married Agnes Hasse on August 16, 1899 in Missouri, one child.

George William Barnes, born September 15, 1880, died July 16, 1885.

James Albert Barnes, born April 8, 1883, Centerville, Missouri, died April 20, 1925, Taft County, California, married Olga Haase in Missouri, four children.

Second marriage of Cynthia Elizabeth (Crownover) Barnes to James Marion Cudniff (born July 28, 1848, died November 14, 1919 in De Soto, Missouri), on January 6, 1878, Centerville, Missouri, one child:

Lucy Alice Cudniff, born April 8, 1889, Centerville, Missouri, died August 25, 1979 in Festus, Jefferson County, Missouri, married first William Alexander Gray (born October 22, 1873 in Salem, Missouri), six children:

George William Gray, born November 23, 1907, in St. Louis, Missouri, married Dorothy Lee Spangler on August 29, 1925, in Hillsboro, Jefferson County, Missouri, three children.

Mamie Letitia Gray, born December 28, 1910, Victoria, Jefferson County, Missouri, married first Lewis, second Billings, third Jack Nengel, four children, three marriages.

James Emmett Gray, born November 5, 1913, in Herculaneum, Missouri, died April 2, 1976, in St. Louis, Missouri, married Ruth Arlene Lambert on July 29, 1933 in Hillsboro, Jefferson County, Missouri, three children.

Alta Lorene Gray, born April 1, 1916, Hematite, Jefferson County, Missouri, married first and third Earl Buford Riley on January 5, 1931, second marriage to R. Davis, three children by first marriage.

Pearl Arline Gray, born March 9, 1920, Victoria, Missouri, married John Le Roy White, three children.

Dorothy Mae Gray, born July 26, 1923, Victoria, Missouri, married first A. Govero, second Earl Robert Stahl on June 8, 1940 in Hillsboro, Missouri, four children.

Second marriage of Lucy Alice (Cudniff) Gray to Leonard Jackson Scott on December 31, 1923 at Farmington, St. Francois County, Missouri, two children:

Doris Marie Scott, born November 5, 1924, Victoria, Missouri, died July 1, 1925, De Soto, Missouri.

Jacqueline (Jackie) Louise Scott, born April 21, 1930, in Festus, Missouri, married Stanley Lee Parks (born June 20, 1928 in Herculaneum, Missouri) on May 23, 1948, Crystal City, Missouri, three children:

Russell Lynn Parks, born September 19, 1949, in St. Louis, Missouri, married Denise Michelle Elliott on January 24, 1970, in Festus, Missouri, two children.

Vicki Lee Parks, born December 16, 1951, St. Louis, Missouri, married George Ulrich Hermes on June 29, 1973, one son.

Dale Stanley Parks, born May 23, 1956, in St. Louis, Missouri, married Joyce Evelyn Dickson on July 24, 1976 in Burkburnett, Texas.

After the death of Sally (Jordan) Crownover in 1848, James Crownover married Eliza Ann Davis (born March 28, 1826, in Tennessee, died before 1870 in Centerville, Missouri). Five children were born of this union:

I. Mahola Jane (Crownover) Callahan, died ? , children ? .

II. Julia Ann Crownover, born March 13, 1856, in Centerville, Missouri, married Christopher C. Callahan in 1873, died April 1, 1882, three children:

Eliza Ann Callahan, born in 1874, Centerville, Missouri, died after 1880.

Laura Bell Callahan, born May 28, 1876, Centerville, Missouri, died September 9, 1932, in Centerville, married Robert Lee Neely on February 24, 1895, in Missouri, seven children.

John Morgan Callahan, born August 23, 1879, in Centerville, Missouri, died September 17, 1979, McCall, Valley County, Idaho, married Cecily Ann Burnham in April of 1908, Van Buren, Reynolds County, Missouri, two children.

III. Margaret Emily Crownover, third child of James and Eliza Ann Crownover, born September 25, 1858, Centerville, Missouri, died November 27, 1935, Reynolds, Missouri, buried in Sutterfield Cemetery, Reynolds County, Missouri, married Joseph C. Jackson (born October 20, 1856, died December 27, 1932) on April 25, 1878. Ten children were born of this union:

James Richard Jackson, born February 17, 1879, Reynolds County, Missouri, died February 17, 1879.

Anna E. Jackson, born September 25, 1879, died September 25, 1879.

William Charles Jackson, born May 16, 1881, died January 20, 1922, married Anna Amy McNail, six children.

Neomi Bell Jackson, born February 2, 1884, died April 28, 1958, buried in Sutterfield Cemetery, Reynolds County, Missouri, married first George Lavern Lay (born March 4, 1880, died April 7, 1902), one child, second marriage to Robert Lee Black (born July 31, 1872, died June 21, 1944) married in 1907, thirteen children.

Edward L. Jackson, born September 23, 1886, died June 27, 1966, Bunker, Reynolds County, Missouri, married first Nancy Alice Clark (born February 27, 1893, died August 11, 1947) on December 31, 1910, Olhom, Missouri, nine children, second marriage to Jenny Ellen Tucker (born March 30, 1891, died August 14, 1968).

Allen F. Jackson, born December 18, 1888, died December 18, 1889.

Sarah Eller Jackson, born August 5, 1890, Reynolds County, Missouri, died October 17, 1921, married Walter George Sutterfield on June 7, 1909.

Robert Theodore Jackson, born July 31, 1893, died October 16, 1921, married Harley Enman (Inman).

Elder Rado Jackson, born November 1, 1896, died July 7, 1959, married first Grace Climie Snlee, second Grace Stulce on December 23, 1915, nine children.

James Loran Jackson, born January 28, 1902, died March 23, 1913.

IV. James Harrison Crownover, fourth child of James and Eliza Ann Crownover, born September 18, 1860, Centerville, Reynolds County, Missouri, died February 22, 1865.

V. William Allen Crownover, fifth child of James and Eliza Ann Crownover, born January 22, 1864, Centerville, Reynolds County, Missouri, married Rebecca Dillard December 29, 1884, Centerville, Missouri, died January 25, 1889, buried in Sutterfield Cemetery, Reynolds County, Missouri, no record of children.

Eliza Ann (Davis) Crownover was the daughter of William A. Davis and Abigal (maiden name unknown) Davis. William A. Davis was born in 1806 in Tennessee. Abigal was born in 1815 in Tennessee. Fifteen children were born of this union:

Mahala Jane Davis, born 1839 in Tennessee, died ? , married ? .

Eliza Ann Davis, born March 28, 1826, died in 1870, married James Crownover in Centerville Missouri.

James H. Davis, born in 1836, died ? , married Matilda ? in 1869.

Elizabeth Davis, born in 1838, in Missouri, died ?, married ? .

John B. Davis, born in 1840 in Missouri, died ? , married ? .

Rachal J. Davis, born in 1849 in Missouri.

Martha Davis, born in 1844, died ? .

Easter Davis, born in 1846, died ? .

Julia Ann Davis, born in 1848, died ? .

Cornelia Davis, born in 1844, died ? .

William H. Davis, born in November of 1850 in Centerville, Missouri, died ? , married Sarah M. ? .

Althia Davis, born in 1853 in Centerville, Missouri (twin).

Dora Davis, born in 1853 in Centerville, Missouri (twin).

Thomas Davis, born in 1856 in Centerville, Missouri.

Lucina Davis, born in 1859 in Centerville, Missouri.

The original Crownover was Van Kouwenhoven. Wolphert Gerretse Van Kouwenhoven, came to this country from Amersfoort, Holland in 1625. He was hired by the Dutch India Company to help establish farms in New Amsterdam, New York. Wolphert came with his wife, Neeltje Jans, whom he married January 17, 1605, in the Dutch Reformed Church at Amersfoort, and their three surviving sons, Gerret, Jacob and Pieter. Wolphert Gerretse Van Kouwenhoven was one of the founders of New Amsterdam, New York, and the founder of our family in America. There are many variations of the family name, to name a few; Van Couwenhoven, Van Couvenhoven, Kouwenhoven, Cowenhoven, Conover, Cownovr, and Crownover.

From an article published in New York, "Records of the Conovers, Schecks and Vanderveers":

The name Van Couwenhoven, as the Dutch language yielded very slowly but surely to the English tongue, underwent several changes both in spelling and pronunciation. Our early court and church records show some of these changes. The "Van" was dropped and the name was spelled Couwenhoven or Kowenhoven. Then Cowenhoven, next Covenhoven or Covenoven, and finally Conover.

This family have been in America nearly three centuries. Very few families in the United States of Netherland blood can show such an ancient lineage, about which there can be no doubt. Neither can any family show greater fidelity in obedience to the scriptural injunction "to increase and multiply in the land". If all the male and female descendants of Wolphert Garritson Van Couwenhoven now in the United States could be gathered together in one place, it would be a mighty multitude.

Neither do I know of any of this name who has been convicted of an infamous crime. Their family history is remarkable, free from all dishonorable stains. While none of them have achieved fame as authors, ministers, presidents, generals, or millionaires, yet on the other hand they have generally occupied respectable positions, led useful lives and been good citizens. That is, the Conovers or not found at either extreme of the social scale but on the safe middle ground. This portion of the article was written about 1900.

From an article by "The Van Kouwenhoven Conover Family Association":

Descendants of Wolphert have taken part in every important phase of America's development, giving their lives in every war, helping expand the frontiers by pushing west into New Jersey, Pennsylvania, Ohio, Indiana, Kentucky, and Illinois, crossing the Mississippi, the Great Plains, and over the Rockies to the Pacific. Many became leaders in local and national affairs, others in professions such as education, engineering, law, medicine and religion. Still others were craftsmen, skilled in the various trades, while many became successful farmers and businessmen.

Note:
I am deeply indebted to Mrs. Jackie Parks, 1002 Arthur St., Burkburnett, Texas, 76354, who furnished much of the above material.

Floyd F. Crownover
4291 N. Parkway Dr.
Fresno, California 93711

MISCELLANY

MOUNTAINS

The St. Francis Mountain Range covers the greater part of seven counties, and within their boundary is found the most rugged terrain in Missouri.

These beautiful mountains and hills are very old, perhaps twelve hundred to fourteen hundred million years. Many changes have taken place during this time, as lava poured upward at different intervals, forming layers of rhyolite and granite, which ultimately became mountains. The seas came and receded and came again, covering all but the tallest peaks and molding the mountains into a shape not too dissimilar from what we see today.

All of these mountains and hills were covered with trees, with only a few openings where solid granite out-croppings are completely void of any soil. These forests have been an asset to this county since the first settlers arrived. They built their cabins, cooked their food, heated their cabins, used sap from the maple trees for sugar and syrup, split rails to fence their land, and fed their hogs acorns from the oak trees. Meat, which furnished the major part of their diet, came from the forests where the animals and birds felt safe and protected in the many giant trees or beneath their spreading branches. All of these were products or by-products of the forest which almost completely covered Reynolds County.

The forest had a variety of trees with each one having its unique characteristics which could be used to fill the needs of the frontiersman. Walnut, hickory, oak, maple, pine, cedar, cottonwood, gum, ash, sycamore, elm . . . all competed for space in the forest, with oak and pine being the greater in number.

Proffit Mountain, the site of Union Electric's upper reservoir for their Taum Sauk Pump Storage Generating Plant, lies near the center of the St. Francois Mountain Range. Proffit Mountain spreads over 6,000 acres and consists of three major peaks, the tallest being 1656 feet above sea level. Taum Sauk Mountain, located three miles to the northeast and rising 1772 feet above sea level, is the tallest mountain in Missouri.

Almost every mountain in Reynolds County is named for an early settler. Proffit Mountain, undoubtedly, got its name from either James or Pattrick Proffit, two brothers who lived near the base of the mountains in the 1850's. Their parents, Rev. Robert and Jane Kirkpatrick Proffit, had settled in Washington County, Missouri, in about 1820.

Bell Mountain, which was designated a wilderness area in 1980, covers 8500 acres and its highest peak reaches 1702 feet above sea level. The mountain range is located in northern Reynolds County and western Iron County. Like most of the St. Francis Mountain Range, Bell Mountain has many out-croppings of red granite rock.

This mountain got its name from Henry Bell, who came to St. Francois County, Missouri, in about 1835 with his parents, John (August 1, 1789-October 3, 1869) and Elizabeth Harbison (June 28, 1790-April 13, 1875) Bell. They were married January 13, 1811, and had eight known children; Susan, Henry, Mary "Polly", Elizabeth, Margaret, Moses Harbison, Anna, and James Stacy Bell.

Ottery Creek winds its southeasterly course just to the west of Bell Mountain and before joining the Middle Fork of the Black River, runs through a picturesque shut-in.

Goggin Mountain, an extension of Bell Mountain, with only a low gap dividing the two ranges, was once used by early settlers who traveled from the Emboden Area to Black River.

Goggin Mountain has four major peaks with the tallest being 1484 feet above sea level. The mountain range is about four miles in length and covers roughly 3000 acres.

Goggin Hollow, running from the Middle Fork of the Black River to the crest of the mountain, was the home of Milton and Nancy Carty Goggin, who came from Cumberland County, Kentucky, in 1829.

RIVERS, CREEKS, AND HOLLOWS

The Black River, known by the first French explorers as Leau Noire, is fed by hundreds of small springs that form branches and flow into the main trunk, which is Black River. Almost all of Reynolds County is a basin for the Black River, and, in times of heavy rains, flooding can reach gigantic proportions, releasing massive destruction to everything in its path.

The East Fork of the Black River is fed mainly by Shut-in, Imboden, Big Taum Sauk, and Little Taum Sauk Creeks. High Top Mountain divides the headwaters of the East Fork from Emboden. This mountain has two significant peaks in Reynolds County, the highest one rising 1590 feet above sea level. Church Mountain lies between the two Taum Sauk Creeks, extending 1648 feet skyward. Cope (Cape) Hollow is believed to be named for Maston Cape, who came here as a young man before 1820. Walker Branch, which starts on the eastern slope of Goggin Mountain, was probably named for Mary Walker's descendants. She came to Reynolds County in the 1860's from Arkansas, accompanied by her four sons: Thomas, James, William and Henry. She married Jacob Eliott before 1870.

The Middle Fork of the Black River has its source in Iron County, where we find: Neals, Strother, Clayton, and Ottery Creeks. Big Brushy and Little Brushy Creeks join the Middle Fork at Black, Missouri. Dry Fork Creek feeds into Big Brushy Creek and Thorny Branch may be the largest branch on Little Brushy Creek. Padfield, Carty, Long, Paynes and Baker Branches have big water basins and flow into the Middle Fork of the Black River.

The West Fork of the Black River has its beginning near Dent County, where Johnson, Radford, Moore, Parker, Kay and Nelson Creeks come together. Henpeck, McMurty, Bill and Small Creeks soon join, as each contributes to or supports the flow of the East Fork. Bee Fork probably has the greatest watershed of any creek which feeds into East Fork of Black River. Some familiar hollows are: Stillwell, McLean, McNab, Hunter, Brooks, Ellington, Parks, Russell, Harrison, Adams, Hawk, Middle and Barn.

The three forks join near Lesterville, making a sizable river which continues to increase in volume as many small streams like Mills, Hyatt, and Goose Creek dump their cool spring-fed water into the Black River. Mayberry, Brawley, Low, Hackworth, and Whizenhunt Hollows all have small branches feeding the Black River.

Sinking, Logan and Webb are the major creeks in the southern part of Reynolds County. Logan Creek headwaters reach into the area of Shannon County and it is fed by Sweetwater, Dickens Valley, Dry Valley, Ellington, Darr Valley and many small streams like Christian, Coleman, Snow, Bay and Boyd Hollows.

There is only one stream of any consequence in Reynolds County which does not flow into Black River. This is Pine Valley, which winds its way to the Current River.

EARLY LAND OWNERSHIP

Henry Sloan; section 25, township 31, range 2 east.
John Johnson; section 25, township 31, range 2 east.
James T. Dobbins; section 6, township 32, range 2 east.
Daniel Lester; section 7, township 32, range 2 east.
Jesse Lester; section 18, township 32, range 2 east.
Elijah Wadlow; section 19, township 32, range 2 east.
Marshall Parks; sections 17 and 21, township 32, range 2 east.
John Buford; section 17, township 32, range 2 east.
Ely Shy; section 21, township 32, range 2 east.
George Adams; section 18, township 32, range 2 east.
William Buford; section 15, township 32, range 2 east.
William Carty; section 15, township 32, range 2 east.
James Stout; section 6, township 33, range 2 east.
Joseph Stout; section 6, township 33, range 2 east.
Abiel Stricklin; section 5, township 33, range 2 east.
William Andrew; section 5, township 33, range 2 east.
Jordan Hasty; section 5, township 33, range 2 east.
William Goggin; section 5, township 33, range 2 east.
Elizabeth Rhodes (sister to William J. Goggin); section 5, township 33, range 1 east.
Elizabeth (Carty) Goggin; section 4, township 33, range 1 east.

Newton Bell; section 4, township 33, range 1 east.
Edward Latham; section 3, township 33, range 1 east.
William Love; section 3, township 33, range 1 east.
George Gallaher; sections 3 & 10, township 33, range 1 east.
Henry Miner; section 10, township 33, range 1 east.
James Carty; sections 15 & 22, township 33, range 1 east.
Laban Miner; section 22, township 33, range 1 east.
Lazaras C. Miner; section 22, township 33, range 1 east.
Califurnia Buford; section 28, township 33, range 1 east.
Redmond Black; section 6, township 30, range 1 west.
James P. Carty; section 12, township 31, range 1 west.
Isaac Mann; section 1, township 30, range 2 east.
Zimri Mann; section 1, township 30, range 2 east.
John Dale Copeland; section 8, township 29, range 2 east.
Belinda Copeland; section 8, township 29, range 2 east.
Sina Ellington; section 32, township 30, range 1 east.
Thomas Barnes; section 32, township 30, range 1 east.
Gabriel Johnston; section 32, township 30, range 1 east.
William Copeland; section 27, township 30, range 1 east.
William Thornton; section 27, township 30, range 1 east.
George W. Mills; section 35, township 30, range 1 east.
John Brawley; section 36, township 30, range 1 east.
Nancy Morris; section 36, township 30, range 1 east.
Green B. Goggin; section 3, township 32, range 1 east.
William B. Cape; section 2, township 32, range 1 east.
William King; section 2, township 32, range 1 east.
William Rayfield; section 11, township 32, range 1 east.
Joseph P. McNail; section 2 & 11, township 32, range 1 east.
John Boyd; section 12, township 32, range 1 east.
Theodore Crownover; section 29, township 32, range 1 east.
James Crownover; section 32, township 32, range 1 east.
Levi Crownover; section 31, township 32, range 1 east.
Greenberry; section 5, township 33, range 1 east.
William Copeland; section 8, township 33, range 2 east.
James Edmond; section 8, township 33, range 2 east.
Samuel Edmonds; section 17, township 33, range 2 east.
Charles Edmond; section 17, township 33, range 2 east.
John Johnston; section 16, township 33, range 2 east.
Robert Johnston; section 16, township 33, range 2 east.
Marion Johnston; section 16, township 33, range 2 east.
Benjamine McNail; section 4, township 33, range 2 east.
Marvin Munger; section 2, township 33, range 2 east.
William Parker; section 22, township 33, range 2 east.
James A. Proffit; section 23, township 33, range 2 east.

Jacob Stout; section 33, township 33, range 2 east.
John Stricklin; section 29, township 33, range 2 east.
Jacob Elliot; section 29, township 33, range 2 east.
Joseph Stout; section 13, township 28, range 1 east.
John Copeland; section 13, township 29, range 1 east.
Cary Copeland; section 32, township 30, range 1 east.
Dale Copeland; section 8, township 29, range 2 east.
Moses Copeland; section 8, township 29, range 2 east.
Moses Copeland; section 15, township 29, range 2 east.
Morgan D. Bailey; section 34, township 29, range 2 east.
William Copeland; section 5, township 29, range 2 east.
Lorenzo Thorpe; section 5, township 29, range 2 east.
Louis Copeland; section 31, township 30, range 2 east.
John Rayfield; section 35, township 30, range 2 east.
Henry Coil; sections 3 & 10, township 31, range 2 east.
Pate Buford; section 3, township 31, range 2 east.

 ERRATA

In the chapter on Ripley County, we quote, "A History of the Black River Baptist Church" compiled by Flora Angel Estep. This quotation states "Black River Baptist Church had twelve charter members." Mrs. Estep intended for the book to state, "twenty charter members as stated by R.S. Duncan in his book, "History of the Baptists of Missouri."

Francis Valle, first commandant of Ste. Genevieve, probably came from Quebec, Canada, to Kaskosia, Illinois, and not from Louisiana as was indicated in the Andrew Henry story.

We were confused about Andrew Stuart Dickey and Andrew L. Dickey in the chapter, "Growth and Development." We now believe the census enumerator intended for the middle initial to be "S.", which would solve the problem. Andrew Stuart Dickey married Elizabeth Gortner October 1, 1818 in Batetourt County, Virginia. One daughter from this marriage, Mary Jane, married William Hawkins June 18, 1835. A son from this marriage, George Washington, came back to Reynolds County and married Sarah Carty. He was born November 15, 1842, in Washington County. (Information furnished by Jeannine Preston and Ethel White.)

We mistakenly said that Ira Munger was a son of Marvin, when evidence would indicate he was perhaps a brother to Marvin Munger.

In the material on the Dennisons, we indicated that Daniel Dennison's wife's maiden name was not known. We have now been informed her name was Nancy Vandiver, thanks to Marcella Appleton, Springfield, Missouri.

Henry Bell, for whom the Bell Mountains was named, was born May 20, 1814, in Kentucky. The Bell family came from Augusta County, Virginia, via Barren County, Kentucky, before coming to Missouri. This information was furnished by Jan Marrs Huston, Newberg, Oregon.

John Rice Jones was married at least two times. His oldest son, Rice, was born Sept. 28, 1781, from his first marriage. Rice Jones was killed by Dr. James Dunlap who was a second for Shadrach Bond in a duel connected to Illinois politics. Shadrach Bond would later become Governor of Illinois. This happened Dec. 7, 1808. Another son, named John Rice Jones, Jr., was born Jan. 8, 1792, to his second marriage.

The author of this book, when doing research on the Maxwell Reserve, came to the conclusion that Rev. James Maxwell never made any attempt to settle the 96,000 acre grant he had obtained from the Spanish government in 1799.

Glenda Stockton, a persistent researcher, has discovered that he indeed had established a small settlement near the three forks of Black River.

Testimony that John Buford gave when he was seventy-six years old states, "that he came to the Maxwell claim in 1815 on Black River. His father bought the land in 1817 or 1818 and his family moved on the land in 1820.

There had been a clearing and improvements on it many years before. There were several houses on it, one a store house, where a store had been kept. There were none of Priest Maxwell's men living there when he first knew the place, but always heard of his having men there at work and intended to have a colony."

Other records indicate Rev. James Maxwell came to the Reserve on several occasions and spent two or three weeks at this remote settlement at different intervals.

On the Chapter "Andrew Henry" we inadvertently forgot to say that Patrick Flemming's wife was Marie L. Tibbeau (Tabeau).

INDEX

175

176

180

De Celle
  Joseph
  Marianne
De Celle Dudos
  Judie
De Gaston
  Elizabeth 61
De La Grange
  Patsy A. 159
Delassus
  Charles D. 104
  Don Carlos 103
Dement
  Mary J. 86
Dennison
  Anna 54
  Charles 54
  Daniel 54, 144, 173
  Elizabeth 54, 145
  Isabelle 129
  James 54
  Joel 54, 70
  John B. 144, 146
  Lucinda 146
  Lucinda J. 146
  Lydia 144
  Martha 54
  Nancy 54, 173
De Soto
  Hernando 5
Dentherage
  Alfred 40, 46, 47
  Amanda 46
  Jasper A. R. 46
Dettmer
  Alma 160
Dickey
  Adeline 32
  Andrew L. 32, 173
  Andrew S. 32, 173
  Caroline 32
  Easter 40
  Elizabeth 173
  Jane 32
  Joseph 32
  Robert 32
  Mary J. 173
Dickson
  Amanda 62
  Frances C. 61, 62
  Giebert 85
  Hiram C. 61
  John C. 61
  John W. 61
  Joyce E. 164
  Lydia 86
  Malinda 61
  Mary 61, 85
  Nancy E. 61
  Rebecca 61
  Sarah J. 61
  Temperance 61
  Thomas 61
  Westly 86
  William 61

William D. 61, 62
Dillard
  Adaline 138
  George W. 138
  Ollie 138, 139
  Rebecca 165
Dillon
  Rose 123
Dobbins
  Amy A. 59
  James T. 59, 91, 170
  Minerva 59
Dodge
  Augustus C. 12
  Christina 12
  Clara 12
  Henry 12
  Israel 12
  Nancy A. 12, 15
Dotson
  James
Douglass
  Margaret 41
  Polly 41
  Thomas 41
Driskill
  Jesse 25
Duncan
  Deanna 34
  R. S. 71, 173
Dunkin
  Allen 39
Dunklin
  Daniel 8, 9, 16, 77
  Pamelia 16
Dunlap
  James 173
Dunn
  Isabelle
Duty
  Phyliss P. 158
Eads
  Abraham 9
  William 9
Earles
  Mary 53
Eaton
  Joe 87
  Margaret 87
Eddings
  Esther M. 89
Edgar
  Marie 58
Edmonston
  Argyle 51
  Elizabeth 51
  Thomas 51
  William 51
Edmunds
  Abigail 27
  Amanda 27
  Andrew 27
  Charles 27, 171

Elizabeth 27
  James 27, 63, 171
  Lavender 27
  Minerva 27
  Moriah 27
  Moses 27, 48
  Nancy 27
  Permela 27
  Rebecca 27
  Samuel 171
  Sarah 27
  William 27
  Willis 27, 30
Edward
  Gov. 49
Eidson
  Elizabeth 51
  Henry 9, 51, 92, 107
  Lucy 92
  Mary 51, 92, 107
  Mary J. 40, 108
  Wanda 92
Eliot
  Jacob 31
  Mary 169
Ellington
  Artimissa 41
  Elizabeth 85
  Harriet 41
  Helen 86
  James 41, 85
  John 41, 86
  Mary 41, 85
  Sina 41, 42, 85
Ellinghouse
  C. R. 153
Elliot
  Aaron 76
  Arlotta 31
  Cassie 31
  Denise M.
  Jacob 31, 169, 172
  Jane 31
  Joseph 31
  Mary 169
  Samuel 31
  Thomas 31
  Unity 31
Engelthal
  Elmo 4
Enoch
  Anne
  Benjamin Jr.
  Benjamin Sr.
  John
  Rees
  Sarah
Earls
  Hannah A. 160
  Rebecca J. 156, 160
Estep
  Flora 38, 44, 82, 153, 173
Estes
  Patrick 9

182

Evans
Effie B. 157
Thomas W. 157
Evarts
Dorothy 112
(family) 113
James 112
Lydia 112
Fagan
Gen. James F. 69
Fakes
Rebecca 160
Willie 160
Farries
Carter
Farris
Anne 59
Lucian 20, 59
Nancy 59
Faulkenberry
Doshia V. 130
Hugh P. 108
James 130
Martha 108
Mary J. 130
Fears
Louisa A. 86
Luther J. 86
Ferguson
Bob 156
Daisy P. 156
Elva O. 156
Martha E. 156
Orbie C. 157
Ferrel
James 30
Ferris
Nancy 59
Lucien N. 59
Finley
A. W. 100
Finn
Robert 60
Fisher
Sarah 44
Fitzgerald
Bessie M. 119
Bula I. 119
Buren F. 119
Charles L. 119
Doyle L. 119
Elsiema 118
Golden 119
Goldia 119
Hartford 119
Hazel 119
John 118
Paul W. 119
Rhona 118, 119
Robert Mrs. 22
Russell T. 119
Watson M. 119
Woodrow M. 119

Fitzpatrick
Dennis 76
Minerva 27
Fitzwater (Fritzwater)
Jasper 160
John 160
Mary A. 160
Sintha 160
Uriah 16
Fleming
Mary 77
Patrick 77
Flowers
Millie 21
Foley
Catherine 128
William E. 7
Ford
Charles 54
Elisah 54
John 161
Joseph 54
Iphey 54
Mary
Sarah J. 161
Forehand
Elizah 62
Jemima 62
Fort
Mitilda 41
Fortinberry
Cynthia 27, 61
Francis
Mrs. O. E. 122
Franzwa
Gregory M. 7, 18
Freeman
Jesse 163
Sarah J. 163
Frizel
Joseph 18
Sarah 18
Front
Lettie 55
Frost
Gen.
Fry
Abraham 73, 74
Anna 73, 74
Elizabeth 72
Emeline 74
Henry 19, 72, 73, 74, 75
Henry Jr. 73, 74
Marie M. 73, 74
Mary 74
Nancy 73
Polly 73
Rebecca 19, 73
Rhoda 73
Sally 73
Tarlton 73, 74
Gage
William B. 48

Galbraith
Rebecca 88
Sam 88
William 88
Gallaher
Charles H. 146
Cyrenia 61, 111
David 9, 43, 146
Drucillia 146
Eliza 43, 62
Ella B. 144
Frank F. 144, 146, 147
George 43, 111, 114, 171
James H. 146
John T. 146
Lillian M. 144
Lydia 43
Mahala E. 146, 147
Milton 111, 146
Nancy 146
Nancy C. 144, 147
Robert N. 146
Sarah 146
Serena 144, 146
William
Gann
Ulay 161
Gardner
James A. 18
Garret
Jacob 24
Garrison
Adie 161
Gastineau
Elizabeth 62
Gatewood
Charles C. 50
Gay
Alexander 162
Rebecca L. 162
George
Andrew L. 40, 50, 51
Catherine B. 40, 51
Elizabeth 51
James 51
John 40, 51
John P. 108
John W. 40, 51
Lucy 108
Lucinda 51
Mary J. 40, 108
Nancy 51
Sarah 40
Soloman 9
Zorilda 131
Gibault
Father 105
Gibbons
James 9
John 9
Joseph 9
Robert 9
Samuel 9
Gibson
Elizabeth 39

184

Sarah A. 126, 136, 147
Sarah C. 144, 149
Sarah E. 129, 145, 150, 151
Sarah J. 120, 124, 129, 141, 146, 147, 148, 149, 150
Sarah S. 149, 150
Sidney H. 146
Stella J. 148
Sterling P. 102, 141, 142
Steven 140
Steven Jr. 140
Steven Sr. 140
Susanna 140
Thomas G. 144, 147, 148
Tony O. 145
Tressie M. 152
Verd N. 148
Vianna M. 148
Viola M. 136, 147
Viola V. 152
Walles T. 136, 147
Walter 145
Willard W. 141
William 29, 54, 70, 140, 142, 143, 146, 148, 170
William H. 148, 150, 151
William J. 61, 95, 98 , 141
William L. 142
William O. 126, 136, 147, 149
Willie C. 144
Winnie D. 142
Zona P. 136, 147

Goldham
Frances 112
Henry 112

Gooding
Mary 69

Goodson
Jake 82, 83

Gordon
John 46, 50, 51, 56

Gortner
Catherine 54
Elizabeth 173

Gorza
Luis 158
Tammy S. 158

Govero
A. 163
Dorothy 163
Eliza 38

Graham 67

Gray
Alta L. 163
Dorothy 163
Dorothy M. 163
George W. 163
James E. 163
Lucy A. 163
Mamie 163
Pearl 163
Ruth A. 163
William A.

Green
Whiley B. 40

Greer
Huston R. 159
Thelma R. 159

Greggs
John 39

Grien
Elizabeth 145

Gringa
Louis 9

Grizzle
Iphey 54

Guess
Eula V. 36, 90

Guilliam
Iowa 110
William H. 110

Guttridge
family 113
Lydia 112

Hackley
Lt. 66

Hackworth
Lettie 55
Thomas 55
Tolbert 55

Haley
Pamelia 16

Hall
Sarah 112
William 112

Halloway
Thomas 75, 79

Hamilton
Elizabeth 89

Hammon
Bro. 100

Hampton
Barbara 55
Elizabeth 34, 55, 89
Henry
James 34, 55
Irene 34
Mary 55
Selina 55
Turner 55

Hand
Jane 112
Joseph 112
Sarah 112

Hanger
David 45
Jane
Samuel 83

Hann
Mary L. 18

Harbison
Elizabeth 54

Hargrove
Essie 86
Frank 86

Harmosen
Peter 25

Harper
Aubery 161

Harris
Angeline 78
Ava
Elizabeth 38
Issac 38
James 66
John A. 79
Lavena 38
Mary 79
Nancy 83
Permela 27
Rankin 78
Sarah 48
Vicy 78
Washington 40

Harrison
Benjamine 102
Carrie C. 144
Charles 144
Diana 101
Elvis 59
Everett F. 144
James C. 144
Jesse R. 130
John R. 144
Lavada 144
Linnie 143
Lucy 101
Lucy B. 143
Lucy J. 144
Mary E. 59
Minerva 59
Nancy 144
Rose E. 130
Sarah 48, 101
Theodosia 130
Thomas B. 59
Thomas D. 124
Thomas E. 144
Thomas W. 143
William H. Pres. 102
William M. 143
William R. 143

Hart
Albert H. 156, 157
Amy A. 85
Delia 157
Hannah L. 156, 157
James L. 156
John C. 157
Joseph 156
Mable 156
Martha 156, 157
Nora 156

Hartman
David H. 143, 148
Donna 143
Ebenezer 143
Ethlinda 143, 148
family 143
John D. 143
John G. 143
Leona 143
Margaret 143
Mary M. 143
Minnie 143

185

Philip D. 143
Rose E. 143
Sarah 143
Sarah I. 143
Vianna M. 143, 148
William 143
Hasse
Agnes 163
Olga 163
Hasty
Jordan 170
Hatter
Mettie I. 89
Hawk
Anna 28
Caroline 145
Elizah 28
George 28
Nelson 28
Hawkins
Arthur C. 150
George W. 130, 150, 173
James. L. 150
Jane 32, 130
John 8, 9
Mable 150
Mary J. 173
Sarah 150, 173
William 32
William J. 160
Hayles
Gladys G. 152
Hazel H. 152
Nancy 152
Raymond 152
Rhoda B. 152
Wesley Y. 152
William 152
Haynes
Clarance O. 160
Jessamine 160
Hays
Nicholas 9
Haywood
Amy A. 85
Edmund G. 85
Head
Martha 69
Hearnes
Warren E. 18
Hedspeth
Joanna 28
Milly 28
Helms
Hay T. 25
Helvey
Archie T. 138
Barbara 55
Fannie D. 138
Jacob 55
Jacob Jr. 55
James 138
John 53
Lucy E. 138

Mary 55, 138
Otho O. 138
Serethy 55
William G. 138
Hemptead
Edward 6
Stephen 7
Henderson
Isabella 30
Samuel 9
Sarah 135
Sarah L. 135
William 9
Hendrick
John W. 67
Henry
Andrew 13, 19, 20, 74, 76, 77, 78
Angeline 78, 79
Carrie 79
Georganna 79
George 19, 76, 78, 79
Grace 79
Jane 78
Lucetta 79
Margaret 19, 76
Marie 76
Mary 77, 78, 79
Missouri 79
Nevada 79
Patrick 79
Hermes
George U. 164
Vick L. 164
Hertick
Clara 12
Hewitt
Elizabeth 9
James 9, 20
Hickman
Elizabeth 32
James 32
Hicks
Ruthy 31
Hickson
Ingealeo 67
Higginbotham
Miss Valle 15
Highley
Nancy A. 48
Nathanial 48
Hight
Alfred D. 20
Henry 20
Hill
John F. 97
Mary E. 128
Olive 26, 128
Polly 26
Sarah 90
William A. 128
William R. 128
Hillen
Angeline 43
Emeline 43

Hodges
Anna 73, 74
John B. 132
John W. 132
Lena S. 132
Lucy E. 132
Mildred 132
William 73, 74
Willard 132
Hodkins
Sarah M. 132
Hogan
William 71
Hoggard
Frank R. 71
Holbert
Hethy 28
Holland
Clara 36
Holloway
Thomas 75, 79
Holmes
John 24
Holt
Mary 38
Honea
Columbus 161
Lucy E. 161
Hopkins
Charles 161
Edith 161
Leonard 161
Pirgie E. 161
Horney
Daniel 108
Mary 108
Hoskins
Roxie 87
Houck
Louis 7, 10, 18, 75, 79, 106
Hough
(Family) 114
Howe
Mary 87
Howard
Gov.
John 25, 39
Howell
Alice 137
Antonia 137
Benjamin 136
Benjamin M. 137
Choloe 137
Clinton 162
Cordelia S. 137
Gideon 137, 162
Henry 162
Laura 162
Margarette 136
Martha 162
Sarah 162
Sarah J. 137
Walter 162
William G. 162

Huddleston
Charles 40
Hudspeth
Ahijah 48
Ayres 47, 48
George 48
James H. 48
John 48
Lewis 48
Malinda 48
Nancy 48
Sarah 48
Susan C. 48
Huett
J. Loyd 36
Huff
Joseph 41, 85
Sina 41, 85
Hughes
Elizabeth 27
Ellen 31
John 9
Mark 31
Susanna 31
William 46
Huitt
Mary A. 99
William 99
Hull
Uriah 9
Hulsey
James 66
William 66
Humphreys
William 9
Hewt
Carrie 127
Ford T. 127
Nancy J. 127
Hunter
Alvin R. 125
Capt. 70
George W. 115
Leora M.
Mable C. 125
Martha A. 135
Mary S. 115
Nancy A. 12, 15, 125
Nancy J.
Phelissanna 135
Samuel 125
Thomas M. 135
William A. 125
William J. 125
Huntley
(Family) 114
Hunziker
Elizabeth 18
Sarah 18
Hurt
Jane 30
Huston
Jan Marrs 173
Hutching
John 9

Hyatt
Lovey 20, 59
Nancy 20
Seth 9, 19, 20, 59
Hyder
Samuel 46
Imboden
Eliza 108
Thomas D. 108
Ingethron
Elmo 71
Ingram
William 24
Inman
Harley 165
Vada 160
Irvin
Alexander 107
Elizabeth 28, 107
John F. 127
Madilena 116
Mary 27, 127
Samuel 27, 127
Sterling P. 116
Jackman
Drucilla 29, 140
Mary 140, 141
Richard 140, 141
Jackson
Allen F. 165
Andrew 94
Anna A. 164
Anna E. 164
Clairbore Gov. 64, 65
Edward L. 165
Elder R. 165
Grace 165
Grace C. 165
Harley 165
James R. 164
Jenny E. 165
Joseph C. 164
Margaret E. 164
Nancy A. 165
Neomi B. 164
Pres. 12, 16
Robert T. 165
Sarah E. 165
William C. 164
Jacobs
Clara 58, 79
James
John 9
Thomas
Jamison 21, 29
Alexander 23
Andromache 110
Ida E. 135
James J. 136
John 22, 23, 44, 110
John H. 70, 153
Julia 110
June 70
Lucy 135, 136
Martha 22

Mary 97
Nancy 131
Patsy 22
Susanna 22, 23
Zerelda 120
January
Alfred 125
Carl C. 125
Ella C. 125
Elmer 125
Isabelle C. 125, 129
Jacob F. 125
Mary M. 125
Minnie V. 125
Nancy A. 129
Otto J. 125
Richard I. 125, 129
Jarrot
Nicolas
Jaycox
June 23, 44, 70
Jeffrey
Christine 56
Johnson
Cassie B. 142
Dallas 82
Edward 9
Elva O. 156
Emma 161
Ida M. 85
James 9
James Jr. 161
James Sr. 9, 73
John 9, 170
Lucinda
Mark 156
Nancy 73
Richard 63
Johnston
Celinda 82
Curincy 31
Elizabeth 31, 81, 82
Emeline 31, 82
Frances 31, 82
John 31, 82
Marion 171
Reuben 31, 82
Robert 30, 31, 171
Ruthy 31
William 25, 40
Jones
Augustus 56
Augustus F. 14
Elizabeth 14
Eva 152
Frank 152
George W. 14
Harriet 14
John 33
John P. 9
John R. 14, 173
John R. 9, 12, 13, 14, 105, 173
Laura 161
Miers 14
Nancy C. 152
Rice 173

187

189

McMullen
Edward 46, 50, 51
McNail
Allan 28
Anna A. 164
Benjamine 28, 171
Daniel 28
Elizabeth 49, 118
Jane 49
Joe
John T. 10, 28, 49
Joseph 49, 50, 59, 60, 86, 118, 171
Mary 28, 49, 118
Rachel 48
Ruth 81
Savannah 28
Sarah 28
McNair
Gov. 13
Madden
Honore 16
Thomas 16
Mahan
James 66
William 66
Mallory
Joseph T. 60
Mallow
Charlotte 54, 61, 98, 110
Catherine 54
Elizabeth 54
Jacob 54
Martha 54
Phillip 50, 54
Mann 42
Andrew 34
Arnold 34
Deanne 34
Ethel L. 86
Elizabeth 34
Finas 34
George 34
Isaac 22, 34, 171
Jacob 34
James 34, 54
John 34
Mary 34
Milly 22, 34, 54
Rachael 34
Sarah 54
Susanna 34
Thedosia 30
Thomas 34
Zimri 54, 171
Mansfile
Mary 34
Margreiter
Don L. 71
Marmaduke
John D. 69
Martin
Benjamine 94, 99, 101
Cynthia 161
Diana 101

James H. 161
Laura 161
Louisa 161
Sarah 161
Walter 161
Mason
Arlotta 30
Georgia A. 131
Latty 30
Nimrod 30, 51
Massie
Alfred N. 89
Anderson 86
Artimissa 86
Charles 86
Delphia A. 86
Elizabeth 86
Emma O. 86
Isaac E. 86
Laura J. 86
Louisa A. 86
Mary E. 86
Mary J. 86
Mollie H. 86
Matthews
Edward H. 24
Margaret 48
Maulding
West 40, 46
Maxwell 50
Catherine 98
Diego 104
Ferdinand 106
Hugh P. 21, 106
James Rev. 7, 11, 21, 76, 103, 104, 106, 174
John P. 21, 106, 174
Lucian B. 106
Sophie A. 106
Mayberry
James 88
Minerva 88
Mayes
Jack F. 71
Medley
Joseph 139
Rosa B. 139
Mefford
Dessie 86
Edward R. 86
Menard
Pierre 76
Mercer
Charles F. 92
Mary E. 92
Merrifield
Calphurnia 23, 122
Fred R. 122
Merrill
Douglas 25
Meyer 19
Duane 7
Middleton
Agness 53
Allen 53

Catherine 53
Ephe J. 53
John 53
Mary 53
Rachel 53
Rhebecca 53
Sarah 111
William R. 111
Miller
Edna 87
Gov. 33
John 47, 48, 96
Margaret 48
Ray 87
Sarah 48
Mills
Bascom 82
Emeline 82
George 31, 82, 171
John 82
Lafayette 82
Miner
Cyrenia 61
Elizabeth 144
Henry 171
John E. 124
Labon 23, 171
Lazaras 171
Lydia 23, 28, 61, 128
Martha 54, 149
Martha J. 124
Mary E. 128
Milton 61
Nancy 38, 61
Serena 43, 144
William 23, 61, 124, 128
William H. 124
Minter
Mildred 63, 111
Mitchell
Rose A. 102
Monday
Louisa 161
William 161
Monroe
James Pres. 95
Mooney
Daisy P. 156
Walter 156
Moore
Adella 79
Alice 120
Alexander 62
America 108
Belle 161
Clara 58, 79
Creed 62
David 50, 51, 60
Doris J. 157
James 85
John W. 120
Maranda 85
Mary 62, 85
Nancy 120
Newt

190

Patsy 62
Polly A. 86
Sina 85
Ursula B. 157
William 62
Zerelda 120
Moran
Lydia 23
More
John S. 25
Morgan
George 6
Morris
Abraham 84
Caleb 83
Curtis 10
George 82, 83
Hannah 83, 84
Hettie 57, 83, 88
James D. 50, 51
Joshua 20, 83
Nancy 83, 171
Morrison
William 76
Morton
Lucy 81
Moss
Elizabeth 13
Mund
Alice 119
Effie 119
Fritz 118, 119
Josie 119
Lillie 119
Mary O. 118, 119
Maud 119
Ruth 119
Munger 21
A. 117
A. J.
Abigal 113
Adeline 117
Alfred 116
Alfred A. 116
Alfred J. 114, 117, 118
Alfred T. 118
Alice N. 120
Amy 117
Andrew J. 118
Ann 112
Annie F. 115
Archie 121
Bessie 118
Beulah 113
Cecil C. 117
Charles M. 116
Clara C. 117, 119
Clarissa 113
Clark 113, 114
Clyde E. 118
Cordelia 117
Daisy 118
Demaris J. L. 121
Deliverance 112
Dorothy 112, 113

Dudley 115
Elizabeth 113, 118
Elizabeth M. 115
Elnathan 113
Elsie 113
Elvina 115, 116
Ephrim 113
Essie L. 118
Ester 113
Ethel L. 117
Eugene M. 122
Eugenia 116
Eunice 113
Fear 113
Frances 112, 122
Frances A. 120
Frances M. 114, 119, 120, 137
George R. 121
George W. 119, 122
Georgia P. 120
Goldie V. 118
Grace A. 118
Harrie L. 116
Harry S. 120
Harvey E. 117
Helen E. 117
Helen M. 117
Ichabod 113
Ida O. 115
Ira 46, 50, 52, 56, 113, 114, 173
Ira C. 114, 117, 118, 119
James 112
James A. 115
Jane 112
J. B. 112, 153
Jehiel 113
Jessee 113
John 112, 113
Jonathan 113
Joseph 112, 113
Lana M. 115
Laura A. 117
Lemuel 118
Letha M. 119, 120
Lewis D. 118
Lewis P. 114, 115, 116, 119, 136
Lloyd Rev. 122
Lois 122
Lola B. 118
Lottie 120
Lottie B. 118
Lottie C. 121
Lucille 121
Lydia 113
M. M. 121
M. W. 117
Madilena 115, 116
Malinda 115, 124
Majorie 122
Marshall 116
Marshall M. 116, 117, 119, 120, 121, 126, 153
Martha 113, 114, 115
Martha J. 115
Marvin 21, 27, 46, 49, 50, 52, 112, 113, 114, 153, 171, 173

Marvin F. 115
Marvin M. 117, 120, 122
Mary 113, 115, 122
Mary C. 114, 119, 120
Mary D. 119, 121
Mary L. 121
Mary O. 117, 118
Mary S. 115, 116, 119, 120, 137
Minnie 118
Minnie 117
Minnie L. 117
Minnie M. 121
Mont 115
Moses 52, 113
Moses W. 114, 117
Myra I. 120
Myra J. 116, 136
Nathaniel 112, 113, 115, 122
Nellie 117
Nicholas 112
Olive 113
Oscar M. 118
Orrin 114, 115, 124
Orrin L. 119, 121, 122
Othal H. 118
Paul M. 122
Polly 113
Preston C. 116, 117
Rebecca 113
Rhona 118
Robert O. 122
Rosanna O. 116
Roy L. 117
Salina 21, 113
Salina C. 116
Samanthia 117
Samuel 112, 113
Sarah 112, 113, 118
Sarah A. 118
Sarah E. 120, 121, 153
Sarah J. 115
Soloman 113
Submit 112
Thomas O. 120
Ulissus S. 116
Watson M. 117, 119
Will
William A. 118, 119, 120
Murphy
Scout Capt. 66
Murray
Verneal 86
Myres
Artie 156
Cynthia E. 156
Elva 156
Lewis 156
Naile
Corina N. 159
Napeoleon 6
Neal
Benjamine 33
Elias 33
Elizabeth 33
Jacob 10

191

192

193

194

195

Ruby M. 129
Sally 129
Samuel 123
Samuel G. 132
Samuel S. 132
Sarah 123, 124
Sarah A. 37, 124, 126, 136
Sarah C. 129
Sarah E. 120, 121, 124, 126, 129,
   131, 153
Sarah J. 124, 133
Seaborn 123
Sebrum 123
Simeon 123
Stella 132
Stella J. 129
Thelma 130
Thomas 123
Thomas A. 126
Thomas D. 128, 129
Thomas J. 121, 124, 125, 135
Walter O. 128
Willard 127
William 132
William A. 130, 132
William F. 37, 124, 126, 137
William H. 128, 129
Willie S. 124
Wilma 125
Zimrier 129
Zoa M. 129

Simpson
Rebecca

Sinclair
John 10
Miriah 97
Miss 111

Sininore
Silas M. 40

Sizemore
Elizabeth 118

Skunkwiler
Sarah A. 85
Will 85

Slade
Ellen K. 52
James A. 51, 52, 60
John W. 52

Sloan
Fergus 10
Gentry 125
Henry 170
Mary L. 150
Robert 10
Samuel 10
Thomas 10
William 8, 10

Smith
Amy A. 87
Barbara 58
Billie H. 44
Emily 86
Ethel C. 129
Freda 157
Hazel 86
Isaac 56

Jackson 129
Jim 87
John 8, 35, 52, 56
Martha 52
Mary 61
Mary A. 129
Mary E. 37, 115
Nancy 35, 36
Sam 157
Wilson 27

Smith T.
Ann 16
Francis 15
Francis Sr. 15
John 15, 16, 27
Lucy 15
Nancy 15, 16

Snlee
Harley
Grace 165

Southwort
Mary

Spangler
Dorothy L. 163

Speck
Preston M. 60

Speer
Rebecca 161
William 161

Spencer
Jesse 25

Sprawle
Letty 90

Stafford
Ernest 150
Fayette E. 150
Lee R. 150
Lora 150
Mable E. 150
Monta 150
Sarah S. 150
Verna B. 150

Stahl
Dorothy M. 163
Earl R. 163

Stalcop
Andreiss 123
Christina 123
John A. 123
Sarah 123
Swain
Tobias 123

Stanton
John 8

Stark
Charles A. 156
Edna J. 156
Ethel M. 157
Freda P. 156
Lucinda E. 156
Martha E. 157
Viola 156

Stephens
Jack 66
Miles 65, 66

Stephenson
Joseph 46

Stevens
Cora B. 131
Elmer 131
Gladys 131
Lowell 131
Mart 131
Nancy E. 131
Paul J. 131
Rebecca 70
Ruby 131
William H. 131

Stevenson
Robert M. 10
William O. 10

Stewart
Lucy B. 143
John 10

Stewbeck
Agatha 17
Daniel 17

Stilwell
Polly 30

Stinson
Polly 88, 89, 90

Stockton
Glenda 4, 10, 23, 36, 44, 56, 58,
   63, 153, 173

Stoner
Lettie S. 110

Stopp
Betty 29

Story
Jesse 66
William

Stout
Cynthia 27, 61
Delsa 36
Elizabeth 86
Ephraim 27
Franklin M. 27
Jacob 26, 61, 172
James 170
Joseph 170, 172
Rachel 26, 30
Samuel 26
Sarah 27
Savanna 28

Strader
Otho 76

Street
Samuel 24
William Sr. 24, 63

Stretch
Connie 36, 58

Stricklin
Abial 30, 51
Abigail 27, 30
Able 30, 63, 170
Cynthia 30
George 70
Henry 30
Isabella
Jane 30, 63

196

197

Vann
Agnes 86
Tolitha A. 137
Varner
James 24
Vassey
David 99
Eliza 99
Vaugh
Eula M. 160
Vendle
Margaret 72
Vernon
Catherine 49
James 25
Volner
Lurena 63
Vickery
Kathryn 63
Villars
Louis D. 11, 76
Marie 76
Marie L. 7
Vinson
Elvina 116
John 116
Vinyard
Nancy 43
William 43
Vistage
Mary
Thomas
Wadlow
Charles C. 135
Cintha 31, 135
Edgar 135
Elijah 42, 50, 170
Elish 42
George W. 135
Holla 135
James 31
John 31, 135
Lucy
Nancy 31, 42
Otho 135
Robert 44
Sarah 31
Thomas 31, 135
William 31, 42, 135
Wakely
Samuel 10
Walker
Henry 169
James 169
John 10
Mary 169
Nancy 15
Sanders 15
Sarah 15
Thomas 169
William 169
Wilmer 151
Waller
Sarah 105
Gertrude 152

Ward
Mary M. 125
Warner
Catherine 62
Jane 43
Lydia 43
Warren
Bill 156
Caswell 55
Elva 156
Mary A. 55
Ronald E. 71
Watkins
David 99
Patsy 22
William 22
Wayne
Anthony 24
Wear
Laura 87
Weaver
Edna 157
Pyrtle 157
Webb
Amy A. 81
Anna M. 81
Cary J. 81
Della L. 81
Dessie 86
Elizabeth 81
Floyd L. 81
James 81
Jim 86
John P. 81
John T. 10, 81
Joseph A. 81
Lott 81
Lou 81
Louisa 86
Lucy F. 81
Lucy J. 81
Mary A. 86
Polly 81
Pricalla 81
Richard 81
Ruth 81
Sarah 81
Sarah E. 81
William 10, 81
William C. 86
Weeks
Gamblin 53, 54, 59
Garret 53
Gideon 53
Julia 54
Martha 57
Susan 57
Weems
Elizabeth A. 84
James 84
Weiher
Anna 161
Welch
Eunice 113
Martha 130

West
Cynthia 162
John 162
Westmoreland
Mary 62
Whaley
James 22
Rebecca 22
Wheelan
Mariam C. 159
Wheeler
Alfred 25
White
Ancel 131
Ann 16
Anna 131
Edwin 131
Ethel 173
Georgia A. 131
Helen M. 117
Herman L. 160
Hilda C. 160
James M. 16
Lyle N. 131
Norman R. 131
Pearl A. 163
Sarah E. 131
Susan 117
William T. 117
Whitley
Mary 87
Ruthay 87
William 87
Wilcox
Elizabeth 13
Wilcoxson
Agnes 100
David 100
Isaac 100
Nancy 100
Wilhelm
Otha 102
Wilkinson
Benjamin 76
Gen. 15
William
Joseph
Margaret 37, 133
Mary 37, 61, 116
Mary H. 133
Raul 10
Ruel L. 134
Theaphilus 37, 133, 134
Thomas 134
Williamson
Elizabeth 69
Wilson
Alfred H. 115
Elizabeth 62
Hangford 115
Jacob 62, 115
James 25, 62, 68, 69
James S. 68
James W. 115
Jemima 62, 115

198

199

CPSIA information can be obtained
at www.ICGtesting.com
Printed in the USA
JSHW021216050522
25580JS00002B/242

9 781681 623689